A LITERARY COMPANION
TO FLORENCE

FRANCIS KING

PENGUIN BOOKS

PENGUIN BOOKS

Published by the Penguin Group
Penguin Books Ltd, 27 Wrights Lane, London W8 5TZ, England
Penguin Putnam Inc., 375 Hudson Street, New York, New York 10014, USA
Penguin Books Australia Ltd, Ringwood, Victoria, Australia
Penguin Books Canada Ltd, 10 Alcorn Avenue, Toronto, Ontario, Canada M4V 3B2
Penguin Books India (P) Ltd, 11 Community Centre, Panchsheel Park,
New Delhi – 110 017, India
Penguin Books (NZ) Ltd, Cnr Rosedale and Airborne Roads,
Albany, Auckland, New Zealand
Penguin Books (South Africa) (Pty) Ltd, 5 Watkins Street, Denver Ext 4,
Johannesburg 2094, South Africa

Penguin Books Ltd, Registered Offices: Harmondsworth, Middlesex, England

First published by John Murray 1991
Published in Penguin Books 2001
1

Printed in England by Clays Ltd, St Ives plc

To the memory of Anita Ryan
first and most entertaining of companions in Florence

Contents

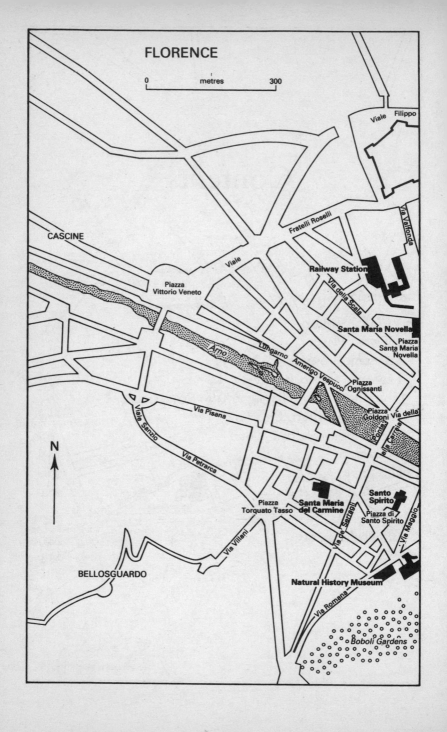

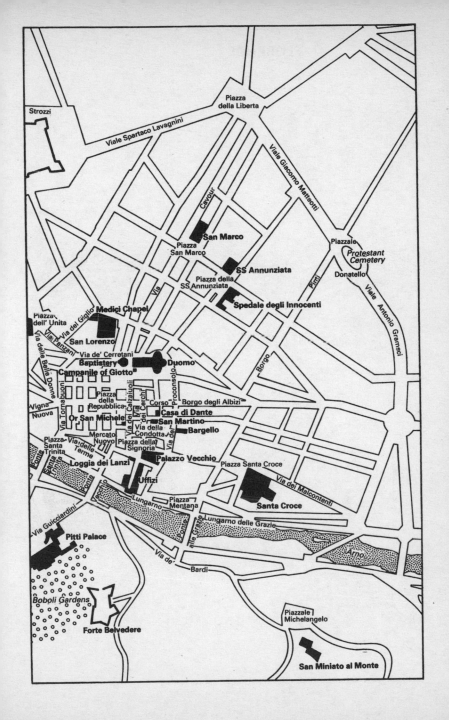

Introduction

O Foster-nurse of man's abandoned glory,
Since Athens, its great mother, sunk in splendour . . .
                    Percy Bysshe Shelley (1792–1822)

I first visited Florence, a young man in the immediate after-math of the last War, in order to fulfil a commission to write a book entitled *The Brownings in Italy*. That book never reached completion. But my research, half-heartedly carried on when I was not gawping at buildings and works of art, chatting with my contemporaries at café tables, or being entertained by members of the 'community', often elderly and often eking out impoverished and improvident lives in once sumptuous but now dilapidated villas, provided, after an interval of more than forty years, the basis for this book. As people reminisced to me, with a typically Florentine mixture of tolerance and malice, not merely about such writers as D. H. Lawrence, Norman Douglas, and Aldous Huxley in the inter-war years, but also about Henry James, E. M. Forster, Anatole France, and even, in the case of one octogenarian Englishwoman, Ouida, I felt the literary past of Florence to be constantly interpenetrating its literary present. With that feeling came another: in some way that literary past – so various, so strenuous, so distinguished – still had the ability to instruct and, far more important, to inspire. Other expatriate writers or would-be writers clearly felt the same. Florence at that period was full of them, from a prematurely aged and drink-sodden Sinclair Lewis, fumbling his way to long-delayed completion of the least successful of his novels, *World So Wide*, to a youthfully ardent Lettice Cooper.

In the first part of this book, I have attempted to describe the lives of these expatriate writers, whether, like the Brownings, Charles Lever, or Fanny Trollope and her son Thomas, as long-time residents, or whether, like George Eliot, Nathaniel Hawthorne, or D. H. Lawrence, as mere transients on whose creativity the city nevertheless exerted a profound influence. In the second part, I have attempted to illustrate how these expatriate writers and such indigenous writers as Dante, Boccaccio, and, in our own times, Pratolini, have viewed the city. As in the case of Michelangelo's *David*, by turns execrated as 'disproportionate', 'brutal', and 'hideous', and lauded as the supreme depiction of youthful masculinity, such writers have often violently disagreed with each other. D. H. Lawrence loved the 'maleness' of Florence; his friend and disciple Aldous Huxley came to hate its maidenly primness. After her turbulent and emotionally ravenous early years, Violet Trefusis found peace and contentment in her villa in Bellosguardo; Dylan Thomas loathed the spot, as he loathed the rest of the city.

Since the fifth century, when Sidonius Apollinaris left his native Lyons on what was in effect a Grand Tour, the things which have lured writers to Florence are generally those which have also lured non-writers. There has always been the beauty of situation, buildings and works of art. Until the nineteenth century there was also the conviction that in culture and civilization Florence was ahead of the cities of northern Europe. As Addison wrote of Italy as a whole:

It is the great school of music and painting, and contains in it all the noblest productions of statuary and architecture, both ancient and modern. It abounds with cabinets and curiosities, and vast collections of all kinds of antiquities. No other country in the world has such a variety of governments, that are so different in their constitutions and so refined in their politics. There is scarce any part of the nation that is not famous in history, nor so much as a mountain or river that has not been the scene of some extraordinary action.

Ruskin's hyperboles about Florentine architecture and art were echoed by innumerable lesser Victorians: for him the Campanile was 'the last building raised on the earth by the descendants of workmen taught by Daedalus'; the Bardi Chapel in Santa Croce 'the most perfect and interesting little Gothic chapel in all Italy'. If human nature could be redeemed through beauty, as Ruskin believed, then Florence was the ideal location for such a miracle.

Increasingly people also came to Florence in search of health. The fruitlessness of such a search in a climate so cold in winter, so hot in summer and so damp in every season is cruelly illustrated by the many nineteenth-century graves of young foreigners in the Protestant Cemetery. D. H. Lawrence was one of the last and arguably the most distinguished of consumptives to discover that, so far from bettering his condition, Florence merely worsened it. No doubt this high incidence of premature mortality had much to do with the foreign community's intense interest in spiritualism during the nineteenth and the first half of the twentieth centuries.

Many people also settled in the city either because it was so cheap that they could live there in a style far grander than would have been possible at home, or because it was so tolerant of their sexual foibles and practices. Thus, in the first half of this century, a number of sexual heretics – among them Radclyffe Hall and Una Troubridge, Vernon Lee, and that old reprobate Norman Douglas – found it far easier to exist at peace not merely with their bank managers but with society and themselves in Florence than in England.

In addition to all these reasons for visiting, even settling in Florence, there was for expatriate writers yet another one. When I arrived there in 1947 there was a feeling, as I have indicated, that Florence was not merely an artists' city but also a writers' one. Just as in the 1920s and 1930s foreign writers had flocked to Paris as to some gigantic forcing-house for literary talent, so for centuries, not merely two decades, writers had similarly flocked to Florence. All that past striving and achievement must, they felt, have somehow impregnated the gold of the air, the grey-brown of the Arno, the greenery of the surrounding hills, the ever-changing colours of the stones.

In *Childe Harold* Byron with justice exclaimed 'Ungrateful Florence!' because it had failed to provide a last resting place for 'the all-Etruscan three' of Dante, Petrarch, and Boccaccio. But to a host of subsequent expatriate writers Florence has provided a home in which they have been able to be both happy and creative.

PART ONE

VISITORS

MONTAIGNE, LASSELS, MILTON, EVELYN, ADDISON,
GRAY, WALPOLE, MRS PIOZZI, MADAME DE STAËL

The first expatriate writer of note to visit Florence – their
Italian travels took neither Chaucer nor Cervantes there – was
the French moralist and essayist, Michel Eyquem de Montaigne (1533–92) in 1580. A sufferer from calculus, he had
heard that the waters of Tuscany were particularly efficacious
in curing or at least alleviating this malady. His *Journal du
voyage*, first published in France in 1774 after having lain
undiscovered for almost two centuries, and published in
England in 1842 in a translation by the son of William Hazlitt,
also named William, is much taken up with trivialities about
health, diet, and the discomforts of travel. There is little about
scenery, since a taste for it was then as uncommon in France as
in England; and (as Stendhal noted) there is not even a mention
of Michelangelo or Raphael.

Richard Lassels (1603–68), an English Roman Catholic,
made a number of tours of Italy as tutor and guide to young
noblemen. His *The Voyage of Italy*, an invaluable account of
his travels, which included Florence, was posthumously published in 1670. The travels themselves took place in the years
1630–40. As when he describes Italian women looking like
'haycocks with armes and heads' or Genoa as looking 'like a
proud young lady in a straight bodyed flowered gowne, which
makes her look tall indeed and fine, but hinders her from being

at her ease and taking breath,' he writes with humour and
vivacity.

The first English writer of real note to visit Florence was
John Milton (1608–74). An interesting letter from Sir Henry
Wotton, poet and diplomatist, close friend of Donne, for-
merly agent and secretary to the Earl of Essex and at the time
Provost of Eton, is printed in the second edition of Milton's
Comus. Milton received it shortly before his departure for Italy.
After having thanked the poet for his 'dainty piece of entertainment,' Wotton tenders some advice: 'I should think your
best line will be through the whole length of France to
Marseilles, and thence by sea to Genoa, whence the passage
into Tuscany is as diurnal as a Gravesend barge.' He goes on to
'tell you a short story from the interest you have given me in
your safety.' The story is as follows:

> At Siena I was tabled in the house of one Alberto Scipioni,
> an old Roman courtier in dangerous times, having been
> steward to the Duca of Paglioni, who with all his family
> were strangled, save this only man that escaped by fore-
> sight of the tempest. With him I had often much chat of
> those affairs, into which he took pleasure to look back
> from his native harbour; and at my departure toward
> Rome (which had been the centre of his experience) I had
> won his confidence enough to beg his advice how I might
> carry myself there without offence of others or of mine
> own conscience. '*Signor Arrigo mio*,' says he, '*I pensieri
> stretti ed il viso sciolto* [honest thoughts and guarded looks]
> will go safely over the whole world,' of which Delphian
> oracle (for so I have found it) your judgement doth need
> no commentary.

Wotton was British ambassador in Venice for three separate
periods between 1604 and 1624.

Having set out with letters of introduction from Wotton,
Milton arrived in Florence in the autumn of 1638. There are
rival claims that he stayed at the house of one Jacopo Daddi, 11
Via del Griglio, and at the house of one Vicenzo Viviani, on
the Via Sant' Antonio. Then thirty, he received a hospitable
reception from the learned Academies, in the minute book of

one of which he is described as *molto erudito*. There are a few
references to Italy in his prose works and in his poetic works
the famous reference to the autumn leaves in Vallombrosa and
the hardly less famous one to Galileo – whom he met in 1639.
Landor wrote an Imaginary Conversation between the two
men.

John Evelyn (1620–1706), whose diaries cover the years
1641–1705, arrived in Florence in 1644. He lodged in the house
of a Signor Baritiere in the Piazza di Santo Spirito – now the
site of a colourful market during the day and a resort of drug
addicts and dealers during the night. Passionately interested in
the fine arts, he has left some vivid descriptions of both
buildings and objects of *vertu*. Since, at that period, the value
of a painting or a statue was usually only assessed in relation to
the building of which it formed a decorative detail, he often
writes of 'divers good pictures' and leaves it at that. The
merit of his observations lies in the fact that he was a man both
erudite about the past and passionately interested in the
present.

Largely because of the Civil War, there was something of a
hiatus in English travel to Italy between Evelyn and Addison.
John Addison (1672–1719) was still in his twenties when he
spent the two years in Italy which resulted in his *Remarks on
Several Parts of Italy*. Dr Johnson summed up this work, so
popular in its own day, as follows: 'As his stay in foreign parts
was short, his observations are such as might be supplied by a
hasty view, and consist chiefly in comparisons of the present
face of the country with the descriptions left to us by the
Roman poets . . . Of many parts it is not a very severe censure
to say that they might have been written at home.' Anyone
who has attempted to read the work in question is unlikely to
dissent from this judgement.

Thomas Gray (1716–71) and Horace Walpole (1717–97)
arrived in Florence on 15 December 1739 as part of a Grand
Tour, then obligatory for young men of family and means,
which took them away from England for three years. Having
descended 'through winding-sheet of mist' (the phrase is
Gray's) into the streets of Florence, they were met by their
host-to-be Horace Mann, described by Gray as 'the best and

most obliging person in the world.' Mann was later to become
envoy extraordinary at the Court of Tuscany, and with him
Walpole was to carry on a correspondence for almost half a
century. For much of the time they led a pleasurably indolent
existence in Horace Mann's guest house, Casa Ambrogi in Via
dei Bardi, overlooking the Ponte Vecchio. Florence, Gray
wrote,

> is excellent to employ all one's animal sensations in, but
> utterly contrary to one's rational powers. I have struck a
> medal upon myself; the device is thus O, and the motto
> *Nihilissimo*, which I take in the most concise manner to
> contain a full account of my person, sentiments, occu-
> pations, and late glorious successes. We get up at twelve
> o'clock, breakfast till three, dine till four, sleep till six,
> drink cooling liquors till eight, go to the bridge [the Ponte
> Vecchio] till ten, sup till two, and so sleep till twelve
> again.

But he could not have been as idle as he here makes out. While
in Florence, he wrote in Latin the major part of a long poem on
Locke's philosophy and a number of other poems, also in
Latin, about the beauties of Fiesole, the Arno, and so forth.
During the Carnival Walpole wrote: 'I have done nothing but
step out of my domino and into bed and out of bed into a
domino.'

When the two men finally left Florence on 24 April 1741,
they had decided that it was 'one of the dullest cities in Italy'.
By now they were also on increasingly bad terms. Eventually
they quarrelled – precisely for what reason, it has never been
established, although Walpole always accepted the blame for
their rift – and were estranged for many years.

Mrs Piozzi (Dr Johnson's Mrs Thrale, 1741–1821) spent the
summer of 1785 in Florence, writing about it most enter-
tainingly in her *Glimpses of Italian Society*. She, her Brescia-
born husband, and a group of friends stayed in the English
House (later to become the Hotel New York) in the Palazzo
Ricasoli on the Piazza Goldoni.

Exiled from France by Napoleon, Madame de Staël (1766–
1817) went to Italy in 1804, and there wrote a novel, *Corinne*

ou l'Italie, which was to have a considerable success in its day. Corinne, half-English and half-Italian and blessed with a multitude of talents, is often said to be the woman whom Madame de Staël herself would like to have been. Madame de Staël visited Florence and the result is a section in the novel entitled *Le Séjour à Florence*. Byron wrote of Madame de Staël and her novel: 'She is sometimes right, and often wrong about Italy and England; but almost always true in delineating the heart, which is of but one nation, and of no country, or, rather, of all.'

ROGERS, BYRON, SHELLEY, LEIGH HUNT

It was on 20 August 1814 that Samuel Rogers (1763–1855) 'set sail from the beach at Brighton in a crouded boat'. So began the journey which was to result in the most successful of all the poems written by this acerbic bachelor, noted both for the breakfasts at which, for more than forty years, he entertained the famous, and for an appearance so cadaverous that the caption over a caricature of him in *Fraser's Magazine* in 1830 ran: '*De mortuis nil nisi bonum!* There is Sam Rogers, a mortal likeness – painted to the very death.' A wealthy banker, often accused of social climbing, he predictably put up at Schneider's Hotel on the north bank of the Arno near the Ponte alla Carraia in Florence, at that time the most expensive and exclusive of hotels in the city and so much frequented by English travellers that it was also known as the 'Locanda d'Inghilterra' or 'The Arms of England.' No less predictably, he was entertained by the *gratin* of Florence: by the Countess of Albany, widow of Prince Charles Edward Stuart, the Young Pretender, and mistress of the poet Alfieri; by Lord Holland; by Lord Brownlow. To set beside other such memorable aesthetic experiences as visiting Santa Croce, San Lorenzo, and the Carmine, he could record in his *Italian Journal*: 'Ortolans at dinner. White as snow and wonderfully rich and delicate.' He was a man whose love of art was equalled by his love of food and drink.

Byron (1788–1824) spent only a day in Florence on his first

visit in 1816 and only a few days, in the company of Samuel Rogers, on his second visit in 1821. Despite the briefness of this acquaintance, he was never in any doubt that he had no wish to live in the city. The trouble was the English tourists – 'Florence and Naples are their Margate and Ramsgate, and much the same company too, by all accounts,' he wrote to Thomas Moore. In a letter to James Wedderburn Lester he varied this condemnation – 'Florence and Naples are their Lazarettoes where they carry the infection of their society . . .' Nonetheless it was Florence which inspired one of the finest cantos, the fifth, of *Childe Harold*.

Shelley (1792–1822) first saw Florence in 1818, when he and Claire Clairmont – Mary was in Bagni di Lucca – were obliged to spend four hours there while waiting for the Austrian minister to provide them with a passport to travel on to Padua. Their journey, 'performed in a one-horse cabriolet, almost without springs, over a rough road' had been 'excessively fatiguing' [letter to Mary Shelley].

On 20 September 1819, Shelley and Claire again travelled to Florence together, in search of lodgings, once more leaving Mary, now heavily pregnant, in Bagni di Lucca. The couple were back in Bagni di Lucca on 29 September, and then returned to Florence, with Mary, on 2 October. They put up at the boarding house of Madame Merveilleux du Plantis in the Palazzo Marini on the Via Valfonda. On 13 November Shelley wrote to Leigh Hunt, 'Yesterday morning Mary brought me a little boy. She suffered but two hours pain, and is now so well that it seems a wonder that she stays in bed. The babe is also quite quite well, and has begun to suck. You may imagine that this is a great relief and a great comfort to me among all my misfortunes, past, present, and to come.' Like Florence Nightingale, the child was named after his birthplace – Percy Florence Shelley.

By now Shelley had written 'Peter Bell the Third' and his 'Ode to the West Wind' while resident in the city. In a prefatory note to the latter he recorded: 'This poem was conceived and chiefly written in a wood [the Cascine] that skirts the Arno near Florence, and on a day when the tempestuous wind, whose temperature is at once mild and animating, was collecting the vapours that pour down the autumnal rains.'

The winter surprised Shelley, as it has constantly surprised visitors, with its severity. 'Tuscany is delightful eight months of the year. But nothing reconciles me to . . . such infernal cold as my nerves have been racked upon for the last ten days,' he wrote to Thomas Medwin on 17 January 1820. In the same letter he describes Italy as 'the Paradise of exiles, the retreat of Pariahs'. Shelley left Florence, with Mary and Claire, for Pisa on 26 January.

It was in November 1820 that, always improvident and usually impoverished, Leigh Hunt (1784–1859) set sail with his wife and family for Italy. In the past Shelley had frequently invited him; and now Byron had added his own invitation, suggesting that, once in Italy, Hunt should collaborate in starting a radical periodical with Shelley and himself. At the time Hunt was in a state near to despair: 'I was ill; it was thought by many I could not live; my wife was very ill too; my family was numerous; and it was agreed by my brother John, that while a struggle was made in England to reanimate *The Examiner* [a periodical edited by Hunt], a simultaneous endeavour should be made in Italy to secure new aid to our prospects, and new friends to the cause of liberty.'

Hunt could usually be relied on to take a wrong decision, and he did so on this occasion, opting, on Shelley's advice, for the hazards, delays, and discomforts of a sea voyage in winter, instead of a journey by land. He ruefully confessed that, had Shelley recommended a balloon, he 'would have been inclined to try it.' It was already mid-summer in Leghorn (Livorno) when the Hunts arrived there, to be met by Trelawny and then to be conducted to Monte Nero, where Byron was staying in 'the hottest-looking house I ever saw'. Hunt hardly recognized Byron because he had become so fat, and Byron hardly recognized Hunt because he had grown so thin. Having returned to Leghorn – 'a polite Wapping' in which, he noted, Smollett lay buried – Hunt was joined by Shelley. Soon after, Byron and the Hunts took up residence in Pisa, the Hunts living on the ground floor of the Casa Lanfranchi, said to have been built by Michelangelo, while Byron occupied the rest of

the palatial mansion. There followed the tragedy of Shelley's
death in Lerici, and the Hunts' move first to Genoa – 'where
we received the first number of the periodical work, the
Liberal, which Lord Byron had invited me to set up' – and
then, in 1823, to Florence, where the first two Italian words
which he heard on his arrival were *fiore* [flowers] and *donne*
[women] – a good omen, he decided.

After a brief stay in a hotel, they found lodgings at 1 Via
delle Belle Donne – 'a name which it is a sort of tune to
pronounce'. It was in this street that Hunt, to his delight, heard
an alfresco concert, with music-stands with scores on them
and amateurs performing as though in a room. From there
they moved to lodgings in the Piazza Santa Croce, at the
corner of Via Magliabechi, and then to the Villa Morandi in
Maiano, at that time no more than an isolated village on one of
the hills around Fiesole. Maiano has given its name to one of
the earliest of the Italian poets, Dante of Maiano, to distinguish
him from his far greater namesake. Living close to the Hunts
was another Dante, a badly-behaved little boy, who 'excelled
in tearing his clothes and getting a dirty face and hands'. Hunt
was always delighted when he heard the boy's mother chide
him with some such words as 'Oh, Dante, what a brute beast
you are!' The Jewish family with whom the Hunts were
lodging were great lovers of both Dante and Alfieri. It was of
the latter that Hunt remarked tartly: 'Alfieri loved liberty like a
tyrant and the Pretender's wife [the Countess of Albany] like a
slave.'

Despite the chronic illness of his wife, whose pulmonary
tuberculosis caused frequent haemorrhages, and despite a
chronic shortage of money, Hunt had many moments of sheer
happiness in Maiano. Sadly, his efforts to start a magazine in
succession to the *Liberal*, which had by then expired, met with
no success, because of the fear inspired in the Tuscan authorities by his revolutionary reputation. Hunt has left us an
account of a conversation which he had with the Italian
bookseller whom he had hoped would be his publisher:

'You must submit the publication (said my bookseller)
to a censorship.'

'Be it so.'

'But you must let them see every sheet before it goes to press, in order that there may be no religion or politics.'

'Very well: – to please the reverend censors, we will have no religion. Politics also are out of the question.'

'Ay, but politics may creep in.'

'They shall not.'

'Ah, but they may creep in (say the authorities) without your being aware; and then what is to be done?'

'Why, if neither the editor nor the censors are aware, I do not see how any very vivid impression need be apprehended with regard to the public.'

'That has a very plausible sound; but how if the censors do not understand English?'

'There, indeed, they confound us. All I can say is, that the English understand the censors, and I see we must drop our intended work.'

But even if the censors impelled him to drop the periodical, Hunt could declare:

I loved Florence and saw nothing in it but cheerfulness and elegance; I loved the name; I loved the fine arts and the old palaces . . . I loved the good-natured, intelligent inhabitants, who saw fair play between industry and amusements; nay, I loved the Government itself, however afraid it was of English periodicals; for at that time it was good-natured also and could 'live and let live', after a certain quiet fashion, in that beautiful bye-corner of Europe, where there were no longer any wars, nor any great regard for the parties that had lately waged them, illegitimate or legitimate. The reigning family were Austrians, but with a difference, long Italianized, and with no great family affection. One good-natured Grand Duke had succeeded another for several generations; and the liberalism of that extraordinary prince the first Leopold, was still to be felt, in a general way, very sensibly.

CHARLES LEVER

The most boldly coloured literary personality to settle in
Florence in the nineteenth century was the best-selling Irish
nóvelist Charles Lever (1806–72). Although his books are
now only obtainable, with difficulty, in second-hand book-
shops, his death elicited from *The Times* the comment,
'Thousands of readers of all ages are deploring Lever's loss as a
personal misfortune.'

What chiefly brought Lever to Florence in 1847 was what
brought many expatriates to the city throughout the
nineteenth century and in the twentieth century up to the
Second World War: the possibility of living there both in
comfort and cheaply. Lever's had, in general, been a robust,
rackety life, in which he had, with some difficulty, qualified as
a doctor at Trinity College, Dublin; had taken to literature in
order to extricate himself from imminent bankruptcy as a
result of his fondness for gambling; had edited the then
prestigious *Dublin University Magazine*; and had finally wandered about Europe with his wife and ever-growing brood of
children, often all but penniless and yet always cheerful,
ebullient, and lavish in his expenditure both on himself and on
others.

Having briefly inhabited apartments in the Palazzo
Ximines-Panciatichi on Borgo Pinti, the family moved to
more spacious ones in the Casa Capponi at Arcetri. A guest
there, Edward Dicey, has left this description of one of those
nights spent in cards, conversation, and drinking which Lever
so much loved:

See again the loveliest scene on which one's eyes ever
gazed. ˙We are standing on a vine-clad terrace on the
hillside of San Miniato; the faint rose tints of the sun,
rising behind the Arno valley, can be seen glistening on
the heights of Fiesole, standing out clear and sharp against
the deep blue of the sky; and from the sea of white mist,
billows rolling at our feet, rise the countless domes and
terraces and belfries of the city of the Medici. It is the
terrace of Lever's house outside the walls of Florence, and

our host, after one of the long nights he loved, has hardly consented to let us go as the daylight crept in through the open windows, and has come with us to the garden gate to show us the way Florencewards. Not 'Addio' we can hear him saying, but 'Ariverdersi.'

Soon after this the Levers made another move, to the Casa Standish (Via San Leopoldo, now Cavour), to which – since he had a passion for amateur theatricals – he was delighted to find a small theatre attached. As the capital of Tuscany, Florence then boasted a British minister, Richard Lalor Sheil, a fellow Irishman and a fellow writer, of whom Lever became a confidant and friend, as he did of his successor, Sir Henry Bulwer-Lytton, later Lord Dalling. Another confidant and friend was Robert, later Lord, Lytton, transferred as attaché from Washington to Florence for a period of four years in 1852. In addition to such company, Lever made friends less elevated. As his nineteenth-century biographer W. J. Fitzpatrick puts it, 'It was Lever's lot [in Florence] to be thrown equally into the society of *diplomats* and demireps, swells and snobs, princes and pretenders, wits and worthies, snarlers and social men!' Lever himself commented that the Florence of that time, like the Florence of today,

contained a good sprinkling of well-dressed, well-got-up men, who daily rise with the very vaguest conception of who is to house them, fire them, light them, and cigar them for the evening. They are an interesting class, and have this strong appeal to human sympathy, that not one of them, by any possible effort, can contribute to his own support. They toil not, neither do they spin.

He himself did toil, as he continued to spin out his vigorous, jolly, episodic novels. But he also spent hours sitting out in cafés, surveying the passing scene; dancing and fencing; entertaining guests after dinner on the terrace of his villa; driving *en grande cavalcade* through the Cascine; or playing cards at the Jockey Club or Il Casino del Nobile. Of the people he met at these last two resorts, he tended to be dismissive. 'The Club abroad is a room where men gamble and talk of gambling, and

no more; it is not a Club. . . . Can you find anything less
clubbable than a set of men like this? You might as well set
before me the stale bonbons and sugar-plums of a dessert for a
dinner as ask me to take such people for associates or even
companions.'

In 1849, the Year of Revolution, Florence underwent a
disagreeable change. Lever wrote:

> The streets, once thronged with gay groups intent on
> pleasure, or hastening from gallery to gallery, are now
> filled with beggars, whose demands too plainly evince
> that the tone of entreaty has given way to open menace.
> Burglaries and street robberies take place in open day, the
> utmost penalty for such offences being a few days',
> sometimes a few hours', imprisonment. . . . Thrice
> within one week the diligence from Bologna to Florence
> was stopped, and the passengers robbed of everything,
> and in one instance, for some imprudent expression of
> anger, severely beaten.

In his essays 'The Italian Question' and 'The Tuscan Revolution', he expressed strong support for the Grand Duke
Leopold, 'whose sincere and single-minded desire for the
happiness of his people has been the mainspring of all his
actions'.

In 1850, Lever found himself in serious financial difficulties,
as the result firstly of two friends defaulting on loans and then
of a loss at cards.

> To retrench in Florence, where we have always lived in
> the best and consequently most expensive set, is im-
> possible. To leave it would incur great expense; and so,
> horned by the dilemma, I am alternately fretting and
> hoping, writing, dining, riding and talking away – to all
> seeming the most easy-minded of mortals, but, as Hood
> said, 'sipping champagne on a tight-rope'.

But like all his recurrent financial crises, this finally resolved
itself when in 1858 he was appointed consul at La Spezia.
'Lever's official labours at Spezzia were not proportioned to
the width of its waters,' comments Fitzpatrick. 'He had little

to do but boat and bask on its beautiful Bay.' The historian
William Lecky has a story from this period:

> I well remember how a large tableful of Italian naval
> officers were electrified by his [Lever's] conversation, and
> especially by the fire and vividness with which he told the
> story of how he, his daughter, and his poodle dog were
> one day upset in the Gulf, and how they swam; Miss
> Lever carrying the dog on her back. When Lever left the
> table I was greatly amused by the exclamation of one of
> the officers, who had known him of old. 'What a wonder-
> ful man that is! I have heard that anecdote again and again;
> but it always seems fresh – there are always new
> incidents.'

The approach of each autumn saw Lever back in Florence,
where he would then spend the next six or seven months. On
one occasion a man who, through the influence of eminent
relations, held a high diplomatic post at the English Legation,
said acidly to Lever: 'Your appointment appears to be a
sinecure. How can you be Consul at Spezzia and live entirely at
Florence? You got it, I suppose, in recognition of your
novels?' Lever replied: 'Yes, sir. I got my position in compliment to my *ante*cedents; you got yours in compliment to your
aunts.' (The jibe has most point if spoken in an Irish accent.)

One of Lever's most welcome guests in Florence was
Thackeray. Together, the two friends would often dine at the
Laura Restaurant, on the corner of Via dei Cerchi and Via della
Condotta. Thackeray, a gourmet, was enthusiastic about the
fish soup for which the restaurant was famous, even writing a
poem about it.

In 1867 Lever, so robust, loquacious, and witty, left
Florence, having been appointed to an even more lucrative
sinecure, a consulship at Trieste. In offering the appointment
Lord Derby said: 'Here is £600 a year for doing nothing; and
you, Lever, are the very man to do it.'

In the failing health of his last decade, Lever always looked
back on his Florence years with nostalgia:

> Although no longer a young man, I had not yet felt one
> touch of age, nor knew myself other than I was at five and

twenty; and it was this conscious buoyancy of tempera-
ment, joined to a shrewder knowledge of life, that im-
parted to me a sense of enjoyment in society for which I
have no word but ecstasy. The unceasing business of life
went on before me like a play, in which, if occasionally
puzzled by the plot, I could always anticipate the denoue-
ment by my reading of the actors. Such a theatre was
Florence in those old Grand-Ducal times – times which,
whatever the political short-comings, were surrounded
with a charm of existence words cannot picture. If it were
an obligation on me to re-live any portion of my life, I
should select this part, even in preference to earlier youth
and more hopeful ambitions.

LANDOR

Walter Savage Landor (1775–1864), then forty-six, first settled in Florence in 1821, after several years of wandering
Europe, during which he quarrelled now with his wife and
now with anyone, however innocuous, to whom he took a
dislike or who happened to get across him. His resolute
mother had long since taken over the administration of his
estate, Llanthony Abbey, and he was, in effect, a high-class
remittance man.

For five years he lived in rooms in the magnificent Palazzo
Riccardi, once the Palazzo Medici, on Borgo degl'Albizzi.
When Cosimo de' Medici, then a frail old man, was being
carried through this palazzo immediately after the death of his
favourite son Giovanni, he is said to have murmured fretfully:
'Too large a house for such a small family.' All too soon
Landor was on the worst possible terms with his landlord, the
Marchese Riccardi. The relationship reached its nadir when
Landor accused the Marchese of having lured away his coach-
man with a mixture of threats and promises of higher wages.
Seeking a personal confrontation with Landor, the Marchese
failed to take off his hat when entering his tenant's apartment.
Landor first struck it off and then gave notice.

On leaving the palazzo, Landor established himself in the

Villa Gherardesca, later called 'Villa Landore', in Maiano. He himself wrote of his Florentine homes:

> From France to Italy my steps I bent,
> And pitched at Arno's side my household tent.
> Six years the Medicean palace held
> My wandering Lares; then they went afield,
> Where the hewn rocks of Fiesole impend
> O'er Doccia's dell, and fig and olive blend.
> There the twin streams in Affrico unite,
> One dimly seen, the other out of sight,
> But ever playing in his smoothen'd bed
> Of polisht stone, and willing to be led
> Where clustering vines protect him from the sun,
> Never too grave to smile, too tired to run.
> Here, by the lake, Boccaccio's fair brigade
> Beguiled the hours, and tale for tale repaid.
> How happy! Oh, how happy had I been
> With friends and children in this quiet scene!
> Its quiet was not destined to be mine;
> 'Twas hard tr keep, 'twas harder to resign.

The reason why 'its quiet was not destined to be mine' was an even more acrimonious quarrel than usual with his wife, at the conclusion of which he resolved to quit both villa and Florence, never to return. But before that he had passed some happy, if also tumultuous, years. In a letter to his sister in 1831, he boasted of having planted two hundred cypresses, six hundred vines, four hundred roses, two hundred arbutuses, seventy bays, and sixty fruit trees 'of the best qualities from France'. He had not had a moment's illness since arriving at the villa and neither had his children. But 'My wife runs after colds' – catching them as a result of her frequent descents into Florence, of which he disapproved. 'We have the best water, the best air, and the best oil in the world. They speak highly of the wine too; but here I doubt . . .'

There were the inevitable rumpuses, however. Accused by a neighbour, secretary at the French Legation, of having interfered with an underground stream which provided the Frenchman's estate with water, Landor pursued a nine-year

feud, culminating in a challenge to a duel which an interven-
tion by the British consul fortunately averted. Servants, artisans, and shopkeepers all complained of verbal and even
physical assaults – on one occasion, displeased with a dish
served up to him, the irate poet hurled his cook out of the
window, only to exclaim in horror 'Good God, I forgot the
violets!' After a sequence of rows with the local authorities, his
deportation was only averted by an appeal to the Grand Duke.
The English community, members of which he had often met
in Lady Blessington's palazzo on the Lungarno, now began to
avoid him, since his aggressiveness was as often directed at
them as at the local people.

On his departure – he made over the villa to his son, Arnold,
and settled a sum on his wife – Landor wrote his farewell to the
place in which he had passed some of his happiest, as well as his
most vexatious, hours:

> I leave thee, beauteous Italy! No more
> From the high terraces, at even-tide,
> To look supine into thy depths of sky,
> The golden moon between the cliff and me,
> Or thy dark spires of fretted cypresses
> Bordering the channel of the milky way.
> Fiesole and Valdarno must be dreams
> Hereafter . . .

Clearly he thought that he would never return. But, having
been obliged to leave England after a ruinous libel case over
some Latin verses lampooning a woman of his acquaintance,
he was back at the villa, now eighty-three years old, in 1858.
After a succession of volcanic quarrels with his family, he was
expelled, another Lear, from the villa by his wife and children,
and threw himself on the mercy of Browning. Browning
behaved with the utmost kindness. Having failed to achieve a
reconciliation between the old man and his family, he arranged
for him to board with Mrs Browning's faithful maid Wilson,
now married to an Italian, in the Via Nunziatina, a stone's
throw from Casa Guidi. By now Landor was suffering from
the deafness of old age. Asking for news of Fanny Trollope
from her son Thomas, he received the answer that she had

grown very deaf. 'Dead? Dead? Well I wish I were too,' he answered. 'No, no,' Tom shouted at him. 'Not *dead*! Deaf.'

In his final domicile Landor was visited by a number of literary admirers, the last of them Algernon Swinburne, who wrote a fine elegy when, soon after this meeting in 1864, the old lion died.

Landor himself had written:

> To my ninth decade I have totter'd on
>   And no soft arm bends now my steps to steady;
> She who once led me where she would, is gone,
>   So when he calls me, Death shall find me ready.

FANNY AND THOMAS ADOLPHUS TROLLOPE

It was in 1843 that the strenuous switchback of her life brought Frances Trollope (1780–1863), then sixty-six years old and already the author of a pot-boiling *A Visit to Italy*, to settle in Florence. With her was the older of her two surviving sons, Thomas Adolphus (1810–92), like his mother a novelist of more perseverance than natural talent.

Their first residence was an apartment in the Palazzo Berti in the Via dei Malcontenti – so named because it was at one time the road to the Florentine equivalent of Tyburn. 'Our house was the one next to the east end of the Church of Santa Croce,' Thomas wrote in his memoirs *What I Remember*. 'Our rooms looked on to a large garden, and were pleasant enough. We witnessed from our windows the building of the new steeple of Santa Croce, which was completed before we left the house.'

'Within a few weeks . . . my mother's home became, as usual, a centre of attraction and pleasant intercourse and her weekly Friday receptions were always crowded,' Thomas noted. Among the guests either there, at a subsequent dwelling in the Via del Giglio, or at the Villino Trollope, a sumptuous residence on the huge, ugly Piazza dell' Indipendenza, were the Brownings, Charles Dickens, Harriet Beecher Stowe, Nathaniel Hawthorne, James Russell Lowell, and

George Eliot and G. H. Lewes. (Subsequently the Villino
Trollope became an hotel. In the spring of 1887 Thomas
Hardy and his first wife, Emily, stayed there, spending much
of their time in the company of the writer 'Leader Scott' – Mrs
Lucy E. Baxter, daughter of Hardy's friend the Dorset poet
William Barnes, and a long-time resident of Florence.)

Not all those who were recipients of the Trollopes' hospitality were always gracious about it. One of Elizabeth Barrett
Browning's letters contains the passage:

> Mrs Trollope has recommenced her 'public' mornings
> which we shrink away from. She 'receives' every Satur-
> day morning in the most heterogeneous way possible. It
> must be amusing to anybody not overwhelmed by it, and
> people say that she snatches up 'characters' for her 'so
> many volumes a year' out of the diversities of masks
> presented to her on these occasions.

The circumstances which eventually enabled Fanny, Thomas, and the wife, Theodosia, whom he had married when
well into his thirties, to live and entertain in such style at the
Villino Trollope were piquant enough to provide the expatriate community with ample opportunity for the gossip which
then, as now, it so much relished. Theodosia's swarthy father,
Joseph Garrow, son of an Indian army officer and a high-caste
Brahmin woman, had married a rich, Jewish widow, twenty-
five years older than himself and the mother of two grown-up
children. At the remarkable age of fifty-nine, this wife was
declared to have given birth to a daughter, Theodosia. Since
the self-effacing daughter of the previous marriage, also called
Fanny, showed her 'step-sister' far more attention than did her
generally disagreeable mother, the obvious presumption is
that Theodosia was in fact Fanny's daughter. This presumption is enforced by the fact that, on her premature death, Fanny
left a surprisingly generous sum of money to Theodosia. It
was largely with this money that the Villino Trollope was
purchased and financed as a centre of Florentine literary life.

Florentine gossip did not end there. For five years Thomas
and Theodosia were childless. Then, despite the fact that
during the summer of 1852 Thomas had rarely been in Flor-

ence, Theodosia announced that she was pregnant. Since the child, Beatrice or 'Bice', looked so much like her mother and in no way like a Trollope, there were inevitable whispers and smiles – to which Browning was to allude in a letter written many years later to his wife's Florentine friend and confidante, Isabel ('Isa') Blagden.

It is astonishing that, despite Anthony Trollope's employment as a civil servant, despite the constant entertaining in which Frances and Thomas indulged during their years in Florence, and despite the fact that Frances did not begin writing until she was fifty-one, the sum total of the published works of the trio, indomitable mother and sons, should have reached three hundred and six.

At a period when spiritualism was so much the vogue, the Villino Trollope was the setting for many a seance, with the world-famous medium Daniel Dunglas Home staying there, at the invitation of Thomas Trollope, for almost a month. It was Home who was to be the prototype for Browning's 'Mr Sludge the Medium'. Observers have reported that even at the mention of Home's name the usually equable Browning would grow pale with passion. Elizabeth Barrett Browning was far more credulous.

Anthony Trollope made a number of visits to his mother and brother, during the third of which he began to write *Dr Thorne*. But he only once used Florence as a setting – perhaps because he felt that, as novelists, Mrs Trollope and Thomas had pre-empted the city. It is in the last third of *He Knew He was Right* that the leading characters find themselves in Florence, Siena and a fictional 'Casalunga'. One of these characters is the American minister to Florence (the city was, at that time, the capital of the country), whose residence Trollope describes as follows:

Mr Spalding at this time inhabited the ground floor of a large palace in the city, from which there was access to a garden which at this period of the year was green, bright, and shady, and which as being in the centre of the city was large and luxurious. From one end of the house there projected a covered terrace, or loggia, in which there

were chairs and tables, sculptured ornaments, busts and
old monumental relics let into the wall in profusion. It
was half chamber and half garden, – such an adjunct to a
house as in our climate would give only an idea of cold,
rheumatism, and a false romance, but under an Italian sky
is a luxury daily to be enjoyed during most months of the
year.

This might be the Villino Trollope itself, as other visitors of
that time have described it.

GEORGE ELIOT

George Eliot (1819–80) and her consort G. H. Lewes paid the
first of their visits to Florence in May 1860, putting up, as so
many literary visitors did at that period, at the Pension Suisse,
situated on the first floor of a house directly opposite the
Palazzo Strozzi, at the corner of the Via Tornabuoni and the
Via della Vigna Nuova. (The number, then 20, is now 13 Via
Tornabuoni.) 'We are at the quietest hotel in Florence,' wrote
Eliot to John Blackwood, 'having sought it out for the sake of
getting clear of the stream of English and Americans, in which
one finds oneself in all the main tracks of travel, so that one
seems at last to be in a perpetual noisy picnic, obliged to be
civil, though with a strong inclination to be sullen. My
philanthropy rises several degrees as soon as we are alone.'
Anyone so wishing to escape from his fellow tourists would
hardly choose a hotel on this site today.

In a letter to John Blackwood's brother William, written
nine days later, Eliot reported that 'There has been a crescendo
of enjoyment in our travels; for Florence, from its relation to
the history of Modern Art, has roused a keener interest in us
even than Rome, and has stimulated me to entertain rather an
ambitious project, which I mean to be secret from every one
but you and Mr John Blackwood.' This 'rather an ambitious
project' had nothing whatever to do with Modern Art or its
history, but was the novel about the life and times of Savonarola which eventually appeared in 1863 as *Romola*.

Having first been fired to the theme by a passage about Savonarola in a guidebook, Eliot, aided by Lewes, plunged into research with characteristic perseverance and energy. Since women then, like Romola herself before them, were not admitted to the monastery of San Marco of which Savonarola was elected prior in 1490, Lewes viewed it for his consort, making copious notes. Next they visited the Great Hall or Sala dei Cinquecento of the Palazzo Vecchio, supposedly built at Savonarola's request in 1495 in order to accommodate the Council of the People after the expulsion of Piero de' Medici. With Perrens's *Jerome Savonarola, sa vie, ses prédications, ses écrits* (Paris 1859) and a copy of Savonarola's own poems, Eliot embarked on the kind of hectic course of reading which one associates with an ambitious undergraduate cramming for the First which might otherwise be beyond his or her mental powers.

Eliot and Lewes returned to Florence in May 1861, on this occasion taking up residence at the Hotel della Vittoria, Lungarno Amerigo Vespucci 10 – 'English landlady' notes Baedeker. Despite the influenza to which first Lewes and then Eliot succumbed, the couple bustled about their research, now visiting churches and museums and now holing themselves up in the Maglibechian Library (now the Biblioteca Nazionale) – which, among other treasures, contains Savonarola's Bible, with his written comments in the margin, and his breviary with an inscription by his pupil Fra Serafino. 'Mr Lewes is kept in continual distraction by having to attend to my wants . . . poking about everywhere on my behalf,' George Eliot wrote to John Blackwood, adding: 'I having very little self-help about me of the pushing and enquiring kind.'

Thomas Trollope, whom they had met during their 1860 visit, was absent from the city for much of this second one. 'We have seen no one but Mrs Trollope and her pretty little daughter, Beatrice, who is a musical genius,' Eliot wrote to Lewes's son Charles. 'She is a delicate fairy, about ten years old, but sings with a grace and expression that make it a thrilling delight to hear her.' Once Thomas had returned home, he set about persuading the visitors to postpone their departure and make with him an expedition to the two celebrated Tuscan monasteries of Camaldoli and La Vernia. 'Neither he nor she were fitted by their habits, or indeed by the conditions of their health, to encounter much "roughing", and a certain amount of that was assuredly inevitable – a good deal more than would be the case now. But if the flesh was weak, truly the spirit was willing!' The nature of this 'roughing' becomes more apparent when Trollope records: 'There followed another night in the cow-house for George Eliot and for us in the convent.'

In her Journal, Eliot wrote of this visit, spent in 'looking at streets, buildings and pictures, in hunting up old books, at shops or stalls, or in reading at the Magliabechian Library,' the apprehensive question 'Will it be all in vain?' Such readers of *Romola* as Tennyson, Mazzini, and Gladstone (who was later also to express extravagant admiration for the works of Marie Corelli) were to answer that question by, in effect, vehemently declaring 'No, of course not!' But Thomas Trollope himself was less certain: 'In drawing the girl Romola, her subjectivity has overpowered her objectivity. Romola is not – could never have been – the product of the period and of the civilisation from which she is described as having issued. There is far too much of George Eliot in her.' Twentieth-century critics have tended to take the same view – as they have of Eliot's Savonarola, portrayed as though he were some fiery non-conformist radical of her own time.

THE BROWNINGS, FREDERICK TENNYSON

In April of 1847, having found Pisa intellectually and socially inert, Robert and Elizabeth Barrett Browning (1812–89 and 1806–61) arrived in Florence on a visit in the company of their friend Anna Jameson – famous in her day as the author of a six-volume *Sacred and Legendary Art*. After an unsatisfactory marriage, culminating in a legal separation when her husband took himself off to Canada, Mrs Jameson had increasingly channelled her ardent emotions into friendships with such notable women as Ottilie von Goethe, Lady Byron, and Elizabeth Barrett Browning – the last of whom she had met through an introduction, strenuously pursued, from Mary Russell Mitford. In her search for the Divine as revealed in painting and sculpture, she inevitably spent a lot of time in Florence.

The 'wild poets but wise people' (as Mrs Jameson described them) first found a comfortable apartment in Via delle Belle Donne, near the Piazza Santa Maria Novella. Mrs Browning was delighted, although overcome by the humid heat so characteristic of Florence during the summer months: 'At Pisa we say "How beautiful!" Here we say nothing; it is enough if we can breathe.' In August, in quest of cooler quarters, they moved to a suite of rooms in the Palazzo Guidi, opposite to the Pitti Palace. It was from the famous 'Casa Guidi Window' that Mrs Browning waited on and then watched the liberation and unification of Italy:

> I heard last night a little child go singing
> 	'Neath Casa Guidi windows, by the church,
> *O bella liberta, O bella!* – stringing
> 	The same words still on notes he went in search
> So high for, you concluded the upbringing
> 	Of such a nimble bird to sky from perch
> Must leave the whole bush in a tremble green,
> 	And that the heart of Italy must beat,
> While such a voice had leave to rise serene
> 	'Twixt church and palace of a Florence street.

It was here that in 1858 Nathaniel Hawthorne, accompanied by his wife Sophia, visited the Brownings. 'We found a spacious staircase and ample accommodation of vestibule and hall, the latter opening on a balcony where we could hear the chanting of priests in a church close by.' Browning greeted them in the anteroom, as did the only child of the marriage, christened Robert but nicknamed Penini by his adoring parents. 'I never saw such a boy as this before; so slender, fragile and spirit-like – not as if he were actually in ill health, but as if he had little or nothing to do with human flesh and blood. His face is very pretty and most intelligent, and exceedingly like his mother's.' Hawthorne continues: 'I should not quite like to be the father of such a boy, and should fear to stake so much interest and affection on him as he cannot fail to inspire. I wonder what is to become of him – whether he will ever grow up to be a man – whether it is desirable that he should.'

Mrs Browning greeted the Hawthornes at the entry to the dining-room: '. . . A pale, small person, scarcely embodied at all; at any rate, only substantial enough to put forth her slender fingers to be grasped, and to speak with a shrill, yet sweet, tenuity of voice. Really, I do not see how Mr Browning can suppose that he has an earthly wife any more than an earthly child; both are of the elfin race, and will flit away from him some day when he least thinks of it . . .'

At first the life of the Brownings was reclusive – 'as to Italian society,' wrote Mrs Browning, 'one may as well take to longing for the evening star, for it seems quite inaccessible.' But soon the fame of the couple, hers then greater than his, attracted people to them. Some of these people – Charles Lever, the buoyant and sometimes even brash best-selling Irish novelist, for example – proved not to their taste. But soon they had assembled a loyal circle around them, the chief member of which was Isabella ('Isa') Blagden, a woman of uncertain origin, with possible Indian blood, who acted as a universal aunt to anyone in trouble or in need in the expatriate community. Isa wished to emulate the literary achievement of her heroine, Mrs Browning; but her talent for writing was inferior to her talent for friendship. 'A little volume of her poems was published after her untimely death,' Thomas Trollope records. 'They are not such as could take by storm the careless ears of the world . . . and must, I suppose, be admitted to be marked by that mediocrity which neither gods nor men can tolerate. But it is impossible to read the volume without perceiving how choice a spirit the authoress must have been, and understanding how it came to pass that she was especially honoured by the close and warm attachment to Mrs Browning.'

'We are as happy,' wrote Browning in December 1847, 'as two owls in a hole, two toads under a tree-stump; or any other two queer poking creatures that we let live after the fashion of their black hearts, only Ba [Mrs Browning] is fat and rosy; yes indeed.' Mrs Browning in turn wrote that, although Browning could not be induced to go out in the evening – 'not even to a concert, nor to hear a play of Alfieri's' – nonetheless 'we scarcely know how the days go, it's such a gallop on the grass.' 'When all's said and sighed, I love Italy – I love my Florence,' she wrote to another correspondent. 'I love "that hole of a place" as Father Prout called it lately, with all its dust, its cobwebs, its spiders even; I love it and with somewhat of the kind of blind, stupid, respectable, obstinate love which people feel when they talk of "beloved native lands". I feel this for Italy, by mistake for England. Florence is my chimney corner, where I can skulk and be happy.'

In 1848 the Brownings moved from furnished rooms in the Casa Guidi to the brighter, more spacious ones, described by Hawthorne and other distinguished visitors, with which they are now associated. The mosquitoes in the garden might be 'worse than Austrians', but the couple had little else of which to complain. For both it was a period of triumphant creativity. Apart from *Casa Guidi Windows*, Mrs Browning also wrote the major part of *Aurora Leigh*, *Poems Before Congress*, and a number of other pieces in support of the liberation and unification of the country whose cause, in company with so many of her fellow expatriates, she had so ardently adopted. There is a parallel between this ardour and that with which non-Spanish writers supported the Republican cause during the Spanish Civil War. Posthumously collected in the volume *Last Poems*, Elizabeth Barrett Browning's later Italian political poems were dedicated by Browning to 'grateful Florence'. Browning produced two of his finest monologues, each a miracle of impersonation, 'Andrea del Sarto' and 'Fra Lippo Lippi', along with 'The Statue and the Bust', and 'Old Pictures in Florence'. 'We neither of us show our work to one another, till it is finished,' Mrs Browning confided in a letter to a friend. 'An artist must, I fancy, either find or *make* solitude to work in, if it is to be good work at all.'

It was in 1853 that Elizabeth Barrett Browning became truly interested in spiritualism. 'You know I am rather a visionary,' she wrote to Mary Russell Mitford, 'and inclined to knock round at all the doors of the present world to try to get out.'

This interest was shared by many of the expatriate community: the Trollopes, whose villa was the setting for many a
seance; Sophia Hawthorne, Nathaniel's wife, who recorded in
her Journal 'Mr Browning cannot believe, and Mrs Browning
cannot help believing'; and Lord Lytton, the future English
ambassador in Paris and Viceroy of India – 'visionary enough
to suit me', Mrs Browning wrote.

Lord Tennyson's brother, Frederick Tennyson (1807–98),
also a poet but one far less gifted than the Laureate – 'It's the
smell of a rose rather than a rose – very sweet notwithstand-
ing,' Mrs Browning wrote of his *Days and Hours* – was another
expatriate in Florence (1850–7) who also came to share the
interest in spiritualism so common at that time in 'the colony'.
At first, admittedly, he was sceptical, writing: 'Browning is a
wonderful man with inexhaustible memory, animal spirits
and bonhomie. He is always ready with the most apropos
anecdote and the happiest bon mot, and his vast acquaintance
with out-of-the-way knowledge and the quaint Curiosity
Shops of Literature make him a walking encyclopaedia of
marvels. Mrs B. who never goes out – being troubled like
other inspired ladies with a chest – is a little unpretending
woman, yet full of power and, what is better, loving-
kindness; and never so happy as when she can venture into the
thick of mysterious clairvoyants, Rappists, Ecstatics and
Swedenborgians.' But in no time at all, Frederick Tennyson
himself had also become the most enthusiastic and gullible
devotee of such people.

For a long period he lived in the Villa Torrigiani above
Doccia, being visited there by his less genial but more eminent
brother, Alfred, in August and September 1851.

In *William Wetmore Story and His Friends*, edited by Henry
James, Story (1819–95), a sculptor and writer of talent,
gives Browning's moving account of the last hours of Mrs
Browning at Casa Guidi on 18 June 1861:

At about three o'clock he was startled by her breathing
and woke her, but she said she was better, and reasoned so
quietly and justly about her state that his fears were again
subdued. She talked with him and jested and gave ex-

pression to her love for him in the tenderest words; then, feeling sleepy, and he supporting her in his arms, she fell into a doze. In a few minutes, suddenly, her head dropped forward. He thought she had fainted, but she had gone for ever. She had passed as if she had fallen asleep, without pain, without thought of death. After death she looked, as Browning told me, like a young girl; all the outlines rounded and filled up, all traces of disease effaced, and a smile on her face so living that they could not for hours persuade themselves she was really dead.

. . . We [Story and his wife] went immediately to Florence, and it was a sad house enough. There stood the table with her letters and books as usual, and her little chair beside it, and in her portfolio a half-finished letter to Mme Mario [née Jessie White, an ardent follower of Mazzini] full of noble words about Italy. Yes, it was for Italy that her last words were written; for her dear Italy were her last aspirations. The death of Cavour had greatly affected her. She had wept many tears for him, and been a real mourner. This agitation undoubtedly weakened her and perhaps was the last feather which broke her down. 'The cycle is complete,' as Browning said, looking around the room; 'here we came fifteen years ago; here Pen was born; here Ba wrote her poems for Italy. She used to walk up and down this verandah in the summer evenings when, revived by the southern air, she first began to enjoy her out-doors life. Every day she used to walk with me or drive with me, and once even walked to Bellosguardo and back; that was when she was strongest. Little by little, as I now see, that distance was lessened, the active outdoors life restricted, until walking had finally ceased. We saw from these windows the return of the Austrians; they wheeled round this corner and came down this street with all their cannon, just as she describes it in "Casa Guidi". Last week when we came to Florence I said: "We used, you know, to walk on this verandah so often – come and walk up and down once. Just once," I urged, and she came to the window and took two steps on it. But it fatigued her too much, and she went back and lay

down on the sofa – that was our last walk. Only the night
she went away for ever she said she thought we must give
up Casa Guidi; it was too inconvenient and in case of
illness too small. We had decided to go away and take a
villa outside the gates. For years she could not give up this
house, but at last and, as it were, suddenly, she said she
saw it *was* too small for us and too inconvenient. And so it
was; so the cycle was completed for us here, and where
the beginning was is the end. Looking back at these past
years I see that we have been all the time walking over a
torrent on a straw. Life must now be begun anew – all the
old cast off and the new one put on. I shall go away, break
up everything, go to England and live and work and
write.'

DOSTOEVSKY

Dostoevsky (1821–81) first visited Florence in August 1861, in
the company of the Idealist critic Nikolai Strakhov, whom he
had met in Geneva. The two of them put up in the Pension
Suisse, opposite the Palazzo Strozzi, in the Via Tornabuoni.
This hotel, used three years earlier by George Eliot and G. H.
Lewes, was then a favourite with foreigners because of its
cleanliness, its quietness, and its comparative cheapness. Literally a minute's walk away, in the Palazzo Buondelmonti, once
the home of Ariosto, in the Piazza Santa Trinita, was situated
the famous Gabinetto Letterario-Scientifico Vieusseux, later
Libreria Vieusseux, to which writers as diverse as Longfellow,
Ruskin, Heine, Stendhal, Browning, and Fenimore Cooper
would resort in order to read foreign newspapers and borrow
foreign books. On this brief visit, little in the museums made
a favourable impression on Dostoevsky. Indeed Strakhov
records that almost as soon as he had entered the Uffizi,
Dostoevsky ran out again. Strakhov also records how, in his
passionate xenophobia, the great author, apostle of universal
brotherhood, insulted a humble waiter, who eventually
chided him: 'Don't you realise that I'm a human being too?'
   To the Pension Suisse Dostoevsky returned with his wife
Anna in November 1868, in order to escape the damp and cold

of Milan, where they had been living for two months. From the Pension Suisse they soon moved to No. 8 (now No. 22) Via Guiccardini, opposite the Pitti Palace, a stone's throw from the Brownings' Casa Guidi. A plaque, set into the façade in 1952, announces: *In questi pressi/ fra il 1868 e il 1869/Fedor Dostoevskij/compi il romanzo 'L'Idiota.'* In her fascinating essay 'Dostoevsky in Florence' [*The Russian Review*, 1964], Katherine Strelsky describes the apartment as follows:

> The house is of the late seventeenth or early eighteenth century, and is not particularly distinguished. The stuccoed brick of its facade is dusky honey-coloured, like all Florentine buildings. It has a plain shabby entrance with a worn stone staircase. . . . The whole floor [the second] is an apartment of eight rooms, four on the front and four on the rear looking out on a cluttered service court. Two large, high, squarish rooms on the center front are flanked by a long narrow one on either side. Today there is no means of heating, but there are two sealed-off fireplaces. In the rear is a large kitchen and a tiny cubicle of a toilet. There is no bath. There has been little or no decorating since 1868. The floors are the original reddish-brown *mattoni* or tiles. One of the large rooms has a crudely painted ceiling. The entire apartment is occupied by a philanthropic institution to provide a home for orphaned young workers. The Dostoevskys did not inhabit the whole of this apartment but two or three rooms, as lodgers on demi-pension terms.

Arthur Hugh Clough (1819–61) had put up briefly in the same house a few years previously.

Dostoevsky was working ferociously on *The Idiot*. But in her *Reminiscences* his wife Anna has recorded the pleasures of those first months. 'I remember his ecstatic reaction to the Cathedral, the church of Santa Maria del Fiore, and the small Chapel del Battistero, in which infants are usually christened.' Dostoevsky was also so much delighted by the bronze doors of the Baptistery that he told Anna that, if he should ever happen to get rich, he would buy photographs of these doors, as large as the originals, so that he could hang them in his study. In the Pitti Palace, he was enthusiastic about Raphael's *Madonna della Seggiola*; and he was also enthusiastic about the same artist's *Saint John in the Desert* in the Uffizi. The Medici *Venus* he considered 'a work of genius'. In the evenings he would read Voltaire and Diderot, borrowed from the Libreria Vieusseux, in their original French.

When Anna became pregnant, Dostoevsky was overjoyed. Such was his concern for her that he concealed from her the part of *War and Peace* – sent out to them by Strakhov – in which the death of Prince Andrei Bolkonsky's wife in childbirth is so poignantly depicted. Since the doctor had prescribed a daily walk for the pregnant woman, she and Dostoevsky would each day go up into the Boboli Gardens where, even in January, there were roses to admire. 'Here we warmed ourselves and dreamed of our happiness to come.'

But dreams of happiness to come were now all too often disturbed for Dostoevsky by three increasingly importunate needs. One of these was for his native Russia. In a letter to his niece Sonya in March 1869, we find him writing: 'I cannot write here. For that I must be in Russia without fail, must see, hear and take a direct part in Russian life; whereas here I am losing even the possibility of writing, since I lack both the essential material, namely, Russian reality (which produces the ideas) and the Russian people.' Intensely xenophobic, he was incapable of using Italy and the Italians as his 'essential material'.

Dostoevsky's second need was for congenial company. As Anna records:

We did not know a single soul in Florence with whom we could talk, argue, joke, exchange reactions. Around us all were strangers, and sometimes hostile ones; and this total isolation from people was sometimes difficult to bear. I remember it occurred to me then that people living in such complete solitude and isolation might, in the final analysis, either come to hate each other or else draw close together for the rest of their lives. Fortunately it was the latter which happened to us. Our enforced isolation compelled us to come even closer together.

At that period there was not, of course, any dearth of Russians in Florence, many of them consumptives in search of health. But such people tended to be one of two things: either aristocrats or rich merchants, who would no more have dreamed of consorting with this novelist of genius than with their grocer, barber, or tailor; or spies or *agents provocateurs* of the Tsarist regime, which was, as Dostoevsky well knew, keeping him under surveillance even in exile.

Dostoevsky's third need was for money. In his lighter moods, he would call himself and his wife Mr and Mrs Micawber; but there were times when the torment of waiting for something to turn up so much exacerbated his nerves that his epileptic fits became more frequent than usual.

Poverty eventually drove them out to a single, cramped room in an apartment overlooking the Mercato Nuovo, the precise address of which has never been established. In a letter to his niece Sonya about this room in a 'tiny dwelling' owned by 'a family [presumably Italian] with whom we are friendly', Dostoevsky describes a hellish three months in the ever-increasing heat of Florence in summer:

Our windows gave on a market square with arcades and splendid granite pillars; in the square was a municipal fountain in the form of a gigantic bronze boar from whose throat the water flowed (it is a classic masterpiece of rare beauty). Well, now reflect that all those arcades and the masses of stone by which the whole square is surrounded, drank in and accumulated all the heat of the sun, and got as scorching as a stove-pipe in a vapour bath – and that was the atmosphere we had to live in. The real heat, that is, the real hell-heat, we had to groan under for six weeks; it was nearly always 34 or 35 degrees Réamur in the shade. You must know that the air, despite this heat and drought (it never once rained) was wonderfully light; the green in the gardens (of which there are astonishingly few in Florence; one hardly sees anything but stones) – the green neither withered nor faded, but seemed brighter and fresher every day; the flowers and the lemon-tree had apparently only waited for the heat; but what astonished me most – me, who was imprisoned in Florence by untoward circumstances – was that the itinerant foreigners (who are nearly all very rich) mostly remained in Florence; new ones even arrived every day. Usually the tourists of all Europe throng, at the beginning of the hot weather, to the German spas. When I saw in the streets well-dressed Englishwomen and even Frenchwomen, I could not conceive why these people, *who had money to get away with*, could voluntarily stay in such a hell. I was sorriest of all for poor Anya. The poor thing was then in her seventh or eighth month, and so suffered dreadfully from the heat. Moreover, the population of Florence spends the whole night on its feet, and there's a ghastly amount of singing. Of course we kept our windows open at night; then, at about five o'clock in the morning, the people began to racket in the market, and the donkeys to bray, so that we could never close an eye.

The only advantage of this almost insupportable heat was that it appeared to have a beneficial effect on the novelist's epilepsy.

Eventually the long-awaited funds arrived and, having paid off their debts to their hosts and others, the couple were able to quit Florence for first Prague and then Dresden. In Florence they had endured loneliness, indigence, and extremes of climate; but Dostoevsky could also write of the city 'When the sun shines, it is almost Paradise. Impossible to imagine anything more beautiful than this sky, this air, this light.' It was in Florence that he not merely completed *The Idiot* but also began the gestation of *The Possessed* and *The Brothers Karamazov*.

Although Elizabeth Barrett Browning had died and Robert Browning had quit the Casa Guidi before Dostoevsky's arrival, Browning continued to frequent the Libreria Vieusseux on his rare visits to Florence. The great Russian novelist and the great English poet might therefore have met – although there is no record of their ever having done so. Here would have been a wonderful subject for an Imaginary Conversation by Browning's old friend Landor.

Ouida

It was in 1871 that Ouida (1839–1908) (born Maria Louise Ramé, of a doting English mother and a wayward French father, but later to call herself, more grandiosely, Louise de la Ramée) arrived in Florence, to remain there for twenty-three years. Described by Max Beerbohm as 'that unique, flamboyant lady, one of the miracles of modern literature', this queen of the circulating libraries is now all too often dismissed as merely another bareback performer on the tosh-horse, for extravagant and wholly undeserved sums, in the circus of literature. Nothing could be further from the truth. There was a great deal of exuberant absurdity in both her life and her novels; but Carl van Vechten was right when he wrote of her, 'Ouida was not an artist, but just as surely she was a genius.'

Used to living and entertaining in hotels – for the previous five years she had made the Langham Hotel her London base, placing in the hall of her suite a notice stating 'Umbrellas and morals to be left at the door' – Ouida, accompanied by her mother, first put up in the Hotel de l'Italie, in the Piazza Ognissanti, which today remains under its new name, Excelsior Italia, the Claridge's of Florence. The sort of luxurious, aristocratic, romantic, and often scandalous life of which she had so often day-dreamed in her novels was now in her grasp as, eager for the company of a writer then as internationally famous as George Sand, the foreign colony hastened to make her welcome. Her biographer Monica Stirling, in her admirable *The Fine and the Wicked*, evokes this life as follows

There was a fancy dress ball at the Comte de Talleyrand's to which the majority of the guests went dressed as their most distinguished ancestors; there was the famous hunt 'Corso' to which everyone including Ouida wore pink coats, followed by a huge dinner-party at Doney's; there was an expedition to Milan to see Garibaldi make one of his last public appearances; there was a trip to San Rossore Grand Ducal park near Pisa, where could be seen the last of the camels introduced in the seventeenth century by Ferdinand de' Medici; later there was the excitement

generated by visits from Queen Victoria, the Duke and
Duchess of Teck, and Queen Victoria's fourth son, Prince
Leopold, Duke of Albany, who became one of Ouida's
admirers.

In addition to all these pleasures, there was the even more
thrilling one of falling in love with the handsome, intelligent,
charming Marchese Lotteria Lotharinga della Stufa, unmar-
ried scion of a family which had first settled in Florence at the
beginning of the thirteenth century. Sadly, it was this nobleman who was to be the unwitting author of most of Ouida's
subsequent troubles.

For ten years, however, all went well between the two,
as they discussed politics – both were ardent admirers of
Napoleon III – literature, and art, and together made a number
of excursions in and around the city as well as to Rome. By
now Ouida and her mother had moved from the hotel into a
sumptuous villa with extensive grounds, rented from the
Marchese Farinola, in Scandicci, some three miles south of
Florence. At this period, the Cavaliere Faenzi described Ouida
to the young Vernon Lee (Violet Paget) as '37, buxom, tall,
very robust, haughty, and taciturn'. Ouida's mother he described as 'a charming old lady'. In a letter to a friend, Vernon
Lee passed on, with what one takes to be the gleeful malice of a
literary aspirant envious of the success of a world-famous
author, a story told to her by this same Cavaliere Faenzi of a
visit to the Villa Farinola. 'Are you fond of art?' Faenzi asked
Ouida. 'I love it,' she declared. 'Look there! There are all
my works.' Faenzi gazed in horror at 'the terrible daubs' which
hung on the walls. Even more at a loss, he asked Ouida who
her master was. 'Master! I never had a master! I would not take
a master on any account.'

Other visitors were kinder in their recollections. In addition
to Ouida's own oil-paintings, they noted such treasures as the
cinquecento Venetian writing-table at which, with frenzied
energy, she wrote at a speed which even Anthony Trollope or
Arnold Bennett might have envied; the two huge golden
eagles once the property of Napoleon I; the della Robbia in the
sacristy; and the bibelots which, in the fashion of the time,

crowded every available space on occasional tables and chimney pieces. Everywhere there were flowers. Offering extravagant hospitality in such a setting, Ouida had no difficulty in attracting anyone of any importance in Florence. But she could be cynical about her social success, remarking: 'The chief difference between Ouida at home and Jumbo at the Zoo is that people visit him in order to give him buns and her in order to receive them.'

Unfortunately, after some ten years an acrimonious rivalry had developed between Ouida and Janet Ross (née Duff Gordon), an intellectual *grande dame* long established, with her ex-banker husband, in the magnificent Villa Gherardo in the Via Settignanese. The cause was della Stufa, who had combined paying discreet court to the eminent and often unladylike lady novelist with continuing to act, as he had long done before Ouida's descent on the scene, as Mrs Ross's *cavaliere servente*. Ouida had convinced herself that della Stufa was eager to marry her; Mrs Ross had convinced herself that this vulgar upstart of a popular novelist had enmeshed her own particular friend, an unwilling victim, in her toils. What was the truth? Ouida put her version of it into an over-heated *roman-à-clef* entitled *Friendship*, in which Lady Joan Challoner, all too clearly Mrs Ross, forces her lover to stick with her against his will, through the expedient of blackmailing him over a crooked business transaction into which, in all innocence, he has been lured by her and her complaisant husband. There was talk of a libel action; of Ouida making unseemly public appeals to della Stufa when he was emerging from his club, the most exclusive in Florence; of Mrs Ross being shot at while standing at her bedroom window; even of Mrs Ross, in one carriage in the fashionable Via Tornabuoni, attempting to horsewhip Ouida in another.

Precisely what was the nature of della Stufa's role in this passionate imbroglio has never been precisely established, but the most satisfactory explanation seems that advanced to the author by Bernard Berenson in 1948. It was Berenson's view that della Stufa, who was never to marry, was a homosexual. He was not Mrs Ross's lover – her husband would probably not have countenanced that – but merely her

devoted companion. He subsequently also became Ouida's
devoted companion. The gossip that was aroused by these two
liaisons served to silence for him any gossip of a more unwel-
come kind in the Florence of that time. To that extent he
welcomed such gossip and even encouraged it. But when
Ouida became more and more insistent that he should marry
her, he took fright at the possible sexual demands that she
might make of him. It was safer to stick with Mrs Ross.

The row between these two women divided Florence – so
that, just as in the past there had been Guelphs and Ghibellines, so now there were Ouida-ites and anti-Ouidaites.
Meanwhile, half-demented over her disappointed hopes,
Ouida began to behave with even more recklessness and to
spend money even more extravagantly. For a while she could
appease her romantic yearnings in the company of the fifty-
three year old Robert Lytton, later to become Viceroy of
India, when he came on a visit to Florence. Although his
father, Edward Bulwer-Lytton, had enjoyed far greater fame,
Robert had himself been praised as a poet under the
pseudonym 'Owen Meredith'. At first, the vain, vague, fop-
pish, romantic Lytton enjoyed the company of this well-
known novelist; then he started to be embarrassed by a
devotion which he could not return. Once more Ouida was
courting derision.

Disasters began to close in on her. The bank in which she
had invested much of her money failed. She quarrelled, largely
through her own arrogance, with her landlord and was brut-
ally evicted by his peasants, pitchforks at the ready. She and
her mother took up residence in a dank thirty-room apartment
in the Palazzo Magnani Ferroni (now Palazzo Amerigi) in the
Via dei Serragli, where their extravagant entertaining continued among a host of yapping and often incontinent dogs.
Her creditors eventually drove her out of this haven, to a
succession of hotels and of rented villas and apartments.
Finally, the Villa della Corona (later the Burns Murdoch
Villa) in Bellosguardo became their home. But despite the
frenzy with which she continued to write, debts again
accumulated. Walpurga Lady Paget, one of the most loyal and
long-suffering of Ouida's friends, describes a visit as follows:

Ouida now inhabits the Villa della Corona, which is very large and dilapidated. Her only furniture seemed to be a plaster cast of Gay's bust, for which she asked me years ago. There were only two or three chairs in the many rooms which I traversed, a pink-and-gold paper hung in rags from the wall, there were no fires, no carpets. A troupe of fluffy and rather dirty white dogs barked at me and then rolled themselves under Ouida's feet, amongst the folds of a draggled black-lace skirt. She wore a mantelet of some once bright but now faded colour, out of which her arms and tiny but ugly hands protruded. Her legs were encased in very bright blue stockings, and her feet in very thin white slippers. She insisted on walking through the lanes with me in this costume, with a white-browney hat with many feathers superadded, and a spotty veil.

In another, smaller villa, La Campora, Ouida's sweet-natured, long-suffering mother fell ill and died. Crazed with grief, Ouida would not for a long time allow the body to be moved to the paupers' section of the Allori cemetery. When sympathetic friends sent her cheques, she would often tear them up; when they sent food, she would give it to her dogs. Eventually, once more evicted for non-payment of rent, she took herself off to Lucca, where her tragic situation deteriorated even further. It is in Lucca that she is buried.

According to Lina Waterfield, Janet Ross's handsome and accomplished niece, her aunt placed a copy of *Friendship*, its binding removed, for use in her guest lavatory. On Ouida's death, an English journalist approached her rival for help with an obituary notice. Her by now white hair and her white dress adding to the dignity of her bearing, Janet Ross answered him: 'You want to know about Ouida? But who is Ouida?'

That a woman who led Ouida's kind of existence should have written with greater perspicacity of the Italians than any English novelist with the possible exceptions of E. M. Forster and D. H. Lawrence must be cause for amazement. In her biography, Monica Stirling rightly singles out the 1881 *A Village Commune* as the most remarkable of all

her works. How did she acquire such knowledge and understanding of the lives of peasants struggling against an
oppressive bureaucracy? One can only wonder at a miracle of
empathy.

JOHN RUSKIN

Despite its schoolmarmish tone and despite the passing of
more than a century since its first publication, Ruskin's *Mornings in Florence* remains a golden key to the city and its
treasures. But both his diaries and his autobiography *Praeterita*
give the impression that there were many occasions when,
fretful or even furious, he had no wish to spend another
morning or indeed any other time of day there.

A highly-strung, prudish, talented, and diligent youth of
twenty-one, he had embarked in 1840 on a Victorian version
of the Grand Tour in the company not of the customary tutor
or cicerone but of his doting parents. On his arrival in Florence,
he recorded in his diary: '. . . My present feelings are of
grievous disappointment. The galleries, which I walked
through yesterday, are impressive enough; but I had as soon be
in the British Museum, as far as enjoyment goes, except for the
Raphaels.' The 'Newgate-like palaces' were 'rightly hateful';
the inside of the Duomo 'a horror'; its exterior 'a Chinese
puzzle'. All the sacred art was 'mere zero' – as it was, he
concluded, to the Italians themselves – and the surrounding
countryside, 'dead wall and dusty olive', was equally un-
appealing. Everything, in short, was 'a provocation and
weariness, except for one master, M. Angelo.'

When he returned five years later, this time with no companion other than a Swiss guide, he was more open to the
beauty of the architecture and art. Excitedly 'scribbling notes
on my arm in the galleries', he was overwhelmed by such
'wonderful things' as Gozzoli's *Procession of the Magi* in the
Medici-Riccardi Chapel and the Ghirlandaios in the choir of
Santa Maria Novella. 'Progressive, but much puzzled', he
gazed at building and pictures; he thought; he wrote; he drew
and painted. But the Florentines themselves precipitated in

him a constant undercurrent of irritation, sometimes even hatred. Like visitors today, he was infuriated by the endless restoring that went on – largely as a result of previous neglect: 'They expose their pictures to every species of injury, rain, wind, cold, workmen, and then they paint them over to make them bright again.' The Italians, he concluded in one particularly violent paroxysm of rage, were 'lazy, lousy, scurrilous, cheating, lying, thieving, hypocritical, brutal, blasphemous, obscene, cowardly, earthly, sensual, devilish'. Eventually, in July, he was propelled out of the city and to his beloved Switzerland – so orderly, so calm, so clean – by the 'buzz-buzz-bang-bang' of the innumerable festivals taking place during that month.

Ruskin was to pay other brief visits to Florence during his later years; but these two, in his early twenties, were the decisive ones. From them came his *Mornings in Florence*; and it was as a result of them that he wrote a famous letter to *The Times*, on his return to England in 1845, to urge that no more pictures by Guido Reni or Rubens should be bought by the National Gallery, while it contained not a single work by Ghirlandaio or Fra Angelico and not a single important one by Bellini or Perugino.

JAMES FENIMORE COOPER, NATHANIEL HAWTHORNE, JAMES RUSSELL LOWELL, HARRIET BEECHER STOWE, MARK TWAIN

After a sojourn in England, during which he found at least as much to criticize as to admire, James Fenimore Cooper (1789–1851) and his ailing wife travelled south through Germany and Switzerland to Italy in 1828. Their conveyance was a 'a roomy family carriage, coachman's box in front and rumble behind'. One suspects that it was to escape his women-folk that Cooper often sat on the box. At her first sighting of Mont Blanc in the distance, Mrs Cooper exclaimed: 'What a beautiful cloud.'

Arriving in Florence in the autumn, they stayed briefly at the English York Hotel on Via de' Cerretani, before settling in the

Palazzo Ricasoli (Piazza Goldoni), its rooms so large and damp that they shocked their Italians friends by the extravagance with which they piled wood on every fire. Mrs Cooper wrote to her father: 'Mr Cooper has almost affronted the Lords, the Dukes, and Princes by declining their invitations – but after satisfying Curiosity, we thought it would be quite as wise to stay at Home, and save Purse for other Purposes.' Nonetheless, Cooper consented to a farewell audience, in court dress, with the Grand-Duke Leopold. He also met the Count Saint-Leu, son of King Louis of Holland and husband of Napoleon's sister Charlotte, and Napoleon's mother, Madame Mère. Throughout this period, he was constantly comparing the English and the Italians, to the disadvantage of the former. The Italians, he commented – as people comment even today – take a pride in waiting on others, while the English merely consider that it demeans them; the Italians have a natural aesthetic sense, the English are philistines. With the coming of summer, the Coopers moved up into a villa in the hills.

It was on 24 May 1858 that Nathaniel Hawthorne (1804–64), his wife Sophia, and his three children set off from Rome to Florence. 'We had a nice old vetturino [coachman], Gaetano by name,' Sophia recorded, 'who looked like a good New England farmer, face placid and gentle, and not at all Italian in colour or expression. Our carriage was of the usual long and cumbersome fashion, with seats inside for four, and a coupé in front for two, in the form of a chaise – and in front of the coupé, a box for the vetturino. Our luggage was bestowed upon the top, and behind, reaching out many a rood, so that with four, and sometimes six horses, we have an effect of an endless arrangement of human affairs.' The journey took eight days.

The Casa del Bello, 36 Via de' Serragli, found for the Hawthornes by the American sculptor Hiram Powers, long a resident of Florence, delighted them with its spaciousness. 'We have the first *piano*,' Sophia wrote, 'which opens at the back upon a broad terrace, leading down into a garden full of roses, jessamine, orange and lemon trees, and a large willow-tree, drooping over a fountain in the midst. We have thirteen rooms on the one *piano*, beside four kitchen rooms beneath.

The Casa is three rooms wide, and four deep – (*five* in one of the rows) – and we are, each one, perfectly accommodated, and each can be alone and remote from each other.' The price was 'only fifty dollars per month (entirely furnished even to silver and linen)'. She concluded, with good reason: 'It is the very luxury of comfort.'

The next morning, she and her husband visited Powers's studio at 111 Via de' Serragli: 'I had hurried glimpses of a bust of Mr Sparks, of California, and Mrs Ward, as Psyche, with a butterfly as a jewel, clasping the bands of her hair.' That Powers should be plying his vocation in Florence of all cities was rather as though one's favourite American aunt were to be discovered making Brownies in the Tour d'Argent. Despite the heat and despite the increasing boredom and irritability of their daughters, Una and Rose, the family spent day after day in sightseeing. 'Florence', Sophia declared, 'is a place to live and be happy in – so cheerful, so full of art, and so *well paved*.' There were old friends to see. Among new friends there were the Brownings – 'a grasp of Mr Browning's hand gives a new value to life', and Mrs Browning's 'fairy fingers seem too airy to hold'.

On 29 June there was a horse race through the city, to which Sophia took Una and Rose. The royal carriage was obliged to stop for three or four minutes precisely opposite the place where the Hawthornes were seated, so that Sophia was able to 'stare straight into the faces of the Grand Duke and the Duchess'. She did not like what she saw. 'The Grand Duke looked like a monkey, with an evil expression, most ugly and mean. The lady has not a ray of beauty left.' Later she reverts to the Grand Duke's unattractiveness: 'The Grand Duke has that frightful, coarse, protruding under lip, peculiar to the court of Austria, and formerly of Spain. It is worth while to extinguish the race, for the sake of expunging that lip and all it signifies. No man with such a mouth can love liberty or spiritual things.'

For August and September, when the heat would be at its worst, the Brownings' ever-helpful friend Isa Blagden persuaded the Hawthornes to move up to the Villa Montuato, close to her own villa on the Bellosguardo hill. Here were

'multitudinous halls and chambers – with deeply shaded avenues; clear, smooth lawn and semicircular terraces – a strong,
old, gray-stone tower, at one end, where owls do whoop and
hoot and sit, "to warm their wit", and in which Savonarola
was imprisoned.' This was the 'Monte Beni' of Hawthorne's
The Marble Faun. At peace, no longer distracted by sightseeing
or too many visits and visitors, Hawthorne was at last able to
settle down to writing. 'Would that he had been able to stay
there for years,' his son Julian was later to remark, 'for had he
continued in an atmosphere which so admirably suited him,
there might have been not just one more romance to be
published but a whole series.'

In his Life of Hawthorne, Henry James estimates what must
have been the effect of Italy on a fellow New Englander and a
fellow novelist:

> Hawthorne's experience had been narrow. His fifty years
> had been spent, for much the larger part, in small Amer-
> ican towns . . . and he had led exclusively what one may
> call a village life . . . In other words, and to call things by
> their names, he was exquisitely and consistently prov-
> incial . . . I know nothing more remarkable, more
> touching, than the sight of this odd, youthful-elderly
> mind, contending so late in the day with the new op-
> portunities for learning old things, and, on the whole,
> profiting from them so freely and gracefully.

There then follows the barb, which James administered with
all the skill of a master dentist sticking a hypodermic needle
into a gum. 'His Italian notebooks are very pleasant reading,
but they are less interesting than the others; for his contact
with the life of the country, its people and its manners, was
simply that of the ordinary tourist – which amounts to saying
that it was extremely superficial.'

While Hawthorne pressed on with the novel that was
to become *The Marble Faun*, Sophia continued to take the
refractory children sightseeing. Finally, on 1 October, the
Hawthornes 'threw a parting glance – and rather a sad one –
over the misty Val d'Arno' and made their way, once more by
easy stages, back to Rome.

James Russell Lowell (1819–91) paid three visits to Flor-
ence: in 1851, when he and his first wife, Maria, rented Casa
Guidi from the Brownings; in 1856 after his first wife's death,
when he stayed for about two months at the Hotel Europe in
Piazza Ferroni; and in 1873, with his second wife, Fanny,
when he stayed for several months at the Hotel du Nord in the
Palazzo Bartolini-Salimbeni, Via delle Terme. This last visit
coincided with one by Henry James, so that the two New
Englanders were able to take wary stock of each other.
Lowell's letters rarely produce a comment of any interest
about the city; and his *Leaves from my Journal in Italy and
Elsewhere* is equally barren.

Harriet Beecher Stowe (1811–96), as famous in Europe as in
America after the success of *Uncle Tom's Cabin*, was in
Florence in 1857, staying in a large apartment in the Casa
Boccini. The Brownings, who were far from sure whether
they would like her or not, at once succumbed to her energy,
directness and palpable decency. She disclaimed all credit for
her book, saying to Elizabeth Barrett Browning: 'I, the author
of *Uncle Tom's Cabin*? No, indeed! The Lord Himself wrote it,
and I was but the humblest instrument in His hand. To Him
alone be all the praise.'

She and Elizabeth Barrett Browning soon found a
shared interest in spiritualism On 16 January 1860, she
wrote to her husband in America about the consolation
which a medium had brought her for the loss of their son,
Henry:

What you said about your spiritual experiences in feeling
the presence of dear Henry with you, and, above all, the
vibration of that mysterious guitar, was very pleasant to
me. Since I have been in Florence I have been distressed by
inexpressible yearnings after him, – such sighings and
outreachings, with a sense of utter darkness and separation, not only from him but from all spiritual communication with my God. But I have become acquainted
with a friend through whom I receive consoling impressions of these things – a Mrs E., of Boston, a very
pious, accomplished and interesting woman, who has

had a history much like yours in relation to spiritual manifestations.

Mark Twain (1835–1910) paid four visits to Florence, two of them as a transient and two as a resident. The result of his first visit in 1867 was his gruff, bluff, no-nonsense *The Innocents Abroad*. In September 1892 he rented the Villa Viviani (now Belvedere) in Settignano. Both delighted and embarrassed by its twenty-eight rooms – emotions shared by many expatriates when first entering their rented apartments or villas – he named the Grand Salon 'the Sahara Desert'. It was during this stay of a little over a year that, in a manner reminiscent of the characters in the *Decameron*, he entertained Janet Ross's guests at the Villa Gherardo in Settignano with a succession of stories, while an influenza epidemic raged in the city below them.

In 1903 he returned to Florence with his by then seriously ailing wife, in the ineffectual hope that the climate would somehow bring about a cure. He rented the Villa di Quarto and began to write *A Year at Florence*. He was negotiating to buy a villa when his wife died.

HENRY JAMES

Henry James (1843–1916) first arrived in Florence, as a twenty-six-year-old tourist, in October 1869, staying at the Hotel de l'Europe in the Piazza Santa Trinita. He had deliberated about going into a *pensione* but had decided against it, since, with the self-consciousness and shyness of youth, he wished to avoid 'public tables', i.e. being obliged to eat in the company of others. An apartment, he decided, would be 'lonesome' and also too costly for his means.

When not writing enthusiastically to his family about the marvels of the city (the Uffizi and the Pitti Palace were '*incroyables*'), he wrote to complain, in anxiety and depression, about the state of his digestion. To his sister, Alice, for example, he reported: 'I am very sorry to say (if you'll allow me to mention the topic) that in spite of the most religious prudence (and I have learned many things) my digestive organs are the bane of my existence and so long as this state of things continues I must ensure myself the best conditions in the way of food and lodging.' After three weeks of 'communing with the immortals' in picture galleries and churches, he was still no better, writing to his father

> . . . I have been in a very bad way. Shortly after getting here I was so knocked up that I had to take to my bed and have the doctor and have since been in his hands. He plies me with drugs, but to no purpose: I only seem to get worse. . . . I don't know whether to think that the Italian air has anything to do with the matter . . . I feel as if I couldn't live a week longer in my present pernicious condition. I'm not impatient: I have given the thing a fair chance and my present condition, which is all that has come of my patience, is quite unendurable. . . . My malady has done a great deal towards spoiling Florence for me . . . The question is of course what to do, inasmuch as I've pretty nearly exhausted expedience. I've almost made up my mind to depart straight from Italy and take refuge at Malvern again.

From all this, the reader might naturally assume that James had fallen victim to the disorder to which travellers to the Mediterranean countries are most susceptible. The revelation contained in a subsequent letter to his philosopher brother William therefore comes as a surprise: 'My back . . . is so chronically affected by my constipated state that there are times when I can hardly drag myself about. Half the week I can eat not a single meal a day; I can't possibly find room for more – and this in spite of getting very tired and passably hungry with all my poking about.' What William, somewhat heartlessly, referred to as his novelist brother's 'moving internal drama' – perhaps 'unmoving' would have been a more a suitable epithet – was finally solved by a Dr Duffy, who prescribed what sounds like an extraordinarily drastic remedy: 'sulfuric acid' pills.

James was back in Italy three years later in 1872. Initially he settled in Rome, where he began to plan what he habitually called his first novel, *Roderick Hudson*, even though *Watch and*

Ward was written earlier. May 1873 found him once more at
the Hotel de l'Europe in Florence. But he was undecided
whether to stay in the city or to 'shuffle off'. On the one hand
there was 'little heat to speak of'; but on the other the
'obstinately relaxing' atmosphere had resulted in another bout
of 'perfect torpor and inaction of the bowels', so that he had
become 'as yellow as an orange'. In addition, Rome – 'so
wondrous in retrospect' – had murdered Florence for him: 'her
great smiting hands have snapt the tender cords to which
Florence appeals.' Within two weeks, he had departed for
Switzerland.

Back in Florence in October of that same year, he was now
delighted with it. Most of the people whom he met were New
England friends of his family, either briefly in Florence in the
course of a European tour or as temporary residents. Soon his
brother William had joined him, their period of cohabitation
eventually providing much of the material for one of James's
least known novels, *Confidence*. William was as indefatigable a
sightseer as his brother, and physically far more robust. His
talk about all that he had seen during his expeditions about the
city was, Henry declared, 'most suggestive'.

After a few weeks in Rome, the brothers returned to
Florence in January 1874. Once again, a comparison with the
capital worked to the detriment of Florence, which now
seemed 'a vulgar little village', 'the region of chapped lips and
chilblains', after the sunshine and warmth of the Pincio, where
they had been living.

However, as the memory of the sonorous music which
Rome played on his imagination began to fade, James once
more succumbed to the smaller city's charms. Among those
whom the brothers now saw were James Russell Lowell and
his wife. Henry had one bout of illness – 'an affair chiefly of the
head', 'a strange and mysterious visitation' – but recovered
after ten days. In February, Willy left to continue his travels to
Germany, but Henry remained, working at his *Florentine
Notes*. By now Henry was *contentissimo*: 'The spring is coming
on bravely and the lights and shadows on the mountain and the
river, the sunsets and the moonlights, the walks in the dim
palace-bordered streets whose shadow is now losing its winter

chill – are all quite worth enjoying.' Unfortunately the *pensione*, the Corona d'Italia, was 'odiously full of new-comers'.

After a spell in Pisa and Lucca, James returned to an apartment, 10 Piazza Santa Maria Novella, on the corner of the Via della Scala, where he declared that he was 'established *à merveille*'. When not working with his usual industry at *Roderick Hudson* – of which he was later to write to Robert Louis Stevenson that it was the work 'in which my little muse first tried to elongate her little legs' – and also at an amazing profusion of articles, he would make solitary excursions around the city or attend this or that hostess's reception. His favourite eating place was Victor's in the Via de' Rondinelli, where he would escape from his own company by conversing with the flower-girl who, like Florentine flower-girls today, would badger men to buy rosebuds either for their button-holes or for the women who were with them. At that time, he confessed to feeling that James Russell Lowell, of whom he was seeing a lot during the American poet's visit to the city, was unlikely to reveal anything new of mind or character to him, and that their friendship was therefore unlikely to develop further. There he was wrong.

In May, he attended 'for information's sake' a 'very brilliant ball' given by the Jockey Club at their Casino in the Cascine. Present was 'a concentration of the elite of Florentine society', with 'more tiaras of diamonds, ropes of pearls and acres of *point de Venise*' than he had ever seen before.

Soon after that, the intense heat of summer had driven away most of the expatriate colony. Looking out through the shutters of his apartment on to the wide, glaring piazza below, he recorded: 'It [the sun] shines so as to scorch the eyes: in the shade on one side is huddled a cab-stand with the drivers all asleep on their boxes and a collection of loungers of low degree and no costume to speak of lying flat on their faces on the stones and courting the siesta.' Within days, fleeing this heat like his American friends before him, he had arrived on Lake Como.

James was briefly back in Florence in the spring of 1880, now staying at the Hotel de l'Arno. Everything seemed to him 'quite too lovely', as he enjoyed 'a holiday pure and simple' before embarking on his long novel *Portrait of a Lady*, for much of which Florence and its environs provide the setting. From his open bedroom window he could look out at the yellow-green Arno and 'the little overhanging cabins of the Ponte Vecchio' directly below him. It was all 'divinely beautiful'. From here he wrote to J. W. Cross, to express his 'sympathy' on his recent marriage to George Eliot. Since Cross, twenty-one years George Eliot's junior, was to attempt to drown himself in a canal during their honeymoon in Venice, the choice of word was perhaps, as so often with James, the right one.

The most enjoyable and, perhaps for that reason, the most productive of all Henry James's journeys to Italy was that which he made from December 1886 to June 1887. For the most part he stayed as the pampered guest or the tenant of friends in their luxurious palazzi or villas. In Florence he was briefly at the Hotel du Sud; but his usual address was the Villa Brichieri in Bellosguardo, in which he had taken a three weeks' let of an apartment belonging to Constance Fenimore Woolson, an 'almost impracticably deaf', fussy American spinster, herself a novelist of indifferent talent, and which he and Miss Woolson were subsequently to share for a brief period. Her shy, yearning involvement with him was far stronger than his decorous, wary involvement with her, and it was no doubt largely because of this disparity that she eventually took her life, leaving him a legacy of puzzlement and remorse. In the Villa Brichieri he wrote *The Aspern Papers* and worked on a number of stories and essays and his study of Robert Louis Stevenson.

Looked after by 'a queer old melancholy male cook', he would 'go out' to be 'lionized' (he himself used the inverted commas) by 'a very thin and flimsy society'. 'My poor clever, tactless and tasteless (intellectually) friend Vernon Lee lives here with a paralyzed step-brother (from the legs down) formerly in diplomacy, and she and he are altogether the best people for talk – and indeed the only ones,' he wrote to one correspondent, Grace Norton. In a later letter to her, he wrote that:

The most intelligent person in Florence is Violet Paget (Vernon Lee) who has lived here all her life, and receives every day from 4 to 7, and as often in the evening as people will come to her. She is exceedingly ugly, not 'well off', disputatious, contradictious and perverse; has a clever, paralysed half-brother, Edward Hamilton [in fact, Eugene Lee-Hamilton (1845–1907), who eventually recovered from a paralysis clearly psychosomatic in origin], formerly in diplomacy – who is always in her salon, bedridden or rather sofa-ridden – and also a grotesque, deformed, invalidical, *posing* little old mother and a father in the highest degree unpleasant, mysterious and sinister, who walks *all day*, all over Florence, hates his stepson, and hasn't sat down to table with his family for twenty years. Yet in spite of all these drawbacks, Miss Paget's intellectual and social energy are so great, that she attracts all the world to her drawing-room, discusses all things in *any* language, and understands some, drives her pen, glares through her spectacles and keeps up her courage. She has a *mind* – almost the only one in Florence.

In 1893, Henry James's brother William was again in Florence on a visit, during which he expressed to Mary Berenson, wife of Bernard Berenson, his disgust at the manner in which Vernon Lee had portrayed his brother Henry in her novel *Vanitas*. Branding Lee 'a most dangerous woman' and seemingly unaware that his brother had similarly used friends as prototypes for characters in his fiction, William James expressed the intention of writing to tell her that he wished to have no more to do with her.

By the time that he came to write the second of his letters to Grace Norton, Henry James was living in the Palazzo Giustinian-Recanati, which formed a kind of guest annexe to the even more sumptuous mansion in which his American hostess, Mrs (Katherine De Kay) Bronson had been living for a decade. Browning had also been a guest of Mrs Bronson in the same guest annexe, so that James could boast of writing at the same desk at which the poet had composed 'crabbed verses'.

Browning and his son Pen were now looking for a Florentine palazzo of their own, James reported.

James's other hostesses – 'rather entertaining women' – included a niece of Byron's Teresa Guiccioli; Janet Ross (1842–1927) at her magnificent Villa Gherardo; and the splendidly named Baroness Zunch, a kind of Florentine Madame Verdurin, whose *salon* attracted people with literary, artistic, and musical aspirations.

In April, James was back at the Villa Brichieri from Venice. He had now made it a rule not to accept luncheon engagements, since 'it is necessary to my salvation to make a *long* morning' and so 'to deny myself the pleasure of a festive noon'. During this second spell in Florence, he took part in the fête to celebrate the unveiling of the completed front of the Duomo. In the course of these festivities, he committed 'the fatuity' of cladding himself in scarlet and black quattrocento dress before attending a ball, given to the King and Queen, in 'a wonderful tapestried hall' of the Palazzo Vecchio. He also met the then highly popular but now almost wholly forgotten English novelist Rhoda Broughton (1840–1920), who was on a visit to Italy. He decided that, in spite of her 'roughness', he liked her – and liked her even more for her liking Florence so much. There is, incidentally, more than a little of Rhoda Broughton in the lady novelist, Miss Lavish, in E. M. Forster's *A Room with a View*.

E. M. FORSTER, D. H. LAWRENCE, NORMAN DOUGLAS

In October 1901, E. M. Forster (1879–1970) and his indomitable mother arrived in Florence during the course of what he was later to call 'a very timid outing' from England to Italy. They stayed briefly at the Albergo Bonciani, Via de' Panzani, before moving on to the Pensione Simi, 2 Lungarno delle Grazie. Of the Cockney landlady of this pensione Forster was to write to the musicologist E. J. Dent: 'She scatters Hs like morsels and calls me "the young gentleman".' Oliver Stallybrass, editor of the Abinger Edition of the works of

E. M. Forster, writes in his notes to *A Room with a View* that the Simi must have been located within the present Hotel Jennings-Riccioli. Forster himself declared of the *pensione* in *A Room with a View:* 'The Bertolini=the Pension Simi'.

Since Forster's three stays in Florence in 1901, 1902, and 1903 can be totalled in weeks and during those years he spent only a few months in Italy as a whole, it is remarkable that his two Italian novels, *A Room with a View*, its first part set in Florence, and *Where Angels Fear to Tread*, much of it set in Tuscany, should have defined the Italian national character for so many English people of his generation and of two or three generations after. *A Passage to India*, the fruit of a not much longer stay in India, did the same thing for that country and its inhabitants.

D. H. Lawrence (1885–1930) and Frieda von Richthofen, then not his wife, had twice lived in Italy before the First World War; but it was not until 1919 that they first visited Florence, putting up at the Pensione Balestri, Piazza Mentana 5, at the suggestion of Norman Douglas, who was already himself living there. In *Aaron's Rod*, the protagonist, Aaron, arrives in Florence to enter, on a whim, the 'pension Nardini', 'a big old Florentine house, with many green shutters and wide eaves' in the Piazza Mentana (Lawrence was little bothered about concealing his literal transcription of his immediate experiences).

Having asked about a room, Aaron is shown by a 'bewildered, wild-eyed servant maid' into 'a heavily gilt, heavily-plush drawing-room with a great deal of frantic grandeur about it.' He there cools his heels for half an hour before the arrival of the proprietress: 'a stout young lady – handsome, with big dark-blue Italian eyes, but anaemic and too stout.' She leads him up the rambling house to the top floor; then along a passageway; and finally into 'a big bedroom with two beds and a red-tiled floor – a little dreary, as ever – but the sun was just beginning to come in, and a lovely view of the river towards the Ponte Vecchio, and at the hills with their pines and villas and verdure opposite.' It is a perfect evocation of the kind of *pensione* – Miss Godkin's, Miss Plucknett's, Mme Jenny Giachino's, the Jennings-Riccioli, the Levelis-Marke, the Bertelli-Scott – in which foreign visitors put up in the days before package tours and 'en suite facilities'.

Aaron is contented with his accommodation, as Lawrence was.

He rather liked the far-off remoteness in the big old Florentine house: he did not mind the peculiar dark, uncosy dreariness. It was not really dreary: only indifferent. Indifferent to comfort, indifferent to all homeliness and cosiness. The over-big furniture trying to be impressive, but never to be pretty or bright or cheerful. There it stood, ugly and apart. And there let it stand. Neither did he mind the lack of fire, the cold sombreness of his big bedroom. At home, in England, the bright grate and the ruddy fire, the thick hearth-rug and the man's arm-chair, these had been inevitable. And now he was glad to get away from it all. He was glad not to have a cosy hearth, and his own arm-chair. He was glad to feel the cold, and to breathe the unwarmed air. He preferred the Italian way of no fires, no heating. If the day was cold, he was willing to be cold too. If it was dark, he was willing to be dark. The cosy brightness of a real home – it had stifled him till he felt his lungs would burst. The horrors of real domesticity. No, the brutal Italian way was better.

Many expatriates in Florence at that period – whether writers and artists, retired folk, or people living on slender unearned incomes – had fled their native countries precisely because, like Lawrence and his Aaron, they had wished to escape 'the cosy brightness of a real home' and preferred 'the brutal Italian way'.

One of Aaron's acquaintances in Florence is a young, upper-class Englishman, Francis, obviously homosexual – although, at that period, Lawrence had to convey this merely by implication. Francis talks, with his over-expressive flamboyance, about the English community: 'Oh, they are such queer people! Why is it, do you think, that English people abroad go so very *queer* – so ultra-English – *incredible!* – and at the same time so perfectly impossible? But perfectly imposs-

ible! Pathological, I assure you. And as for their sexual behaviour – oh, dear, don't mention it. I assure you it doesn't
bear mention. And all quite flagrant, quite unabashed – under
the cover of this fanatical Englishness. But I couldn't begin to
tell you all the things. It's just incredible.'

Francis takes Aaron to a party at which many of the guests
are literary, artistic, or musical. Among them are James
Argyle, based on Norman Douglas; Walter Rosen, based on
Bernard Berenson; and Algy Constable, based on Reginald
(Reggie) Turner, an adoring acolyte at the altar of Oscar
Wilde, to whom he had remained loyal at a period when so
many of those who had once relished his company were either
spitting or turning their backs on him. It was Reggie Turner, a
justly unread novelist, who, when Somerset Maugham was
boasting about the rarity of his first editions, piped: 'It's my
second editions which are so rare. They simply do not exist.'

At the party, Argyle–Douglas launches an attack on
chastity.

Where's the soul in a man that hasn't got a bedfellow – eh?
– answer me that! Can't be done, you know. Might as
well ask a virgin chicken to lay you an egg. But believe
me, there's far more damned chastity in the world, than
anything else. Even in this town. Call it chastity, if you
like. I see nothing in it but sterility. It takes a rat to praise
long tails. Impotents set up the praise of chastity – believe
me or not – but that's the bottom of it. The virtue is made
out of the necessity . . .

When Argyle–Douglas 'lays into' poor little Algy–Turner –
he describes him as one of those 'little old maids who do their
knitting with their tongues' – Aaron–Lawrence cannot help
being charmed by 'a certain wicked whimsicality'. 'He must
have been very handsome in his day,' Aaron–Lawrence decides, 'with his natural dignity, and his clean-shaven strong
square face. But now his face was all red and softened and
inflamed, his eyes had gone small and wicked under his bushy
eyebrows. Still he had a presence. And his grey hair, almost
gone white, was still handsome.'

Anyone who knew Douglas in his later years will at once
recognize the accuracy of this portrait.

Lawrence had gone to Florence ahead of Frieda, who joined
him a few days later. Meeting her train at four in the morning,
he insisted on showing her the city at once. For this purpose he
hired one of the open carriages, then so common and so cheap,
outside the station. Frieda, far too robust to feel tired despite
her long journey, describes the experience as follows:

> I saw the pale crouching Duomo and in the thick moon-
> mist the Giotto tower disappearing at the top into the sky.
> The Palazzo Vecchio with Michelangelo's *David* and all
> the statues of men, we passed. 'This is a men's town,' I
> said, 'not like Paris, where all the statues are women.' We
> went along the Lungarno, we passed the Ponte Vecchio,
> in that moonlight night, and ever since Florence is the
> most beautiful town to me, the lily town, delicate and
> flowery.

All the English were kind to the couple: they still had, wrote
Frieda, 'a sense of true hospitality, in the grand manner.'
Nonetheless, 'it all struck me as being like "Cranford", only it
was a man's "Cranford". And the wickedness there seemed
like old maids' secret rejoicing in wickedness. Corruption
is not interesting to me, nor does it frighten me: I find it
dull.'

Almost against her will, Frieda warmed to Douglas. Fluent
in her own native language of German, he was transformed
when he was speaking it and not English to her. She was
'thrilled at the fireworks of wit that went off' between
Lawrence and him.

Frieda was far less thrilled than Lawrence with Maurice
Magnus, a European-American friend of Douglas also resident at the Balestri. A sly, persuasive conman, who had been
both Isadora Duncan's manager and a journalist, Magnus now
lived on his wits and his friends – among whom Lawrence was
at once enlisted. Having 'borrowed' money from the impoverished Douglas or Lawrence, on the pretext that otherwise he would starve or be thrown into prison, he would then
go off and order a suit from an expensive tailor, eat in one of

the best restaurants of the city, or make a journey first class. After Magnus had committed suicide in Malta, Douglas and Lawrence were to quarrel over his *Memoirs of the Foreign Legion*, which Lawrence substantially rewrote and for which he provided a lengthy preface in order to achieve its publication and so to earn money to pay off Magnus's creditors. Douglas unjustly accused Lawrence of having exploited their highly exploitative friend. If Lawrence did, in a sense, exploit Magnus, it was in using him as Mr May, the disreputable and slithery American theatrical manager in his story *The Lost Girl*.

Back in Florence early in the next year, Lawrence met Rebecca West through an introduction by Norman Douglas. West would tell the story of how Douglas had remarked, as they set off to see the younger man, that Lawrence had no sooner to arrive in a place than he would at once set about writing about it. Shown up to Lawrence's room in the Balestri, they found him hammering out an article about Florence on his typewriter. 'There – what did I tell you, my dear?' Douglas demanded of West. Lawrence looked furious.

August 1921 found the Lawrences back in Florence for a visit of three weeks. In her absence in Venice, a friend of theirs, Nellie Morrison, had lent them her roomy flat at 32 Via de' Bardi – the house which, so tradition had it, George Eliot's Romola had inhabited. Although, by his own confession, 'feeling tired and seedy', Lawrence was writing away as feverishly as ever in the 'rather dark and cool' room which he occupied above the din of the street below. J. M. Barrie's former wife, Mary, now married to the novelist Gilbert Cannan, visited them in the flat and fell so much in love with it that she herself wished to rent it. Lawrence was happiest when he, Frieda, and Mary would sit out on the terrace in the evening, as the sun sank behind the Carrara mountains and the hills grew dark. 'On the Ponte Vecchio the windows of the little houses shine yellow, and make golden points on the water.'

In the spring of 1926, Lawrence and Frieda settled in the Villa Mirenda, San Paolo Mosciani, Scandicci, a few miles outside Florence, to make of this 'square big box of a house' their home for what was, for two such nomads, the unprecedentedly long period of two years. What was then in effect a village has now become one of the grislier and glummer suburbs of the city. It was in Scandicci that Lawrence wrote one of the most famous and feeble of his novels, *Lady Chatterley's Lover*. It was here that Lawrence's friendship with Aldous Huxley, whom he first met when they were both guests of Lady Ottoline Morrell at Garsington during the War, became close and intense. It was here too that the feud between Lawrence and Douglas over Magnus was resolved. At the bookshop of Pino Orioli, the Lawrences were chatting to Orioli when, to their embarrassment, Douglas, one of Orioli's cronies, burst in. In no way embarrassed himself, Douglas held out his snuff-box to Lawrence with the invitation: 'Have a pinch of snuff, dearie.' Dearie took some snuff.

Frieda has left a vivid account of the journey by tram from Scandicci into Florence.

The handsome Tuscan girls with their glossy, neatly done hair . . . A chicken, sitting, tenderly held by its owner in a red hankie, its destiny either a sick friend or the mercato. Bottles of wine are hidden from the Dazio [toll-gate] men, men friends embrace each other, somebody sees a relation and yells something about the 'pasta' for midday, and so on, while we sail gaily on for Florence.

She has also left a no less vivid account of Florentine shopping:

Shopping in Florence was still fun, not the dreary, large-store drudgery . . . There are paper shops, leather shops, scent shop, stuffs; one glorious shop sells nothing but ribbons, velvet and silk, all colours and sizes, spotted and gold and silver. Another shop, all embroidery silks. Then to have your shoes made is so comfortable . . .

In June and July Lawrence was severely ill, with a series of bronchial haemorrhages. When he was convalescing, Osbert and Edith Sitwell arrived on a visit from their father's Tuscan mansion of Montegufoni. 'They moved us strangely,' Frieda wrote. 'They seemed so oversensitive, as if something had hurt them too much, as if they had to keep up a brave front to the world, to pretend they didn't care and yet they only cared too much. When they left, we went for a long walk, disturbed by them.' Another, less distinguished writer who at that time wandered, a diminishing planet, into their orbit was Michael Arlen, whom Lawrence met on one of his by now rare descents into the city. He wrote of the Armenian-born author of the best-selling *The Green Hat* that he was 'quite a sad dog, trying to be rakish'.

Although he first resided in Florence in 1917 – declaring in a letter 'I don't much like the place; never did; I don't like the Tuscan character' – it was not until 1919 that Norman Douglas (1868–1952) began to make it the one fixed point in his restless life.

When D. H. Lawrence joined him there, he was at the Pensione Balestri. Subsequently he moved to the top floor of the Nardini Hotel, into 'two microscopic rooms' – too small, Reginald Turner remarked, even to swing a boy in. In 1922 he met the bookseller and publisher Pino Orioli, with whom he was to share a love not merely for food, drink, literature, and talk, but also for what Orioli used fondly to call *pulcinini* ('chickens') and Douglas himself 'crocodiles'. Orioli encouraged Douglas, more scholar than professional author, to write – as he could do superlatively well, when he gave his mind to it; and then, through the issue of limited editions, to ensure that his writing brought the maximum returns.

It was Orioli who eventually found for Douglas a flat in the Via San Niccolo – 'a tumble-down sort of place', with no kitchen and 'prehistoric' plumbing such as might well have deterred anyone more fastidious. Ejected from this, which he was renting, he moved first into rooms, also rented, in the Borgo dei Greci, then a red-light district – not that that worried him – and then into a bought flat at 14 Lungarno delle Grazie. Once there, he was soon again in trouble. 'Florence is taboo to me,' he wrote to Lytton Strachey, having been obliged to flee to Prato. 'I . . . only venture in for an afternoon now and then, thickly veiled and wearing blue glasses and a carroty beard.'

Douglas had little interest in the art and architecture of Florence. 'Isn't all that rather *Cinquecento*, my dear?' he derided

Nancy Cunard, when she began to gush to him about Benozzo
Gozzoli, Piero della Francesca, and Signorelli. He had even
less interest in the conventional world of expatriates hobnob-
bing with each other and with anglophile members of the
Florentine aristocracy. 'I never go to the British Institute,' he
wrote to Edward Hutton, a remorselessly industrious
journeyman of letters, who became his friend, occasional
collaborator, and unpaid agent. 'It is crowded day and night,
with frowsy old pension-cats, who occupy all the chairs and
read, each of them, five newspapers at the same time.' The
people with whom he consorted could usually be divided into
three groups: Italian eating and drinking companions; resident
or visiting authors who either shared or were tolerantly
amused by his sexual tastes; and a multitude of youths, some
of whose parents could become so censorious and even finan-
cially demanding that he would have to flee from them to
other parts of Italy or abroad.

Eventually, what drove Douglas from Florence in 1937,
never again to become a permanent resident, was a scandal
involving not a boy but a young girl, Renata. 'They always
turn to little girls in the end,' Compton Mackenzie remarked,
when hearing news which clearly did not surprise him,
although it surprised almost all of Douglas's other friends. In
fact, Renata was eventually found to be still a virgin; but there
seems little doubt that Douglas must have indulged in some
kind of affectionate love-play with her.

Through all these years Douglas suffered, Job-like from an
extraordinary assortment of painful ailments, ranging from
toothache to erysypelas. But, as in the case of his many brushes
with irate parents or the police, his pagan robustness and
stoicism always enabled him to surmount them.

ALDOUS HUXLEY

At first Aldous Huxley (1894–1963) had no reason to feel
affection for Florence. In June 1916, while still an undergraduate at Balliol College, Oxford, he had written to his brother
Julian that he had 'at last discovered a nice Belgian: wonders
will never cease.' This 'nice Belgian' was Maria Nys, de-

spatched by her parents to England to escape the worst of the First War. Initially she had lived at Garsington Manor as the guest of Philip Morrell and his flamboyant wife Lady Ottoline, and it was there that Huxley had met her. But at about the time that Huxley, classified as physically unfit for military service, had himself taken up residence at Garsington, Maria had moved to London, where she gave French lessons to support herself. In 1917, Maria – with whom Huxley had fallen in love – was (as he put it in a letter to Lewis Gielgud, uncle of the actor John Gielgud and a writer of modest talent) 'hustled out remorselessly to her ghoulish mother in Florence', with the result that two years were to pass before the lovers were once more to meet.

In March 1921, by now married for two years and the parents of a baby son called Matthew, Maria and Aldous arrived in Florence to stay in the wing of the Villa Minucci, 4 Via Santa Margherita a Montici, almost opposite to Castel Montici, the residence of the Fasolas, an Italian family who had offered hospitality to Maria and her mother during the war. The flat was 'hideously', albeit adequately, furnished, there was no electricity, all cooking had to be done on a tiny range fed with charcoal, and prices in the immediate aftermath of the war were 'fantastic'. But the great consolation was the view from the western windows: 'A valley sloping away from the house in the foreground, planted with olives and vines, with the church of San Miniato on the opposite side; to the right, looking down the valley, we see almost the whole of Florence lying in the plain, a sort of Oxford from Boar's Hill effect, only very much more so.' [Letter to Leonard Huxley].

After this stay of three months, the Huxleys returned to Florence in 1923, this time for a stay of only one month, at the Castel Montici itself. Once again Huxley complained of the discomforts: because of a failure of the electric water pump, all water had to be laboriously carried in pails to the kitchen and bathroom; the architecture was ugly; recent decoration had been shoddily carried out. But once again there was the compensation of a 'marvellous position', with extensive views down over Florence, up the Arno Valley, and on to the Appenines. With four living rooms, six bedrooms, a tower

room, and a fifty-foot balcony terrace, running the whole
length of the house, the family had ample space. [Letter to
Leonard Huxley]. It was here that Huxley began *Antic Hay*,
completed in Siena and the seaside resort of Forte dei Marmi.
Sharing Dr Johnson's contempt for those authors who write
more than they read, Huxley read strenuously through this
month of increasing heat; but he also wrote strenuously, often
putting in eight hours a day – which he would compare,
unfavourably, with Balzac's 'herculean' eighteen.

In June, the Huxleys returned to the Castel Montici, to
remain there, with breaks for visits to London, Tunis, and
other parts of Italy, until June 1926. Florence was, he recorded
in a letter to his father Frederick on their arrival, packed with
English visitors; but he and Maria rarely ventured down from
their eyrie to see them. Among those whom they did see were
'funny old' Vernon Lee (Violet Paget), John Mavrogordato
(later to achieve fame as the translator of Cavafy into English),
Norman Douglas (then lodged at 24 Via dei Benci), and
Geoffrey Scott, author of *Portrait of Zélide*, and his wealthy
American wife Lady Sybil Scott (Cutting), mother of the
writer Iris Origo. This last couple lived in luxurious splendour
in the Villa Medici in Fiesole. Of *Portrait of Zélide* Huxley
was to write that 'it is full of that kind of exquisitely good
writing that is, one feels instinctively, only another kind of
bad writing.'

Huxley was now working on the short stories which make
up the collection *Little Mexican* and also cogitating *Those
Barren Leaves*. Of the latter he wrote to his father that the mere
business of telling a story interested him less and less. 'The
only really and permanently absorbing things are attitudes
towards life and the relation of man to the world.'

Through these eighteen months he was for the most part
grateful: 'the greatest luxury of this existence is the feeling and
being well – *unberüfen*.' But by 25 April he was beginning to
fret. He and Maria would probably look for something in
Rome in the autumn, he wrote to his brother Julian – 'After a
third-rate provincial town, colonized by English sodomites
and middle-aged Lesbians, which is, after all, what Florence is,
a genuine metropolis will be lively.'

Shortly before their departure, the Huxleys had 'a curious taste of fascist methods.' Huxley had already had cause to complain of the officiousness of the Italian police over speeding; but this was far more disagreeable. 'Four of the most sinister looking gallows' birds you ever saw' burst into the house and insisted on searching it for either the person of, or documents belonging to, Professor Gaetano Salvemini, an eminent historian and an opponent of Mussolini, who was a friend of friends of the Huxleys. In the event, the police found neither professor nor documents and left with embarrassed apologies.

In October 1926, Huxley was once more back briefly in Florence, from the mountain resort of Cortina d'Ampezzo, in order to have treatment for a painfully abscessed tooth. Once again he was overwhelmed by the beauty of the city:

> . . . I regret having to go up again to the mountains, where I shall miss the delicate colouring of the Tuscan landscape, the grand yet noble forms of the hills, the white villas with their gardens, the patiently elaborated terraces on the slopes with their grey olives, their vines and strips of ploughland, and here and there the black cypresses and the clumps of ilex and bay tree.

In February 1929 the Huxleys paid a last brief visit to Florence. On this occasion, they stayed at the Hotel Moderno, which Huxley warmly recommended in a letter to his brother Julian: 'No nonsense about having to take half pension with your room . . . and the water's hot, the radiators work.' Most of Huxley's novel *Time Must Have a Stop* (1944) is set in Florence. But, like so many expatriate novels set there, it contains virtually no Italian characters who are not either aristocratics or menials.

HAROLD ACTON, BERNARD BERENSON, SINCLAIR LEWIS, VIOLET TREFUSIS

The doyen of expatriate writers in Florence has, for the past half-century, been Sir Harold Acton (1904–   ). For a long period he and Bernard Berenson (1865–1969) were the twin peaks to be scaled by any energetic social or cultural climber on a visit to the city. Now he stands alone.

Having amassed a vast fortune by acting as adviser, in an increasingly uneasy relationship, to that black prince of art dealers, Lord Duveen, Berenson settled in his magnificent villa, I Tatti, in Settignano. There he was surrounded by a small but obsequious court to which museums, libraries, and dealers would send their reverential ambassadors. An increasingly frail octogenarian and then nonagenarian, he would rouse himself to totter forth, a living relic of aestheticism sought out in worship, to greet yet another busload of tourists who would wave, stare, and click their cameras at him. Sadly, this supreme proponent of style – according to one story, his manservant would be obliged each morning to warm his wristwatch so that the touch of metal should not administer too violent a shock to his skin – was cruelly fretted by the consciousness that, despite his friendships with such writers as Edith Wharton, often a visitor at I Tatti, and Logan Pearsall Smith, whose sister he married, and despite the help which he received from such of his colleagues as Kenneth Clark and Raymond Mortimer, his own literary style remained turgid and graceless.

Acton, at once far more kindly, despite his sometimes abrasive tongue, and far less ruthless, despite an energy and a drive amazing for a man of his years, has extended the hospitality of his Villa La Pietra to innumerable writers over the years, so that it is rare for any book about Florence not to contain at least one grateful and admiring reference to him.

In the late forties, at the same time as myself, Sinclair Lewis (1885–1951) was resident in Florence. By then saturated in alcohol and puffing asthmatically at the fag-end of what had once been a brilliant career, he had grown so crude and irascible that, so far from seeking him out, people now avoided him.

In 1927 the parents of Violet Trefusis (1894–1972) bought the Villa dell'Ombrellino in Bellosguardo. Described by Trefusis herself as having 'quality, beauty, spaciousness, but no intimacy,' the house enjoys magnificent views, overlooking both the city and the countryside. It was the latter view that Trefusis preferred – 'just like a Florentine primitive' her guests would remark.

Trefusis's mother, Mrs Keppel, had been the mistress of Edward VII. Of this fact Trefusis was inordinately proud. Summoned, an ingenuous and timid young man, to the Villa dell'Ombrellino to meet Trefusis, I was asked as soon as I had seated myself: 'Do you know who I am?' I was about to stammer in bewilderment: 'You're Mrs Trefusis, aren't you?' when she announced, 'I am the illegitimate daughter of Edward VII.' When I recounted this to Harold Acton, he said that it was 'bosh': the dates did not fit. It was no doubt because she so often talked 'bosh' that Harold Acton subsequently wrote of her, in the course of a review in the *Spectator* of *Violet to Vita: The Letters of Violet Trefusis to Vita Sackville-West*: 'In a spacious villa on the hill of Bellosguardo she bombinated in her aura of luxurious fantasy.'

Trefusis's first acquaintance with Florence in 1921 had not endeared the city to her:

This is a pestilential place, smug little hills domed over with villas, and museums and churches that have been so much photographed and written about that one is fed up to the eyes with them long before one sets foot inside. It amuses me that I have been brought here to be 'reformed'. The Italian Society here is the most corrupt I have ever run across, except perhaps Rome. They are mercenary, vicious, lewd, stupid. If one lived here long enough, I tremble to think what one would become. So much for the *Italian* set. The *foreign* set – Russian, Greek, French, American, English – is worse.

Yet eventually the city so much won her over that she would spend long periods of her life there.

In 1944, when the Second War was drawing to a close, an English major, Hamish Erskine, hurried round to the Ritz in London, where Mrs Keppel was then staying, to tell her excitedly that the Villa dell'Ombrellino was safe. 'Everything is intact, even the Chinese pagodas!' he assured her.

Mrs Keppel replied with frigid hauteur: 'Those, my dear Hamish – those were the *common* pagodas!'

Like many of the English expatriates, Mrs Keppel had a passion for gardens; and for her, as for them, a garden, even in Italy, meant an English garden. She would first point with her parasol in this or that direction and then prod with its ferrule at her aged gardener. '*Bisognia begonia!*' she would command. Eventually the Villa dell'Ombrellino was surrounded with as many begonias as had been any of the palaces once inhabited by her royal paramour.

PART TWO
PLACES

A Distant Prospect

The most distant of all distant prospects of Florence is that of the adolescent narrator of Proust's *A la recherche du temps perdu*. His father has proposed an Easter journey to Florence, and at once, so vivid is his imagination, the boy sets off for the city in his mind. Since, never having been there, he is unable to 'introduce into the name of Florence the elements that ordinarily constitute a town', he is obliged to 'let a supernatural city emerge from the impregnation by certain vernal scents of what I supposed to be, in its essentials, the genius of Giotto'. The vision is, as it were, a diptych. In one half of this diptych, he is gazing at a fresco, over part of which 'a curtain of morning sunlight, dusty, aslant,' is slowly spreading. In the other half, he is hurriedly moving – so as to arrive at a table laid out for him with fruit and a flask of Chianti – 'across a Ponte Vecchio heaped with jonquils, narcissi and anemones.' This imaginary Florence is so near and yet so inaccessible: a paradox which never fails to move him as he contemplates it.

In fact, the plan of an actual journey to Florence has to be abandoned when an over-cautious physician fears that it will be bad for the ailing boy's health. Years later, grown up, still a stranger to Florence and now in love with the Duchesse de Guermantes, the Narrator recalls his unassuaged longing for the city. Florence for him is forever associated with Easter, since it was for the Easter holidays that the journey was planned. 'I could not prevent my memory of the time during which I had looked forward to spending Easter in Florence from continuing to make that festival the atmosphere, so to speak, of the City of Flowers, to give at once to Easter Day something Florentine and to Florence something Paschal.'

(The fastidious and accomplished translator of these passages, C. K. Scott Moncrieff, was one of the many *stranieri inverti* – as the Florentines called them – who could be found in Florence in the period between the wars).

One of the most vivid of real evocations of a distant prospect of the city is that of Shelley, in a letter to Mary Shelley, on his first arrival:

As we approached Florence, the country became cultivated to a very high degree, the plain was filled with the most beautiful villas, and, as far as the eye could reach, the mountains were covered with them; for the plains are bounded on all sides by blue and misty mountains. The vines are here trailed on low trellises or reeds interwoven into crosses to support them, and the grapes, now almost ripe, are exceedingly abundant. You everywhere meet those teams of beautiful white oxen, which are now labouring the little vine-divided fields, and their Virgilian ploughs and carts. Florence itself, that is the Lung'Arno (for I have seen no more), I think is the most beautiful city I have ever yet seen. It is surrounded with cultivated hills, and from the bridge which crosses the broad channel of the Arno, the view is the most animated and elegant I ever saw. You see three or four bridges, one apparently supported by Corinthian pillars, and the white sails of the boats, relieved by the deep green of the forest, which comes to the water's edge, and the sloping hills covered with bright villas on every side. Domes and steeples rise on all sides, and the cleanliness is remarkably great. On the other side there are the foldings of the Arno above; first the hills of olive and vine, then the chestnut woods, and then the blue and misty pine forests, which invest the aerial Appenines, that fade in the distance. I have seldom seen a city so lovely at first sight as Florence.

Dickens was equally overwhelmed by the beauty of the far-off vista:

Oh! How much beauty, when on a fair, clear morning, we look from the summit of a hill, on Florence! See where it lies before us in a sunlighted valley, bright with the winding Arno, and shut in by swelling hills; its domes, and towers, and palaces, rising from the rich country in a glittering heap and shining in the sun like gold!

Entering Florence, Thomas Gray commented, like Shelley, on the vines, but this time in a December bareness which, as he put it, revealed the skeleton of Italy. 'I was able to observe very public and scandalous doings between the vine and the elm-trees, and how the olive-trees are shocked thereon.' Gray was rarely so skittish either in his conversation or in his writing.

The 'shocked' olive-trees were what Lord Macaulay chiefly noticed at his approach:

The sight of the olive-trees interested me much. I had, indeed, seen what I was told were olive-trees, as I was whirled down the Rhone from Lyons to Avignon; but they might, for anything I saw, have been willows or ash-trees. Now they stood, covered with berries, along the road for miles. I looked at them with the same sort of feeling with which Washington Irving says that he heard the nightingale for the first time when he came to Eng-land, after having read descriptions of her in poets from his childhood. I thought of the Hebrews, and their numerous images drawn from the olive; of the veneration in which the tree was held by the Athenians; of Lysias's speech; of the fine ode in the Oedipus at Colonus; of Vergil and Lorenzo de' Medici.

Like so many travellers at a time when Florence was free of industry and therefore of pollution, Stendhal, approaching the city, remarked on two things above all: the small green hills, covered not, as now, by houses and factories but by agriculture; and the blueness of the sky.

While Milan is a circular town, without a river, a town that lies in an unbroken plain except for its many brooks of running water, Florence is built entirely differently in a fair-sized valley that is bounded by rugged mountains.

The town is right against the hill which limits it to the
south, and by the disposition of its streets is not unlike
Paris, being also situated on a river, the Arno, as Paris is
on the Seine . . . If we go to the southern hill in the garden
of the Pitti Palace and then walk around the walls as far as
the Arezzo road, we shall get an idea of the infinite
number of little hills of which Tuscany is made up, and
which, covered with olives, vines and small patches of
wheat, are cultivated like a garden . . . As in the pictures
of Leonardo and of the early manner of Raphael, the
horizon is often bounded by dark trees relieved against a
blue sky.

A half century later, in 1895, André Gide, a French novelist
scarcely less distinguished than Stendhal, provided his own
distant prospect from the Viale dei Colli, San Miniato, 'in the
most radiant weather':

A sky now but softly overcast, now almost azure, which
deepens towards evening because of the abundant mists:
the whole city melts in a golden bake-oven. The roofs are
plum-coloured; the Duomo with its campanile, the tower
of the Palazzo Vecchio rise above the rest; the hills seem
remote; the high mountain opposite Fiesole stands out.
The wonderful Arno appears in places, as it enters and
leaves the city. The sun is setting, bathing with soft and
veiled glory this whole scene that we can see from the
marble terraces of the cemetery, framed in by mortuary
cypresses, almost black, severe and most appropriate to
Florence.

In Somerset Maugham's *Then and Now*, his hero Machiavelli is similarly bewitched by the distant view:

'Look, Messere,' cried his servant Antonio, riding up
to come abreast of him. 'Florence.'
Machiavelli looked. In the distance against the winter
sky, paling now with the decline of the day, he saw the
dome, the proud dome that Bramante had built. He
pulled up. There it was, the city he loved more than his
soul . . . Florence, the city of flowers, with its campanile

and its baptistery, its churches and palaces, its gardens, its tortuous streets, the old bridge he crossed every day to go to the Palazzo, and his home, his brother Toto, Marietta, his friends, the city with its great history, his birthplace and the birthplace of his ancestors, Florence, the city of Dante and Boccaccio, the city that had fought for its freedom through the centuries, Florence the well beloved, the city of flowers . . . Spring had come early that year and the countryside, with the trees bursting into leaf, the wild flowers, the fresh green of the grass, the rich growth of the wheat, was a joy to the eye. To Machiavelli the Tuscan scene had a friendly, intimate delight that appealed to the mind rather than to the senses. It had none of the sublimity of the Alps, nor the grandeur of the sea; it was a patch of the earth's surface, classical without severity, lightly gay and elegant, for men to live on who loved wit and intelligent argument, pretty women and good cheer. It reminded you not of the splendid solemn music of Dante, but rather of the light-hearted strains of Lorenzo de' Medici.

In his *World So Wide*, matching cliché for cliché, Maugham's American near-contemporary Sinclair Lewis shows his hero, Hayden, at first disappointed but soon equally in thrall to the city:

The railway station at Florence had a fine, flaring Mussolini touch, very spacious and inclined to marble and wood panels, but the piazza in front of it was of a suburban drabness, and the back of the church of Santa Maria Novella was a mud-coloured bareness, sullen with evening. He would not be staying here long! His taxi-driver was learning English, and he was willing to make it a bilingual party, but as Hayden's Italian was limited to *bravo*, *spaghetti*, *zabaglione* and the notations on sheet music, this promising friendship did not get far, and he went to bed blankly at the Hotel Excelsior.

But in the bright morning of late autumn he looked from his hotel and began to fall in love with a city.

He saw the Arno, in full brown tide after recent

mountain rains, with old palaces along it and cypress-waving hills beyond. On one side was the Tower of Bellos-guardo and a fragment of the old city wall, and on the other the marvel of the church of San Miniato, white striped with a green that seemed black from afar. Hayden saw a city of ancient reticences and modern energy, with old passageways, crooked and mysterious, arched over with stone that bore carven heraldic shields.

'I like this! Maybe I'll stay out the week.'

It was this city that Coleridge apostrophized as 'Thou brightest star of star-bright Italy!', and of which, more pro-saically, Elizabeth Barrett Browning wrote: 'If you take one thing with another, there is no place like Florence, I am persuaded, for a place to live in – cheap, tranquil, cheerful, beautiful, within the limits of civilisation, yet out of the crush of it.'

The Arno and its Bridges

In his *The Innocents Abroad* (1869) Mark Twain views the Arno with typically Yankee robustness and realism:

> It is popular to admire the Arno. It is a great historical creek with four feet in the channel and some scows floating around. It would be a very plausible river if they would pump some water into it. They all call it a river, and they honestly think it *is* a river, do these dark and bloody Florentines. They even help out the delusion by building bridges over it. I do not see why they are too good to wade.

For Arnold Bennett in 1912, however, the Arno was 'a surging, yellow-brown flood.'

During his stay in Florence in 1895, André Gide was more appreciative. After one of many walks along the Arno, he wrote in his Journals:

> Beautiful hills along the Arno from San Miniato to those opposite the Cascine. I am becoming more and more familiar with their contours of stern softness and their hues of green and grey.
>
> On the edge of the Arno I like to observe at length the powerful wave made by the rolling water of the weir; the weir is on an angle in the river so that the water piles up rather on one side. Against the wall is a fold that hollows out the wall's edge; the water then rolls over itself like a

propellor, forming a constant unmoving wave. Wonderful to look at that fixed form with a fleeting and fluid
matter always passing through it . . .

Even more rhapsodic is one of Gide's subsequent descriptions,
this time of the Arno at sunset on 31 December:

. . . Return along the shores of the Arno – setting sun;
water losing itself in golden sands; in the far distance,
some fishermen; the smoke rising from the roofs, at first
gray, becomes gilded when the sun touches it. That
radiance lasts for a long time; the roofs near San Miniato,
the white walls of the villas become the colour of unripe
apricots; the cypresses around them seem all the darker.
The fall of the Arno has as it were some mother-of-pearl
glints of an extremely pale green and, lower down, of that
same colour with a tint of orange.
   The fishermen in the distance are carrying their bow-
nets and returning to their boats . . . The wonder of these
lengthening days . . .

But the Arno is not always beautiful and benign. In 1269
there was a flood so severe that it swept away both the Ponte
a Santa Trinita and the Ponte alla Carraia and spread so far that –
as Giovanni Villani put it in his *Croniche Fiorentine* – 'the great
part of the city of Florence became a lake.' It was in response to
a similar flooding of the city in 1557 that Cosimo set about
beautifying the city, instead of merely restoring it.

In 1740 Horace Walpole witnessed another, less disastrous
flood:

If you have had a great wind in England, we have had a
great water in Florence. . . . Yesterday, with violent
rains, there came flouncing down from the mountains
such a flood, that it floated the whole city. The jewellers
on the Old Bridge removed their commodities, and in
two hours after the bridge was cracked. The torrent broke
down the quays, and drowned several coach horses,
which are kept here in stables underground. We were
moated into our house all day, which is near the Arno,
and had the miserable spectacles of the ruins that were

washed along with the hurricane. There was a cart with two oxen not quite dead, and four men in it drowned: but what was ridiculous, there came along a fat hay-cock with a hen and her eggs and a cat. The torrent is considerably abated; but we expect terrible news from the country, especially from Pisa, which stands so much lower and nearer the sea. There is a stone here, which when the water overflows, Pisa is entirely flooded. The water rose two ells yesterday above that stone. Judge! [Letter to Richard West]

Of 'a terrible and unprecedented flood' (the second adjective is inappropriate since there had already been the precedents above), which occurred in 1844, Thomas Trollope has left us an account. Having climbed to the top of Giotto's tower on the morning after a night of torrential rain, Trollope was appalled to find that one-third at least of Florence was under water.

Having descended from the tower, he made his way to the Lung'Arno, where 'the sight was truly a terrible and a magnificent one.'

The river, extending in one turbid, yellow, swirling mass from the walls of the houses on the quay on one side, to those of the houses opposite, was bringing down with it fragments of timber, carcasses of animals, large quantities of hay and straw; – and amid the wreck we saw a cradle with a child in it, safely navigating the tumbling waters! It was drawn to the window of a house by throwing a line over it, and the infant navigator was none the worse.

But very great fears were entertained for the very ancient Ponte Vecchio, with its load of silversmiths' and jewellers' shops, turning it from a bridge into a street – the only remaining example in Europe, I believe, of a fashion of construction once common. The water continued to rise as we stood watching it. Less than a foot of space yet remained between the surface of the flood and the key-stone of the highest arch; and it was thought that if the water rose sufficiently to beat against the solid superstructure of the bridge, it must have been swept away. But at last came the cry from those who were watching it close at hand, that for the last five minutes the surface had been stationary; and in another half hour it was followed by the announcement that the flood had begun to decrease. Then there was an immense sensation, of relief; for the Florentines love their old bridge; and the crowd began to disperse.

Trollope and the friend accompanying him now decided to go to Doney, in the Via Tornabuoni, for a cup of coffee, to make up for the breakfast which they had missed. But since the Via dei Malcontenti and the Piazza di Santa Croce were both still under water, they had to get a lift aboard a large barge, which was carrying bread to people in the most deeply flooded part of the town. This barge took them to the Palazzo Berti, on the second floor of which the Trollopes were then lodged. Trollope was obliged to ascend to this floor by a ladder, placed on the deck of the perilously rocking boat. For years after, as Trollope records, social events in Florence were dated as having occurred before or after the flood.

In her *Diary of Florence in the Flood*, the American novelist Katherine Kressman Taylor recorded the not dissimilar events of 1966, which resulted in an invasion of water-carried mud and silt bearing off the marble revetments of the Duomo, panels from the great doors of the Baptistery, and statues from the Arno bridges.

A tumultuous mass of water stretches from bank to bank, perhaps four feet below the tops of the twenty-five-foot walls, a snarling brown torrent of terrific velocity, spiraling in whirlpools and countercurrents that send waves running backward; and its colour is a rich brown, a boiling *caffè-latte* brown streaked with crests the colour of dirty cream. This tremendous water carries mats of debris: straw, twigs, leafy branches, rags, a litter that the river sucks down and spews up again in a swelling turbulence. Its thunderous rush holds me tense at the window, as any movement of great force can lay a spell on the eyes. All I can think of is that it is as magnificent as it is threatening, a river in spate moving at full stress, its surface twisting with curling ropes of water that smack together and go up in spouts of foam. The flood is as absolute as a forest fire is absolute or a full gale stripping the countryside and bending down all the trees.

Eventually there are three meters of water in the Piazza Duomo, and stranded families are calling for help from second-floor windows. Army helicopters arrive, rescuing the women and children but leaving the men to wait either for a subsidence of the floods or for future rescue.

As always on such occasions of natural disaster, people alternated between feelings of horror and exhilaration; between wanting the waters to subside and wanting them to sweep everything before them. In 'A Letter from Florence' Francis Steegmuller has recorded the behaviour of onlookers by the Ponte Vecchio:

> . . . The wife of one of the jewellers [shop-owners on the Bridge] had said that when she and her husband arrived they found a number of noctambulous Florentines – some of them apparently hoodlums, some in cars with headlights pointed towards the scene – gathered at the end of the bridge, watching, as though hoping to see it break and collapse. The arrival of the jewellers with their suitcases [to carry away the most valuable of their merchandise] was greeted with jeers . . . The water continued to rise and about half the jewellery shops on the Ponte Vecchio are now gaping open – gutted by the tremendous force of a torrent that passed right through them.

Someone has rightly said that the only sure way of avoiding Florentine floods would be to move the city itself.

In his *Mornings in Florence* Ruskin calls the Ponte Vecchio 'the old treasure bridge', adding that it is 'the most precious historical link of all, tottering under the weight of shops and galleries.' The first of these shops belonged, unromantically, to butchers; but by 1644, when the young John Evelyn paid his visit, the jewellers had already taken over. There is a reference to their presence in the twelfth line of Longfellow's sonnet 'The Old Bridge of Florence':

Taddeo Gaddi built me. I am old,
    Five centuries old. I plant my foot of stone
    Upon the Arno, as St Michael's own
    Was planted on the dragon. Fold by fold
Beneath me as it struggles, I behold
    Its glittering scales. Twice hath it overthrown
    My kindred and companions. Me alone
    It moveth not, but is by me controlled.
I can remember when the Medici
    Were driven from Florence; longer still ago
    The final wars of Ghibelline and Guelf.
Florence adorns me with her jewelry;
    And when I think that Michel Angelo
    Hath leaned on me, I glory in myself.

In 1868, when he wrote this poem, Longfellow was staying at the Hotel Arno – as he put it, 'within a stone's throw of the Arno.' Foreign visitors of that period constantly expressed delighted surprise at the size of their rooms, whether in hotels or in rented apartments or villas, and Longfellow was no exception: 'My bedroom looking over the river is thirty-two feet by thirty, and high in proportion, I feel as if I were sleeping in some public square.'

Today the Ponte Vecchio totters even more than when Ruskin saw it, under the weight not merely of its shops, galleries, and the passage built by Cosimo to connect the Palazzo Vecchio with his newly completed Palazzo Pitti, but of the tourists who at the height of the season tend to turn it into a squalid mixture of souk, airport lounge, and dormitory.

In his *Pictures from Italy*, Dickens left a vivid picture both of the bridge and of Cosimo's passage:

Among the four old bridges that span the river [the Ponte a Santa Trinita, the Ponte alla Carraia and the Ponte alle Grazie were the other three], the Ponte Vecchio – that bridge which is covered with the shops of Jewellers and Goldsmiths – is the most enchanting feature of the scene. The space of one house, in the centre, being left open, the view beyond is shown as in a frame; and that precious glimpse of sky, and water, and rich buildings, shining so quietly among the huddled roofs and gables on the bridge, is exquisite. Above it, the Gallery of the Grand Duke crosses the river. It was built to connect the two Great Palaces by a secret passage; and it takes its jealous course among the streets and houses, with true despotism: going where it lists, and spurning every obstacle away, before it.

Writing in her *Italy* (1821) the now-forgotten novelist Lady Sydney Morgan (1783–1859) has left an entertaining account of her tribulations when ordering a *bandeau* from a dilatory jeweller on the Ponte. Today these jewellers are quite as prompt and efficient as any English or American ones.

Having explained most circumstantially the nature of the ornament I bespoke, sketched it with my pencil, and cut it out with my scissors, I left him with the full conviction that my order was understood, and would be well executed – a conviction impressed by the manner in which it was received; for while I stood before him, in all the eagerness of detail suited to the importance of the subject, he was squatted in an easy chair in a fine breathing heat after his siesta! – his thumbs twirling, his eyes closing and his answers laconically confined to '*Sarà fatto!*' (It shall be done!) repeated every second. Calling on the following day to see how '*sarà fatto*' was going on; to my enquiries the only answer I could obtain was, '*Veramente non mi ricordo di niente, Signora mia,*' ('Truly I remember nothing of all this, my lady.') To stimulate his memory for the future, I wrote down the order in the best Italian I could muster; and the day was fixed for the delivery of the article, with a promise of punctuality, which all the saints were called on to witness; but that day, and many a following one passed, and the answer to all enquiries was '*Sarà fatto,*' and '*Pazienza, Signora cara mia!*' My *pazienza* and residence at Florence had nearly however expired together, when, a day or two before our departure, '*sarà fatto*' entered my room with the long-expected *bandeau* glittering between his finger and thumb; and with a look of the most obvious triumph distending his apoplectic

face, he exclaimed, '*Mirate, Signora! che gran bella cosa!!*
*Questa è cosa per far stupire! veramente è degna di nostro
divino Benvenuto Cellini!!!* ('See, Madam, what a beautiful
thing! – a marvellous work! and worthy of our divine
Benvenuto Cellini.') His self-approbation had now
banished the languour of his habitual indolence; and the
naivete and hyperbole with which he applauded his own
work, resembled the very manner, in the self-same
dialect, with which '*Nostro divino Benvenuto*' charms his
readers, and leads them back to the frank simplicity of
the sixteenth century.

Stendhal also had an encounter with one of the jewellers on
the Ponte Vecchio.

This Nathan [the jeweller, like many of those then and
now plying their trade there, was Jewish], besides being a
fervent devotee of his persuasion, has perfected to an
astonishing degree a sort of philosophy of impassivity,
together with the most useful art of paying as little as
possible for all his daily needs. The accident of our
encounter afforded us sincere delight on either side. Upon
the instant, fearing to lose my company, he promoted me
to the status of a business associate, and bade me follow
him to the house of a client, to whom he proceeded to sell,
for the sum of ten *louis*, an exquisite graved stone by
Pickler. No less than three-quarters of an hour was spent
in bargaining; yet to me the time seemed short. Except for
the actual formulation of an offer, not one single word
was uttered of those which a Frenchman would have
employed in similar circumstances.

Stendhal then comments on the difference between the Italian
and the French collector: the Italian is interested in building a
collection for his descendants; the Frenchman in buying an
object which may eventually be resold at a profit.
Stendhal's jeweller friend later introduced him 'into the
society of a group of wealthy merchants and their wives', so
that he could watch a marionette show. Measuring no more

than five feet across, the theatre was an exact copy of La Scala in Milano.

There were tiny lamps proportionate to all the rest, and each change of set was carried out rapidly . . . I can conceive nothing more enchanting. A company of four-and-twenty marionettes, each eight inches tall, equipped with leaden legs and costing a *sequin* apiece, performed a delicious, if somewhat indelicate, comedy which proved to be an abridged version of Machiavelli's *La Mandragola*. Subsequently these same marionettes proceeded to dance a miniature ballet, with considerable style and elegance.

In 1513 Ariosto stayed for six months in a Hospice of the Knights at the end of the bridge, and fell in love with the beautiful Alexandrina Benucci. Near the Hospice stood the statue of Mars beneath which, in 1215, the body of Buondelmonte dei Buondelmonti was left by members of the Amadei family and their *consorzeria* or allies, who had clubbed and stabbed him to death because he had jilted an Amadei girl in order to marry a Donati one. With an extreme lack of tact, he was crossing the bridge to celebrate his marriage to the second girl on the precise day fixed for his marriage to the first one. In *Il Paradiso* (XVI.140) Dante writes of the tragic incident:

O Buondelmonte, ill dids't thou to flee
Those nuptials when another prompted it!
Glad had been many, who now most mournful be,
If God thy body had into Ema thrown
The first time that the city welcomed thee.
Yet fit it was that to the battered stone,
Which guards the bridge, our Florence should present
A victim in the last peace she hath known.

The murder of Buondelmonte in what at first appeared to be no more than an act of private vengeance for a slight to a single family's honour soon embroiled the whole city, some noble families siding with the youth's family and others banding together in opposition to it. The first faction declared them-selves Guelphs, the second Ghibellines. Thus, but for

Buondelmonte's fickleness and tactlessness, it is possible that the history of Florence would have been much less bloody and Italian literature much less rich.

The original Ponte alla Carraia, made of wood, was erected in 1218 to accommodate an increase in traffic caused by the growth of the wool and silk industry in the area it served, Borgo Ognissanti. In 1304 a dense crowd assembled on it to watch a mystery play enacted on boats in the river. The bridge collapsed beneath their weight, drowning many of the spectators in what Dante called now *il bel fiume* (the beautiful river) and now *la maladetta e sventurata fossa* (the cursed and luckless ditch). By a grim irony, the work being presented was entitled 'Inferno'.

The prolific Scottish novelist Mrs Oliphant (1828–97) – who, with her dying artist husband, spent the winter of 1859 in Florence on the second floor of the Palazzo d'Elci, 28 Via Maggio – has vividly described the scene in her *The Makers of Florence*. Messengers had been sent far and wide to announce that 'whosoever would have news of the other world was to go on the kalends of May to the Ponte alla Carraia and to the banks of the river.' When the day dawned, the Arno was already packed with boats and rafts carrying the performers in the spectacle, disguised either as demons or as their victims. At the collapse of the bridge, many received only too literally 'news of the other world.'

Was this strange scene an unconscious reflection from Dante's *abozzo* [rough draft of the *Inferno*] then reposing in darkness and secrecy in one of Madonna Gemma's strong-boxes? [Gemma, Dante's wife, looked after his papers in Florence when he was in exile.] Or is it merely an indication how the mind of the time was turning, occupying itself with such dramatic guesses into a vivid revelation under the poet's touch? Between the blue skies of May and the glimmering of the Arno, overshadowed by its bridges, what strange phantasmagoria it was which bewildered the crowded spectators on the banks! the red gleams of the fires floating on the dark river, the cries of the fictitious victims, the shouts of the demon-actors, the

smoke and burning that figured hell; and then all at once a
real hell of terror and suffering – the crash, the plunge, the
wild dismay, the fantastic horror come true. Must not the
exile, straining his eager ears outside, have heard some
echo of the great outcry? and felt with characteristic pride
and scorn that nothing less than some unconscious rever-
berations from the visionary world which he alone had
revealed could have conjured up this extraordinary scene?

A week after their arrival in Florence, the Hawthornes
walked beside the Arno in the early evening, after a day of
hectic sightseeing. As so often, it is Sophia Hawthorne, rather
than her novelist husband, who vividly recreates the scene for
us:

As we issued from the dim shade of the court, the golden
light and the transparent mirror of the Arno burst upon us
like a symphony, and now our way was toward the west,
still glowing, with one star brilliant over the central arch
of a bridge, making the apex of an invisible pyramid. All
being reflected, there was also a pyramid below, each
pointed by the star, so that the ovals of the arches and the
pyramids were in lovely struggle together.

The Lung-Arno was lighted with gas along its whole
extent, making a cornice of glittering gems, converging
in the distance, and the reflection of the illuminated
border made a fairy show. No painting, and scarcely a
dream could equal the magical beauty of the scene.

Two weeks later, the Hawthornes drove in an open
barouche beside the Arno to view the illuminations in celebration of the Eve of St John. 'It was,' recorded Sophia, 'a scene of
enchantment', with the Ponte a Santa Trinita and the Ponte
alla Carraia 'hung with globes of light, like huge bubbles'
and everything reflected in the waters.

The parapets, on both sides of the river, were studded
with the same delicate globes, making a glittering cornice, doubled beneath; and lighted boats floated quietly in
every direction, each one a moving constellation of stars,
on the surface of the water, as well as in the pictured

world below. The palaces on the Lung'Arno were kindled up over the facades, and, afar off, the mountains, a dark, waving outline, and above, a black sky, with heavy, windy clouds, were the frame of this radiant pageant.

At that period to walk beside the Arno was not to be jostled by crowds and deafened by traffic. The most sought-after hotels and *pensione* would have at least some rooms with a view of the river, as did the Bertolini in E. M. Forster's *A Room with a View*:

'The Signora had no business to do it,' said Miss Bartlett, 'no business at all. She promised us south rooms with a view, close together, instead of which here are north rooms, looking into a courtyard, and a long way apart. Oh, Lucy!'

'And a Cockney, besides!' said Lucy, who had been further saddened by the Signora's unexpected accent. 'It might be London.' She looked at the two rows of English people who were sitting at the table; at the row of white bottles of water and red bottles of wine that ran between the English people; at the portraits of the late Queen and the late Poet Laureate that hung behind the English people, heavily framed; at the notice of the English church (Rev. Cuthbert Eager, M. A. Oxon.), that was the only other decoration on the wall. 'Charlotte, don't you feel, too, that we might be in London? I can hardly believe that all kinds of other things are just outside. I suppose it is one's being so tired.'

'This meat has surely been used for soup,' said Miss Bartlett, laying down her fork.

'I wanted to see the Arno. The rooms the Signora promised us in her letter would have looked over the Arno. The Signora had no business to do it at all. Oh, it is a shame!'

'Any nook does for me,' Miss Bartlett continued; 'but it does seem hard that you shouldn't have a view.'

Lucy felt that she had been selfish. 'Charlotte, you mustn't spoil me: of course, you must look over the

Arno, too. I meant that. The first vacant room in the front –'

'You must have it,' said Miss Bartlett, part of whose travelling expenses were paid by Lucy's mother – a piece of generosity to which she made many a tactful allusion.

'No, no. You must have it.'

'I insist on it. Your mother would never forgive me, Lucy.'

'She would never forgive *me*.'

The ladies' voices grew animated, and – if the sad truth be owned – a little peevish. They were tired, and under the guise of unselfishness they wrangled. Some of their neighbours interchanged glances, and one of them – one of the ill-bred people whom one does meet abroad – leant forward over the table and actually intruded into their argument. He said:

'I have a view, I have a view.'

Miss Bartlett was startled. Generally at a pension people looked them over for a day or two before speaking, and often did not find out that they would 'do' till they had gone. She knew that the intruder was ill-bred, even before she glanced at him. He was an old man, of heavy build, with a fair, shaven face and large eyes. There was something childish in those eyes, though it was not the childishness of senility. What exactly it was Miss Bartlett did not stop to consider, for her glance passed on to his clothes. These did not attract her. He was probably trying to become acquainted with them before they got into the swim. So she assumed a dazed expression when he spoke to her, and then said: 'A view? Oh, a view! How delightful a view is!'

The real Pension White, at which Arnold Bennett put up at about the same period, is an establishment remarkably similar to Forster's fictional one:

Little tickets in each bedroom stating day of week when room is 'cleaned'. Little bookshelves about, in any case hanging in the worst possible place in the room – just over the washstand so that the books can be well splashed.

Embroidered or chintz covers for things. Everything little, and neat in the arrangements. No provision of writing materials. No spectacular quality at all anywhere. The Italian manageress has become almost English in her very soul. The great quality of the place is the meals. A really A1 dinner last night when we came home at 11 p.m.

Whether a glittering trickle or an opaque flood, the Arno always remains the backbone of the city. As C. Day Lewis put in his 'Florence: Works of Art':

> . . . Where rode Lorenzo, panoplied and plumed,
> Where Savonarola burned, and Ruskin fumed,
> The lady artist sets her easel up,
> The tourist with mild wonder is consumed.
>
> Yet still the Arno navigably flows
> And saunterers past the Ponte Vecchio's
> Jewel shops cast a shadow: here is still
> A taste for life, a market for the rose.

From the Piazza della Signoria to Santa Croce

PIAZZA DELLA SIGNORIA AND PALAZZO VECCHIO

Just as, today, the Acropolis best evokes the whole history of Athens and the Capitol the whole history of Rome, so the Piazza della Signoria performs a similar service for Florence. Many of the approaches to the great square are streets so tall and narrow that one has a feeling of claustrophobia walking up their dimness and dankness. This feeling is succeeded by one of liberation as one emerges into the amplitude and brilliance of the Piazza. It is easy to see this change as symbolic of the emergence of Florence from the artistic and intellectual constriction of medieval times into the freedom of the Renaissance.

Dominating the Piazza, as indeed it dominates the whole of Florence, is the looming bulk of the Palazzo Vecchio – or the Palazzo dei Priori, as it was originally called. At once strong and graceful, it too seems symbolic of a historical transition: its strength, as of a fortress, was necessary in a city where dissension within once posed quite as many dangers as attacks from without; its elegance was desirable in a city that was, at the time the Palazzo Vecchio was erected in the thirteenth century, already setting itself the classical ideal not merely of *mens sana in corpore sano* but of *mens* and *corpus* at perfect ease in surroundings ideally fitted for them. The American novelist W. D. Howells (1837–1920) summed up the qualities of the Palazzo when he wrote of it that it was 'a great, bold, irregular mass, beautiful as some rugged natural object is beautiful, and with the kindliness of nature in it.'

Stendhal was more rhapsodic:

. . . This stark, contrasting incarnation of the stern realities of medieval times, set square amid the artistic glories of the past and the insignificant throng of modern *marchesini*, creates an impression of unparalleled grandeur and truth. Here, for the instruction of the philosophic mind, stand the masterpieces of those arts, whose genius was fired by violence of passion and bore fruit, only to wither in a later century and fade, becoming petty, insignificant and misshapen when the tempest of desire ceased to swell the sails by which alone that frail craft of the human soul, so impotent when passion falters and evaporates, leaving it bereft alike of vice and virtue, is driven across the stormy seas of life.

One evening Stendhal sat out 'on a cane chair in front of the coffee-house in the centre of the great *piazza* facing the *Palazzo Vecchio*.'

Neither the crowd nor the cold – the one as inconsiderable as the other – could prevent my eye from beholding the whole tapestry of incident which had been unfolded on this same *piazza*. Here, on these very stones, Florence had risen a score of times in the name of *liberty*, while blood had flowed in the cause of an unworkable constitution. And now the rising moon, by imperceptible degrees, began to print the massive shadow of the *Palazzo Vecchio* upon the scoured flagstones of the *piazza*, and to lend her magic touch of mystery to the colonnades of the Uffizi, beneath whose arches gleamed the lights of houses, distant beyond the Arno.

Eventually Stendhal had to drag himself away from 'this awesome sight' in order to make his way to *il Cocomero*, the theatre in which he was to see a performance of *The Barber of Seville*.

It is at night that the American hero of Henry James's 1873 short story 'The Madonna of the Future', having arrived for the first time in Florence, wanders by accident into the Piazza:

> A narrow passage wandered darkly away out of the little square before my hotel, and looked as if it bored into the heart of Florence. I followed it, and at the end of ten minutes emerged upon a great piazza, filled only with the mild autumn moonlight. Opposite rose the Palazzo Vecchio like some huge civic fortress, with the bell-tower springing from its embattled verge like a mountain-pine from the edge of a cliff. At its base, in its projected shadow, gleamed certain dim sculptures which I wonderingly approached. One of the images, on the left of the palace door, was a magnificent colossus shining through the dusky air like some young god of defiance. In a moment I recognized him as Michael Angelo's David. I turned with a certain relief from his sinister strength to a slender figure in bronze, stationed beneath the high, light *loggia*, which opposes the free and elegant span of its arches to the dead masonry of the palace; a figure supremely shapely and graceful; gentle, almost, in spite of his holding out with his light, nervous arm the snaky head of the slaughtered Gorgon. His name is Perseus . . .

John Addington Symonds also admired Benvenuto Cellini's masterpiece, writing of it: 'It has something of a fascination, a *bravura* brilliancy, a sharpness of technical precision, a singular and striking picturesqueness which the works of elder masters want. It soars into a region of authentic, if not pure and sublime, inspiration.'

Writing of the Palazzo Vecchio, Dickens noted 'its enormous overhanging battlements and the Great Tower which watches over the whole town.'

> In its courtyard – worthy of the Castle of Otranto in its ponderous gloom – is a massive staircase that the heaviest wagon and the stoutest team of horses might be driven up. Within it, is a Great Saloon, faded and tarnished in its stately decorations, and mouldering by grains, but recording yet, in pictures on its walls, the triumphs of the Medici and the wars of the old Florentine people.

Inevitably, his attention was attracted by the Tetto de'
Pisani, a gaol built by Pisan prisoners in 1364 but demolished,
in an act of unforgivable vandalism, near the close of the
nineteenth century.

The prison is hard by, in an adjacent courtyard of the
building – a foul and dismal place, where some men are
shut up close, in small cells like ovens; and where others
look through bars and beg; where some are playing
draughts, and some are talking to their friends, who
smoke, the while, to purify the air; and some are buying
wine and fruit of women-vendors; and all are squalid,
dirty, and vile to look at. 'They are merry enough,
Signore,' says the Jailer. 'They are all blood-stained here,'
he adds, indicating with his hand three-fourths of the
whole building. Before the hour is out, an old man,
eighty years of age, quarrelling over a bargain with a
young girl of seventeen, stabs her dead, in the market-
place full of bright flowers, and is brought in prisoner to
swell the numbers.

If the Palazzo Vecchio represents a period of transition from
feudalism to oligarchy and from war to peace, the magnificent
arcade of the nearby Loggia dei Lanzi – so called from the Swiss
lancers placed there in attendance on Cosimo I – represents one
of stability and calm. The mixture of round arches with Gothic
design and ornament, so typical of buildings in Florence, has
about it no suggestion of conflict or stress. Indeed, there is an
assurance about the very openness of the structure to every
comer.

As many a tourist soon learns to his surprise, rain is by no
means uncommon in Florence, so that the original reasons for
building the Loggia was to provide a covered space where
public ceremonies could be conducted without any fear of the
elements. But since then the Loggia has fulfilled a variety of
other functions. Less than half a century after its completion,
Leon Battista Alberti, one of those 'universal men' in which
the Renaissance was so rich, commented that its portico
provided a refuge under which old men might pass the heat of
the day. In a letter, Elizabeth Barrett Browning recorded: 'I

often go out after tea in a wandering walk to sit in the Loggia and look at the Perseus' – another reference to Cellini's masterpiece. Some forty years later, in 1896, the Victorian traveller Augustus Hare saw the Loggia as a listening post:

> The predominance of males is striking. Hundreds of men stand here for hours, as if they had nothing else to do, talking ceaselessly in deep Tuscan tones. Many who are wrapped in long cloaks thrown over one shoulder and lined with green, look as if they had stepped out of the old pictures in the palace above.

Arnold Bennett had also remarked, in 1912, on these lounging, loitering men – many of them 'dressed in the most amusing fur-coats.' The Loggia has constantly been a market, whether for flesh, for lottery tickets or, in the years immediately after the Second War, for black market cigarettes sewn into the voluminous overcoats of the sellers.

It was in the Piazza della Signoria that, in 1498, Savonarola presided over his famous Bonfire of the Vanities. In *Romola* George Eliot brilliantly evoked the scene:

> She [Romola] chose to go through the great Piazza that she might take a first survey of the unparalleled sight there while she was still alone. Entering it from the south, she saw something monstrous and many-coloured in the shape of a pyramid, or, rather, like a huge fir-tree, sixty feet high, with shelves on the branches, widening and widening towards the base till they reached a circumference of eighty yards. The Piazza was full of life: slight young figures, in white garments, with olive wreaths on their heads, were moving to and fro about the base of the pyramidal tree, carrying baskets full of bright-coloured things . . .

These 'bright-coloured things' are the objects doomed to incineration.

> There were tapestries and brocades of immodest design, pictures and sculptures held too likely to incite to vice; there were boards and tables for all sorts of games,

playing-cards along with the blocks for printing them,
dice, and other apparatus for gambling; there were
worldly music-books, and musical instruments in all the
pretty varieties of lute, drum, cymbal and trumpet; there
were masks and masquerading-dresses used in the old
Carnival shows; there were handsome copies of Ovid,
Boccaccio, Petrarca, Pulci, and other books of a vain or
impure sort; there were all the implements of feminine
vanity – rouge-pots, false hair, mirrors, perfumes, pow-
ders, and transparent veils intended to provoke inquisitive
glances: lastly, at the very summit, there was the un-
flattering effigy of a probably mythical Venetian mer-
chant, who was understood to have offered a heavy sum
for this collection of marketable abominations, and soaring above him in surpassing ugliness, the symbolic figure
of the old debauched Carnival.

A year later it was in the Loggia dei Lanzi that, as a test of
Savonarola's saintliness, an ordeal by fire was arranged between one of the most faithful of his Dominican disciples, Fra
Domenico da Pescia, and a friar of the rival Franciscan order.
A bonfire, similar to that which had consumed the Vanities,
had been raised. The idea was that, when it had been lit, each
contestant would walk through it. Not surprisingly, there
were repeated delays, as each side found fault with the pro-
cedures of the other. As the nineteenth-century novelist
Mrs Oliphant (1828–97) describes it:

> From half-past twelve to the hour of vespers, this tragi-
> comedy went on . . . A thunderstorm swept across the
> Piazza, then a tumult arose; but neither storm nor tumult
> was enough to disperse the crowd or make a natural end
> to the situation. At last, as the day waned, the Signoria
> finding it impossible to screw the contestants to the
> sticking-point, put a stop to the ordeal altogether and sent
> word to Savonarola to depart with his brethren.

On 23 May 1498, Savonarola's hanged body was inciner-
ated, along with those of two of his closest companions, in the
Piazza.

The Festa degli Omaggi (The Feast of St John) was an annual event in the Piazza della Signoria for several hundred years; in 1581 Montaigne described the celebrations:

It being St John's eve, the roof of the cathedral was surrounded by two or three rows of lamps, and a number of rockets were let off. They say, however, that it is not the general custom in Italy, as in France, to have fire-works on St John's day. The festival came round in due course, on the Sunday, and being, of all the saints' days, the one observed with the greatest solemnity and rejoic-ing, everybody was from an early hour abroad to take part in it, dressed in their best. I had thus an opportunity of seeing all the women, old and young; and I must confess that the amount of beauty at Florence seemed to me very limited. Early in the morning the grand duke took his seat in the palace square, upon a platform which occupied the whole front of the palace, the walls of which, as well as the platform, were hung with rich tapestry. He was seated under a canopy, with the Pope's nuncio at his side on the left, and the Ferrarese ambassa-dor on his right, but not so near him by a good deal as the nuncio. Here there passed before him a long procession of men in various guises, emblems of the different castles, towns and states dependent upon the archduchy of Florence, and the name and style of each, as its representa-tive passed, were announced to the assembled multitude by a herald, who stood in full costume. Representing Siena, for instance, there came forward a young man habited in white and black velvet, bearing in one hand a large silver vase, and in the other an effigy of the she-wolf of Siena. These offerings he laid at the feet of the duke, accompanying them with a suitable address. When he had passed on he was followed, in single file, and as their names were successively called out, by a number of ill-dressed men, mounted on sorry hacks or on mules, some carrying a silver cup, others a ragged banner. These fellows, of whom there were a great number, went on through the streets, without any sort of form or ceremony, and indeed, without exhibiting the slightest gravity or even decency of demeanour, but rather seeming to treat the whole thing as a jest. They took their part in the affair as representatives of the various castles and other places in immediate dependence upon the state of Siena. . . .

By and by, advanced a car, bearing a great wooden pyramid, with steps all up to it, on which stood little boys dressed in different fashions, to represent saints and angels. The pyramid was as high as a house; and at the top of it was St John, bound to an iron bar. Next after this car came the public officers, those concerned with the revenue occupying the first rank. The procession was closed by another car, on which were several young men with three prizes, which were afterwards run for in different sorts of races. On each side of the car were the horses that were about to take part in the races, led by the jockeys, wearing the colours of their different masters, among whom were some of the greatest nobles of the country. The horses were small, but exquisitely formed.

. . . After dinner, everybody went to see the horse-racing. The Cardinal de' Medici's horse won; the prize was worth about 200 crowns. This spectacle is not so agreeable as the chariot-race, for it takes place in the street, and all you see is the horses tearing past where you stand, at the top of their speed, and there is an end of the matter as far as you are concerned . . .

On the preceding Saturday the grand duke's palace was thrown open to all comers, without exception, and was crowded with country people, who by and by nearly all collected in the great hall, where they fell to dancing. As I looked upon them, it seemed to my fancy an image of a people's lost liberty – an all but extinguished light throwing out a flickering gleam once a year, amid the shows of a saint's day.

Almost exactly three hundred years later, in 1858, Nathaniel Hawthorne was depressed, rather than impressed, by the same festival:

The Feast of St John, like the Carnival, is but a meagre semblance of festivity, kept alive factitiously, and dying a lingering death of centuries. It takes the exuberant mind and heart of a people to keep its holidays alive.

These already moribund festivities have long since been abandoned. The Feast of St John, the patron saint of Florence, is now celebrated on 24 June at the Piazzale Michelangelo with a public holiday and a fireworks display. A *calcio in costume* (football match in fancy dress) is also played three times during that week, in the Piazza Signoria, the Piazza S. Croce, and the Boboli Gardens.

In his autobiographical *A Voyage to Pagany* ('Pagany', the place of pagans), the result of a journey made in response to the urging of his friend Ezra Pound, 'You'd better come across [to Europe] and broaden your mind', William Carlos Williams has his forty-year-old American alter ego Dr Evans (Dev) arrive in Florence and eventually make his way into the Piazza della Signoria, to be confronted by Michelangelo's *David*. Dev has already gazed, in the course of his wandering about the city, at Donatello's depiction of the same subject and, inevitably, a comparison follows:

The false crudity of Angelo, the delicate torment drove him wild again. That's Christian, big with mental anguish, the genesis of which is the impossibility of fusing the old power with the new weakness. The pain, the weakening is the charm! Agh! He twisted the Greek; put the anguish of the soul into it. The Christian anguish. But why take *that* to torment the Greek, the quiet, the perfect, the lovely. No, no!

Evans could not frame it. He felt only the offence in the David. The too big hands, the over-anxious Jewish eyes. The neurasthenic size of the thing standing there in the courtyard with the Judith not far off turning her face away.

This is not Italy. The David meant nothing to him. It is lying. It leans on the Greek, which it bastardizes, to give it a kind of permission. Had to have something to lean on –

so it slimes the anguish over that, trying to unite two
impossible themes.

Hazlitt, in 1821, was even less impressed by the *David*,
remarking that it was 'as though a large mass of solid marble
fell on one's head, to crush one's faith in great names. It looks
like an awkward overgrown actor at one of the minor theatres,
without his clothes; the head is too big for the body, and it has
a helpless expression of distress.'

What William Carlos Williams's 'Dev' saw in the Piazza was
not Michelangelo's original statue, long since removed to the
Accademia di belle Arti, but a copy. Hazlitt saw the original.

There are other twentieth-century views of the Piazza della
Signoria in D. H. Lawrence's *Aaron's Rod* and E. M. Forster's
A Room with a View.

Lawrence's Aaron, a flautist, suddenly catches sight

of the long slim neck of the Palazzo Vecchio up above, in
the air. And in another minute he was passing between
massive buildings, out into the Piazza della Signoria.
There he stood still and looked round him in real surprise
and real joy. The flat, empty square with its stone paving
was all wet. The great buildings rose dark. The dark sheer
front of the Palazzo Vecchio went up like a cliff to the
battlements, and the slim tower soared dark and hawk-
like, crested, high above. And at the foot of the cliff stood
the great naked David, white and stripped in the wet,
white against the dark, warm-dark cliff of the building –
and near, the heavy naked men of Bandinelli.

The first thing he had seen, as he turned into the square,
was the back of one of these Bandinelli statues: a great
naked man of marble, with a heavy back and strong naked
flanks over which the water was trickling. And then to
come immediately on the David, so much whiter,
glistening skin-white in the wet, standing a little forward
and shrinking.

He may be ugly, too naturalistic, too big, and anything
else you like. But the David in the Piazza della Signoria,
there under the dark great Palace, in the position

Michelangelo chose for him, there standing forward stripped and exposed and eternally half-shrinking, half-wishing to expose himself, he is the genius of Florence. The adolescent, the white, self-conscious, physical adolescent: enormous, in keeping with the stark, grim, enormous palace, which is dark and bare as he is white and bare. And behind, the big, lumpy Bandinelli men are in keeping too. They may be ugly – but they are there in their place, and they have their own lumpy reality. And this morning in the rain, standing unbroken, with the water trickling down their flanks and along the inner sides of their great thighs, they were real enough, representing the undaunted physical nature of the heavier Florentines.

Aaron looked and looked at the three great naked men. David so much white and standing forward, self-conscious: then at the great splendid front of the Palazzo Vecchio: and at the fountain splashing water upon its wet, wet figures; and the distant equestrian statue; and the stone-flagged space of the grim square. And he felt that here he was in one of the world's living centres, here, in the Piazza della Signoria. The sense of having arrived – of having reached a perfect centre of the human world: this he had.

And so, satisfied, he turned round to look at the bronze Perseus which rose just above him. Benvenuto Cellini's dark hero looked female, with his plump hips and his waist, female and rather insignificant: graceful, and rather vulgar . . .

The great naked men in the rain, under the dark-grey November sky, in the dark, strong, inviolable square! The wonderful hawk-head of the old palace! The physical self-conscious adolescent, Michelangelo's David, shrinking and exposing himself, with his white, slack limbs! Florence, passionate, fearless Florence had spoken herself out. Aaron was fascinated by the Piazza della Signoria. He never went into the town, never returned from it to his lodging, without contriving to pass through the square. And he never passed through it without satisfaction. Here men had been at their intensest, most naked pitch, here, at

the end of the old world and the beginning of the
new . . .

Just as Augustus Hare saw the Loggia dei Lanzi as a place of
men, so does Aaron see the whole of the Piazza della Signoria
and even the whole of Florence: 'He found the Piazza della
Signoria packed with men: but all, all men. And all farmers,
land-owners, land-workers. The curious, fine-nosed Tuscan
farmers, with their half-sardonic, amber-coloured eyes.'

On a day of warm sun in April 1887, Thomas Hardy sat
down for a long time on the steps of the Loggia dei Lanzi and,
as he put it, 'thought of many things'. His diary recorded:

It is three in the afternoon, and the faces of the buildings
are steeped in the afternoon stagnation. The figure of
Neptune is looking an intense white against the brown-
grey houses behind, and the bronze forms round the basin
[of the fountain] are starred with rays on their noses,
elbows, bosoms and shoulders . . .

In the caffè near there is a patter of speech, and on the
pavement outside a noise of hoofs. The reflection from
that statue of Neptune throws a secondary light into the
caffè.

Everybody is thinking, even amid these art examples
from various ages, that this present age is the ultimate
climax and upshot of the previous ages, and not a link in a
chain of them.

In a work of art it is the accident which *charms*, not the
intention; *that* we only like and admire. Instance the
amber tones that pervade the folds of the drapery in
ancient marbles, the deadened polish of the surfaces, and
the cracks and the scratches.

The scene in *A Room with a View* which E. M. Forster – of
whom Lawrence wrote, after a visit, 'his life is so ridiculously
inane, the man is dying of inanition' – sets in the Piazza is the
pivotal one of the novel:

'Nothing ever happens to me,' she [Lucy Honeychurch, the heroine] reflected, as she entered the Piazza
Signoria and looked nonchalantly at its marvels, now

fairly familiar to her. The great square was in shadow; the sunshine had come too late to strike it. Neptune was already unsubstantial in the twilight, half god, half ghost, and his fountain plashed dreamily to the men and satyrs who idled together on its marge. The Loggia showed as the triple entrance of a cave, wherein dwelt many a deity, shadowy but immortal, looking forth upon the arrivals and departures of mankind. It was the hour of unreality – the hour, that is, when unfamiliar things are real. An older person at such an hour and in such a place might think that sufficient was happening to him, and rest content. Lucy desired more.

She fixed her eyes wistfully on the tower of the palace, which rose out of the lower darkness like a pillar of roughened gold. It seemed no longer a tower, no longer supported by earth, but some unobtainable treasure throbbing in the tranquil sky. Its brightness mesmerised her, still dancing before her eyes when she bent them to the ground and started towards home.

Then something did happen.

Two Italians by the Loggia had been bickering about a debt. 'Cinque lire,' they had cried, 'cinque lire!' They sparred at each other, and one of them was hit lightly upon the chest. He frowned; he bent towards Lucy with a look of interest, as if he had an important message for her. He opened his lips to deliver it, and a stream of red came out between them and trickled down his unshaven chin.

That was all. A crowd rose out of the dusk. It hid this extraordinary man from her and bore him away to the fountain. Mr George Emerson [the man whom, at the close of the novel, Lucy marries] happened to be a few paces away, looking at her across the spot where the man had been. How very odd! Across something. Even as she caught sight of him he grew dim; the palace itself grew dim, swayed above her, fell onto her softly, slowly, noiselessly, and the sky fell with it.

She thought: 'Oh, what have I done?'

'Oh, what have I done?' she murmured and opened her eyes.

'You fainted.'

Later, as she is recovering, 'In the distance, she saw creatures with black hoods, such as appear in dreams.' Although she does not know it, these are members of the Misericordia, whose business it still is, in case of accident or sudden death, to assemble and render what assistance may be necessary.

In Anatole France's *Le Lys Rouge* (The Red Lily), set in Florence at almost exactly the same time as *A Room with a View*, there is also a description of the Misericordia:

> Just then they saw lights and heard mournful songs approaching them out of the darkness. And then, like phantoms, driven by the wind, there appeared before them black-robed penitents. The crucifix was carried before them. They were the Brothers of the Misericordia. With their faces hidden by cowls they were holding lighted torches and singing psalms. They were bearing a corpse to the cemetery. It was the Italian custom for the funeral procession to take place at night and to pass along rapidly. On the deserted quay there appeared cross, coffin and banners. Jacques and Thérèse stood against the wall to let pass the crowd of priests, choristers and hooded figures, and, in their midst, importunate Death, whom no one welcomes on this pleasure-loving earth. The black stream had passed. Weeping women ran after the coffin borne by weird shapes in hob-nailed boots.
>
> Therese sighed: 'Of what avail is it to torment ourselves in this world?'

Dickens, having noted that the Grand Duke himself wore the black robe and hood as a member of this body, described its duties as follows:

> If an accident takes place, their office is to raise the sufferer, and bear him tenderly to the hospital. If a fire breaks out, it is one of their functions to repair to the spot and render their assistance and protection. It is also among their commonest offices to attend and console the sick; and they neither receive money, nor eat, nor drink, in any house they visit for this purpose. Those who are on

duty for the time are called together at a moment's notice, by the tolling of the great bell of the tower; and it is said that the Grand-Duke might be seen, at this sound, to rise from his seat at table and quietly withdraw to attend the summons.

W. D. Howells writes of the Misericordia in less matter-of-fact fashion in his *Tuscan Cities*:

While these brothers, 'black-stoled, black-hooded, like a dream,' continue to light the way to dusty death with their flaring torches through the streets of Florence, the mediaeval tradition remains unbroken, Italy is still Italy. They knew better how to treat death in the Middle Ages than we do now. These simple old Florentines, with their street wars, their pestilences, their manifold destructive violences, felt instinctively that he, the inexorable, was not to be hidden or palliated, not to be softened or prettified, or anyways made the best of, but was to be confessed in all his terrible gloom; and in this they found, not comfort, not alleviation, but the anaesthesis of a freezing horror. Those masked and trailing sable figures, sweeping through the wide and narrow ways by night to the long, wild rhythm of their chaunt, in the red light of their streaming torches, and bearing the heavily draped bier in their midst, supremely awe the spectator, whose heart falters within him in the presence of that which alone is certain to be.

Except that now the torches of its members do not flare or stream, that the bell which summons them tends to be that of a telephone, and that they usually sweep through the streets not on foot but in motorized vehicles, the Misericordia today is little different from what it has been over the centuries.

THE UFFIZI

On their first visit to the Uffizi, the Hawthornes enjoyed something unexpected. Their friend, Mrs Mountford, sum-

moned them to the Great Court, where a flower-carpet was in
process of being laid.

> . . . Twenty or more men were at work, weaving a
> wonderful tissue, composed of petals of flowers, and
> leaves of box. The pattern was carefully chalked upon the
> flat flag-stones, and the men were rapidly filling in the
> forms with separate colours. Each of their baskets con-
> tained petals of one hue, and they, being perfectly in-
> structed in what they were to accomplish, moved about,
> scattering blue, or red, or purple, or yellow petals in each
> defined division, so quickly and accurately, that, like a
> vision, the gorgeous carpet soon was spread over the
> stones. Its life was preserved bright and fresh by the
> continual sprinkling of water from many watering-pots
> which also made the petals heavy, so that the breeze
> would not blow them out of place. The fragrance was
> delicious, and can anything be more preciously beautiful
> than such a carpet? for its evanescence in this case added to
> its beauty. Such prodigality of richness just for a few
> hours – at the expense of so much toil! It was like carving
> and painting for the Lord, with the single purpose of
> worship; for it was Corpus Christi day, and the body of
> the Saviour was to pass over it – and the procession would
> inevitably destroy all the cunning workmanship.
> Thousands of wax-candles, in prismatic chandeliers, and
> in candelabras, placed in front of mirrors, with crystal
> pendants, were to light up the scene. As these chandeliers,
> composed of prisms, vibrated, they reflected the crimson
> tints of the surrounding silk hangings, and so looked like
> rubies flashing, even in the daylight.'

Sophia Hawthorne has recorded how, on their last visit to
the Uffizi, she and her husband were distracted by two
Englishmen –

> one a tall red-faced squire and fox-hunter, I fancy, with a
> loud, lumbering voice, like a sledge-hammer, slightly
> modulated by a certain amount of civilisation: the other
> a small, slender, delicately organized, polished, trim,

regular-featured, conceited, cautious gentleman, with silver hair, resembling a shining little minnow in the wake of a porpoise. The porpoise was the introducer of the minnow to the wonders of art before them, and it was a rare spectacle to see how he managed it. He plainly had no perception of art at all, but he was quite sure he had, and that he was an accomplished connoisseur, as he knew the names and reputations of the pictures. He desired a large audience, or more exactly, he felt that he deserved one, and looked about to observe who heard his remarks, as much as to say, 'Listen all who can.' To all his dogmatical assertions in heavy sledgy voice, the silver minnow responded in thin tones of assent, with consummate skill and nicety. Such a precise, immaculate little nonentity of a person! for there was no intellect in his face – he was only well arranged; but the small parlor of his mind was in exact order, and all its minute objects of *vertu* laid out to best advantage. The two friends consulted together about going to the Pitti. The silver minnow said to the red porpoise, in his fine, wee voice, 'It confuses one to see too many things at once.' 'It DOES SO,' replied the other in heavy boulder-tones. They were extremely diverting, yet there was so much for us to see that I could not spend any more time observing them.

After a visit to the Uffizi, E. M. Forster commented in a letter to E. J. Dent:

. . . How flagrantly indecent are the statues in the Uffizi with their little brown paper drawers, I almost feel that the permanent plaster article of the Catholic reaction is preferable. It did know its own mind.

His reaction recalls that of Samuel Butler, a writer whom he much admired, to the prudery of a fig-leaf on a statue in the Montreal Museum ('O God, O Montreal!').

The horror of Saunders McMuckleman, a Scottish clergyman character in *Continental Adventures* by the now forgotten nineteenth-century novelist Charlotte A. Eaton, is very

different: 'Gude Lord, why she's stark naked!' he exclaims of
the *Venus de Medici*.

This statue, found in Hadrian's villa in Tivoli, has inspired a
number of writers. Samuel Rogers, who spent long periods
gazing in absorbed silence at it, declared:

> We must return, and once more give a loose
> To the delighted spirit – worshipping,
> In her small temple of rich workmanship,
> Venus herself, who, when she left the skies,
>   Came hither . . .

Byron wrote of the same statue:

> We gaze and turn away, and know not where,
> Dazzled and drunk with beauty, till the heart
> Reels with its fulness; there – for ever there –
> Chain'd to the chariot of triumphal Art,
> We stand as captives and would not depart.

Even the usually phlegmatic Hawthorne was moved to
enthusiasm:

> Her modest attitude is partly what unmakes her as the
> heathen goddess and softens her into woman. One cannot
> think of her as a senseless image, but as a being that lives
> to gladden the world, incapable of decay or death; as
> young and fair as she was three thousand years ago, and
> still to be young and fair as long as a beautiful thought
> shall require physical embodiment.

Smollett – who in January 1765 'lodged at the Widow
Vinini's, an English house delightfully situated on the bank of
the Arno' – was less enthusiastic about the *Venus*. While
admitting that 'the back parts . . . are executed so happily as to
excite the admiration of the most indifferent spectator,' he
'cannot help thinking that there is no beauty in the features . . .
and that the attitude is aukward [sic] and out of character.'
Leigh Hunt also admired 'the back parts' of the *Venus*,
commenting:

It would be difficult nowadays to convey, in English, the impression of the Italian word *fianchi* (flanks) with the requisite delicacy, in speaking of the naked human figure. We use it only to mean the sides of an army, of a fortified place, or of a beast. Yet the words *rilevati fianchi* (flanks in relief) are used by the greatest Italian poets to express a beauty eminent among all beautiful females who are not pinched and spoilt by modern fashions . . .

But his final conclusion was even more severe than Smollett's:

I must make bold to say, that I think neither the gesture of the figure modest, nor the face worthy even of the gesture. . . . To my mind, the expression of the face (not to mince the matter, now I must come to it) is pert, petty, insolent, and fastidious. It is the face of a foolish young woman, who thinks highly of herself, and is prepared to be sarcastic on all her acquaintance.

Even in Madame de Staël's time the Uffizi was easily accessible to the public at large. In *Corinne* she comments approvingly: 'The fine arts are very republican in Florence. The statues and pictures are on show at all hours, with the utmost ease of entry. Attendants, trained and paid by the government, are on hand to explain the masterpieces.'

Few present-day visitors marvelling at the treasures of the Uffizi can be aware of the extent of their debt to the Archduke Pietro Leopoldo. Writing in the early nineteenth century, Antoine Laurent Castellan makes that debt clear in his *Letters on Italy*:

Under his directions, many more halls were built and a new flight of stairs to ascend them; and he added to the museum the most precious ornaments of the other palaces. He likewise sent to Rome for the statues from the Villa Medici, and more especially for those of Niobe and her children. By his exertions every class of objects had their distinct place, they were found without trouble, and classed so as to satisfy all tastes. He was rigorous in his selection, and admitted nothing that was not worthy of being preserved. The prince himself watched over the execution of his projects, and animated the workmen by his presence. One knows not which to admire most – the grandeur of the enterprise or the celerity of the execution. In 1780, in the space of one year, new buildings were added, and divided into halls; while, by this means, the communication was rendered more easy, and they were ornamented with stuccoes, gilding, paintings, and marbles; the tapestry and other drapery was renewed; the statues and pictures were placed in other situations, cleaned, or restored; whilst everything was ranged according to the system of a library, where every volume had its own separate and distinct place. And this metamorphosis was executed in so rapid a manner, that travellers, ere they had completed the tour of Italy, as they repassed through Florence, thought they beheld a new gallery, and were full of admiration at a change which almost appeared magical.

Via di San Martino to the Porta di San Piero

This street contains both the Casa di Dante, where an inscription records that Dante was born in 1265, and the little church of S. Martino, founded in 786 by the Irish St Andrew, Archdeacon of Fiesole. It was in the church of S. Martino that Dante was married. Augustus Hare writes that the house – subsequently to become a wine-shop frequented by Michelangelo, Cellini, and other notabilities – 'was of great interest as late as 1877, but has since been completely "renovated", to the utter destruction of its value, not a stone of the house which Dante looked upon having been spared.'

Mrs Oliphant describes the Florence of Dante as follows:

The little Florence in which Dante was born was very much unlike the noble and beautiful Florence which is now, like Jerusalem, a joy of the whole earth . . . The high houses that rose in narrow lines closely approaching each other, with a continual menace, across the straight thread of the street, had not yet attained to the characteristic individuality of Tuscan architecture. The beautiful cathedral, which so many a traveller, thoughtless of dates, has contemplated from the Sasso di Dante, with a dim notion that Dante himself must have sat there many a summer evening . . . had not, even in the lower altitude given to it by Arnolfo, begun to be when the poet was born. The old Bargello and the Palazzo Vecchio were still in process of building. Santa Croce, Santa Maria Novella, and Giotto's lovely Campanile were all in the future with their riches. The ancient Badia, or Abbey of Florence, still struck the hour, as the poet records, to all the listening city; and though the bridges, curiously enough, had all been built, there was scarcely as yet any Oltr' Arno. . . . The Baptistery had not even got its coating of marbles, but was still in flint, grey and homely, when the child of the Alighieri was christened there; and little Santa Reparata, with its grave-yard around it, lay deep down as in a well in the heart of the tall houses. The Baptistery, too, was surrounded by graves, its square being filled up by sarcophagi of a still older date, in which – a curious fancy – many of the greater families of Florence buried their dead. The tower of one of the great houses was called *Guarda-morte*, 'watcher of the dead', so closely round that little centre of the buried clustered the houses of the living. But to the old church of the Baptist, the 'bel San Giovanni' of the poet, every child of Florence was carried then, as now, to be made a Christian. That great solemn interior, still and cool and calm amid the blazing sunshine, remains alone unchanged amid all the alterations around. The graves have been cleared away, the great Duomo has been built, the tower of Giotto, airy fabric of genius, defying all its tons of marble to make it less like a lily born of dew and sunshine, has sprung up into the heavens; but San Giovanni is still the same, and still the new Florentines are carried into its serene solemnity of gloom to be enrolled at once in the Church and in the world by names which may be heard of hereafter – as was the infant Durante, Dante, prince of poets . . .

At the corner where the Corso now joins the Via del Proconsolo, there stands the Palazzo Salviati, on the site of the house of Folco Portinari, father of Dante's Beatrice. In the courtyard is the *Nicchia di Dante* (Dante's Niche), from which he is said to have watched for his love. In his *Life of Dante*, Boccaccio tells the story of that first encounter:

It happened that Folco Portinari, a man of great honour in those times among the citizens, had assembled the neighbours in his house to entertain them [*festeggiare*], among whom was the young man called Alighieri, whom (since little children, especially in places of merrymaking, are accustomed to go with their parents) Dante, not having yet completed his ninth year, accompanied. And it happened that, with others of his age, of whom both boys and girls there were many in the house, after he had served at the first tables as much as his tender age permitted, childishly with the others he began to play. There was among this crowd of children a daughter of the above-named Folco, whose name was Bice (though he always named her Beatrice, her formal name), who was about eight years old, gay and agreeable; with habits and language more serious and modest than her age warranted; and besides this with features so delicate and so beautifully formed, and full, beside mere beauty, of so much candid loveliness that many thought her almost an angel. This girl then, such as I describe her, and perhaps even more beautiful, appeared at the *festa* – not I suppose for the first time, but for the first time in power to create love – before the eyes of Dante, who, though still a child, received her image into his heart with so much affection that from that day henceforward, as long as he lived, it never again departed from him.

The *Vita Nuova* is, of course, the story of this strange love. In it Dante himself describes that first meeting. Beatrice's dress was 'of a most noble colour, a subdued and goodly crimson, girdled and adorned in such sort as best suited with her very tender age.' As soon as he had looked on her:

Love ruled my soul . . . and began to take such security of sway over me . . . that it was necessary for me to do completely all his pleasure. He commanded me often that I should endeavour to see this so youthful angel, and I saw in her such noble and praiseworthy deportment that truly of her might be said these words of the poet Homer – 'She appeared to be born not of mortal man but of God.'

In Dante's time the Porta di San Piero, long since vanished, lay just beyond the church of San Piero Maggiore, in the busy little piazza of that same name. Franco Sachetti (c. 1333–1400), best known for his *Trecentonovelle*, tales of Florentine life, recounts the following:

Passing by the Gate of San Piero, Dante saw a smith beating iron upon his anvil, and all the while he sang from Dante's poem, as one singeth a song, and he so jumbled the verses, clipping here and adding there, that he seemed to Dante to be doing him a very great injury. Dante said nothing, but he approached the smith's shop – there where he had many irons with which he plied his trade. And Dante took the hammer and flung it into the street; he took the scales and he threw them into the street; and thus he threw out many of his tools. The smith, turning upon him with a threatening gesture, cried:

'What the devil are you doing? Are you mad?'

Dante asked him: 'What art thou doing?'

'I am doing my own business,' answered the smith, 'and you are spoiling my tools, throwing them into the street.'

Said Dante: 'If thou desirest that I should not spoil thy things, do not thou spoil mine.'

Said the smith: 'What am I spoiling of yours?'

Dante answered: 'Thou art singing out of my book, and are not singing it as I wrote it. I have no other trade but this, and thou art spoiling it for me.'

The smith was taken aback, and knowing not what to reply, he gathered his things together and returned to his work. And now if he wisheth to sing, he singeth Tristan or Lancelot, and leaveth Dante alone.

THE BARGELLO

The Bargello (entrance in Via del Proconsolo) was originally
built as the Palace of the Podestà, the chief criminal magistrate
of Florence. After the abolition of the office of Podestà by
Cosimo I, the palace became the headquarters of the Bargello
or chief of police.

More than a century ago the Bargello became the Museo
Nazionale – a change of which Henry James could not wholly
approve:

> Beautiful and masterful though the Bargello is, it smells
> too strongly of restoration, and, much of old Italy as still
> lurks in its furbished and renovated chambers, it speaks
> even more distinctly of the ill-mannered young kingdom
> that has – as 'unavoidably' as you please – lifted down a
> hundred delicate works of sculpture from the convent-
> walls where their pious authors placed them. . . . The
> Bargello is full of early Tuscan sculpture, most of the
> pieces of which have come from suppressed religious
> houses; and even if the visitor be an ardent liberal, he is
> uncommonly conscious of the rather brutal process by
> which it has been collected. One can hardly envy young
> Italy the number of odious things she has had to do.

In his Journal for December 1895, André Gide describes a
visit to the Bargello where he gazed, enraptured, at the *David*:

> Wonderful *David* of Donatello! Small bronze body!
> ornamented nudity; Oriental grace; shadow of the hat
> over the eyes, in which the source of his glance is lost and
> become immaterial. Smile on the lips; softness of the
> cheeks.
>   His small delicate body with its rather frail and strained
> grace – hardness of the bronze – the figured armor-plate
> on the legs covering only the calf and permitting the thigh
> to rise from it more tender by contrast.
>   The very strangeness of that immodest accoutrement,
> and the taut nervousness of the little arms, which hold
> either the stone or the sabre. I should like to call him up

before me at will. For a long time I observed – trying to memorize, to retain within me those charming lines, that fold of the abdomen immediately under the ribs hollowed out when he breathes, and even that leanness of the muscle joining the top of the breast to the right shoulder – and that somewhat broken fold at the top of the thigh – and that extraordinary flatness of the loins immediately above the sacrum . . .

The rich and elderly connoisseur, Eustace, one of the leading characters in Aldous Huxley's *Time Must Have A Stop* (1945), decides 'to pop into the Bargello for a moment after a visit to Vieusseux's Lending Library':

Ten minutes were enough to whizz around the Donatellos and, his head full of heroic bronze and marble, he strolled up the street in the direction of the bookshop [owned in the novel by a 'Bruno Rontini', based on the real-life Pino Orioli, friend of D. H. Lawrence, Norman Douglas, and many other English writers].

Yes, it would have been nice, he was thinking, it would have been very nice indeed if one's life had the quality of those statues. Nobility without affectation. Serenity combined with passionate energy. Dignity wedded to grace. But, alas, those were not precisely the characteristics that one's life had exhibited. Which was regrettable no doubt. But of course it had its compensating advantages. Being a Donatello would have been altogether too strenuous for his taste. That sort of thing was much more John's cup of tea [a left-wing journalist] – John who had always seen himself as the equivalent of a mixture between Gattamelata and the Baptist. Instead of which, his actual life was . . . what? Eustace cast about for the answer, and finally decided that John's life was best compared to a war picture by one of those deplorable painters who were born to be magazine illustrators but had unfortunately seen the Cubists and taken to High Art. Poor John! He had no taste, no sense of style . . .

SANTA CROCE

The church and cloisters of Santa Croce are often referred to as
the Westminster Abbey of Florence. Madame de Staël wrote:
'This church of Santa Croce contains the most brilliant
assembly of corpses in perhaps the whole of Italy.' Here,
among many other illustrious people, lie Lorenzo Ghiberti,
Michelangelo, Galileo, and Alfieri. It was in reference to such
as these that Leigh Hunt wrote: 'The church of Santa Croce
would disappoint you as much inside as out, if the presence of
great men did not always cast a mingled shadow of the awful
and beautiful over our thoughts.'

In the fourth canto of *Childe Harold's Pilgrimage*, Byron
referred both to the illustrious Florentines who had found their
final resting place in Santa Croce and to those who, scandal-
ously, had failed to do so:

But where repose the all-Etruscan three –
Dante, and Petrarch, and scarce less than they,
The Bard of Prose, creative spirit, he
Of the Hundred Tales of love – where did they lay
Their bones, distinguished from our common clay
In death as life? Are they resolved to dust,
And have their country's marbles nought to say?
Could not her quarries furnish forth one bust?
Did they not to her breast their filial earth entrust?

Ungrateful Florence! Dante sleeps afar,
Like Scipio, buried by the upbraiding shore:
The factions, in their worse than civil war,
Proscribed the bard whose name for evermore
Their children's children would in vain adore
With the remorse of ages; and the crown
Which Petrarch's laureate brow supremely wore,
Upon a far and foreign soil had grown,
His life, his grave, though rifled – not thine own.

Boccaccio to his parent earth bequeathed
His dust, – and lies it not her great among,
With many a sweet and solemn requiem breathed

> O'er him who formed the Tuscan siren's tongue,
> That music in itself, whose sounds are song,
> The poetry of speech? No; even in his tomb
> Uptorn must bear the hyaena bigot's wrong,
> No more amidst the meaner dead find room,
> Nor claim a passing sigh, because it told for *whom*!

One of the most interesting tombs is that of the great Italian poet and dramatist Alfieri (1749–1803), erected by Canova at the behest of Alfieri's lover, the Countess of Albany. Alfieri had declared that the love of fame first came to him as he was walking among the tombs of the illustrious dead in this church. The Countess herself sat to Canova for the figure of bereaved Italy. Her story is told with dry irony by E. V. Lucas:

> This curious and unfortunate woman became, at the age of nineteen, the wife of the Young Pretender, twenty-seven years after the '45, and led a miserable existence with him (due chiefly to his depravity, but a little, she always held, to the circumstance that they chose Good Friday for their wedding day) until Alfieri fell in love with her and offered her his protection. Together she and the poet remained, apparently contented with each other and received by society, even by the English Royal Family, until Alfieri died in 1803, when after exclaiming that she had lost all – 'consolations, support, society, all, all!' – and establishing this handsome memorial, she selected the French artist Fabre to fill the aching void in her fifty-years-old heart; and Fabre not only filled it until her death in 1824, but became the heir to all that had been bequeathed to her by both the Stuart and Alfieri. Such was the Countess of Albany. She herself is buried close by, in the chapel of the Castellani.

Of Alfieri's monument Sophia Hawthorne wrote: 'It is not good for anything to me.' Now it is regarded as one of Canova's greatest works.

In the Palazzo Masetti (Castelbarco), now the home of the British Consulate, on the Lung' Arno, the Countess and Fabre maintained a *salon*, frequented by such literary celebrities as

Chateaubriand, Foscolo, and Von Platen. But increasingly dissatisfied with each other and therefore with life, they became a sour, gloomy couple. One of their writer guests, Massimo d'Azeglio, gave an amusing account of a visit paid to them. Arriving late, he heard the Countess exclaim to Prince Borghese: 'What an hour to arrive!' Overcome, d'Azeglio hurried over to the buffet, to help himself to an ice. The ices on offer were those especially hard ones called *mattonelle* ('little bricks'), on this occasion modelled into the shape of peaches. D'Azeglio takes up the story:

> While I was vainly striving to make an impression on my ice with the spoon, what does it do but slip off from under it, like a cherry-stone that is snapped? I see it now, bounding against the minister's diamond cross (the Sardinian Minister in Tuscany was standing by him), falling to the floor, and rolling straight to the Countess of Albany's feet. I felt as if I should never leave off running. That was my last visit.

It was in the Palazzo Masetti that Alfieri died in 1803. Delirious, his hand in that of the mistress who had finally become his wife, he miraculously recited one hundred verses of Hesiod, read only once in his youth, before he expired. It is a wonder that, during the recitation, the Countess did not herself expire of boredom.

Another interesting monument in Santa Croce is that by Bernardo Rossellino to Leonardo Bruni, known as Aretino. Unlike many of the others in this church, it is contemporary, dating from Aretino's death in 1444. Described by John Addington Symonds as 'the nearest approach to a really great figure in the Florentine literary world of the first half of the fifteenth century', Aretino was the translator of Plato and Aristotle, the author of a Latin history of Florence, and the first biographer of Dante.

In E. M. Forster's *A Room with a View*, the heroine Lucy Honeychurch and her companion Miss Lavish, a novelist who is constantly saying that she knows her Florence 'by heart', lose their way to Santa Croce, as many tourists have done both before them and since. Miss Lavish cries out:

'Lost! Lost! My dear Miss Lucy, during our political diatribes we have taken a wrong turning. How those horrid Conservatives would jeer at us! What are we to do? Two lone females in an unknown town. Now, this is what *I* call an adventure.'

Lucy, who wanted to see Santa Croce, suggested as a possible solution that they should ask the way there.

'Oh, but that is the word of a craven! And no, you are not, not, *not* to look at your Baedeker. Give it to me; I shan't let you carry it. We will simply drift.'

Accordingly they drifted through a series of those gray-brown streets, neither commodious nor picturesque, in which the eastern quarter of the city abounds. Lucy soon lost interest in the discontent of Lady Louisa, and became discontented herself. For one ravishing moment Italy appeared. She stood in the Square of the Annunziata and saw in the living terra cotta those divine babies whom no reproduction can ever stale. There they stood, with their shining limbs bursting from the garments of charity, and their strong white arms extended against circlets of heaven. Lucy thought she had never seen anything more beautiful; but Miss Lavish, with a shriek of dismay, dragged her forward, declaring that they were out of their path now by at least a mile.

The hour was approaching at which the continental breakfast begins, or rather ceases, to tell, and the ladies bought some hot chestnut paste out of a little shop, because it looked so typical. It tasted partly of the paper in which it was wrapped, partly of hair oil, partly of the great unknown. But it gave them strength to drift into another Piazza, large and dusty, on the farther side of which rose a black-and-white facade of surpassing ugliness. Miss Lavish spoke to it dramatically. It was Santa Croce. The adventure was over.

But before the two women can enter, Miss Lavish catches a glimpse of what she calls 'my local colour-box' – an old man with white whiskers – and hurries off in pursuit. Abandoned,

Lucy awaits her return; then, after ten minutes, enters the church alone.

Of course, it must be a wonderful building. But how like a barn! And how very cold! Of course, it contained frescoes by Giotto, in the presence of whose tactile values she was capable of feeling what was proper. But who was to tell her which they were? She walked about disdainfully, unwilling to be enthusiastic over monuments of uncertain authorship or date. There was no one even to tell her which, of all the sepulchral slabs that paved the nave and transepts, was the one that was really beautiful, the one that had been most praised by Mr Ruskin.

Then the pernicious charm of Italy worked on her, and instead of acquiring information, she began to be happy. She puzzled out the Italian notices – the notice that forbade people to introduce dogs into the church – the notice that prayed people in the interest of health and out of respect to the sacred edifice in which they found themselves, not to spit. She watched the tourists; their noses were as red as their Baedekers, so cold was Santa Croce. She beheld the horrible fate that befell three Baptists – two he-babies and a she-baby – who began their career by sousing each other with the Holy Water, and then proceeded to the Machiavelli memorial, dripping but hallowed. Advancing toward it very slowly and from immense distances, they touched the stone with their fingers, with their handkerchiefs, with their heads, and then retreated. What could this mean? They did it again and again. Then Lucy realised that they had mistaken Machiavelli for some saint, hoping to acquire virtue. Punishment followed quickly. The smallest he-baby stumbled over one of the sepulchral slabs so much admired by Mr Ruskin, and entangled his feet in the features of a recumbent bishop. Protestant as she was, Lucy darted forward. She was too late. He fell heavily upon the prelate's upturned toes.

Ruskin did indeed admire some of the sepulchral slabs; but there was much that he did not admire, haranguing his readers:

See those huge tombs on your right hand and left, with their alternate gables and round tops, and the paltriest of all possible sculpture, trying to be grand by bigness, and pathetic by expense.

During the course of the section entitled *Le Séjour à Florence*, the eponymous heroine of Madame de Staël's *Corinne* visits Santa Croce. Corinne is a woman of such a variety of talents – poet, musician, dancer, actress – that it is hardly surprising that a young Englishman called Oswald, travelling in Italy for his health, should fall in love with her, and extremely surprising that he should later abandon her for her half-sister, Lucile.

The sight of this church, adorned with so many noble memorials, reawakened Corinne's enthusiasm. Whereas the faces of the living had discouraged, so now the silent presence of these dead reanimated in her the craving for glory with which she had formerly been seized. She walked with a firmer tread through the church, and thoughts from the past once more traversed her spirit. She saw appear under the vault some young priests, who were chanting in deep voices even as they moved at a slow pace round the choir. She asked one of them what was the meaning of their ceremony. 'We are praying for our dead,' he answered her. 'Yes, you are right to remember your dead,' Corinne thought to herself. 'They make up the only glorious possession left to you. . . . Oh, why has Oswald snuffed out those gifts which I received from heaven, and which I ought to use to awake enthusiasm in souls in tune with mine? Oh, my God!,' she cried out, as she threw herself on her knees, 'it is not at all in empty pride that I beg you to return to me those talents with which you originally blessed me. Undoubtedly the most superior of all beings are those obscure saints who know how to live and die for You and You alone. But the path for ordinary mortals is different, so that the spirit which dedicates itself to generosity and goodness, to all that is noble, humane and true, can surely be admitted at least into the outer courts of heaven.' Corinne's eyes were lowered as she uttered this prayer, and it was thus that she was struck by the inscription on the tomb on which she was kneeling. It ran as follows: 'Alone at my dawn, alone at my setting, I am again alone here.'

'Ah!' Corinne cried out to herself, 'here is the answer to my prayer! What ambition can one feel when one is alone on the earth? Who would share in my success, if I was able to achieve it? Who would be concerned in my fate? What feeling would encourage my spirit to labour? I must have Oswald's approval for reward.'

Another epitaph caught her eye. 'Do not grieve for me,' enjoined a man who had died in his youth. 'If only you knew how much pain this tomb has spared me.' 'What a detachment from life these words inspire!' thought Corinne, shedding tears. So close to all the bustle of the town, there is this church, which teaches people the secret of everything, if only they have ears to hear it. But they pass by without entering, and the marvellous illusion of forgetfulness keeps the world turning.'

The cloister, in which can be found monuments of minor Florentine celebrities, has always appealed to visitors. W. D. Howells wrote of it in his *Tuscan Cities*:

There is nothing more Florentine in Florence than these old convent courts into which your sight-seeing takes you so often. The middle space is enclosed by sheltering cloisters, and here the grass lies green in the sun the whole winter through, with daisies in it, and other sympathetic little weeds or flowers; the still air is warm, and the place has a climate of its own.

Most visitors would regard Santa Croce as a monument both to the Christian faith and to the cultural greatness of Florence. But perversely the hero, Evans (Dev), of William Carlos Williams's 1928 *Voyage to Pagany* finds in it chiefly 'a resurgent paganism'.
Having pushed upon the church's soiled red leather inner doors and then let them close behind him, he is

overtaken by an emotional reaction, striking back upon him across that rolling floor, that lifted him into an enchantment he would never cease to recall thereafter as long as he should live – nor to enjoy.

He escaped wholly at that first moment the feeling of a church. A double row of widely spaced hexagonal columns held up the flat beamed middle ceiling painted with crude colours, a dark and intricate design of blue and red and gold, orange and green and red; it might have been the flat roof of an old temple. But the floor of worn mosaics, uneven, undulant, irregular, the tomb of saints over whose effigies in bronze and marble he walked; and in the side walls other famous tombs – of Dante, the Medici; the Pantheon of Florence; it seemed all to him a savage, spacious present; direct, puissant – overwhelming, free, free somehow of all that which he hated.

Viewing the altar and the chapels on either side of it, Dev – who is, the author tells us, 'unable to tell the Giotto from the Cimabue' – is 'carried away by awe and antiquity,' and feels, exultantly, 'a beauty that by its simplicity, not softened, reached back truly outside of church into a sunlight which he identified by his earliest uncaptured instincts.'

Being so huge, the Piazza Santa Croce has always been a centre for festivities and ceremonies: tournaments, jousts, and games of *calcio* (football) on the one hand, penitential processions of the victims of the Inquisition on the other. In his *Letters on Italy* (1820), the French painter and writer Antoine Laurent Castellan (1772–1838) has left us an account of the celebration there of the annual Carnival:

. . . We have descriptions of many of these festivals; and amongst others, of a magnificent masquerade given by Cosimo I in the carnival of 1565; the carnival of 1615 has been engraved by Callot, and many others have exercised the gravers of La Bella. The taste for these amusements was so great that during the reign of Ferdinand II and in the space of five months, six fetes of different kinds were given, each more magnificent than the preceding.

The square of Santa Croce is surrounded with a boundary of chains, which leave sufficient space for the passage of carriages before the houses. On certain occasions amphitheatres are raised, round which also carriages can drive. The square was thus laid out in 1738 for the last festival of the *Calzio* or foot-ball, which has been engraved by Gioseppe Zocchi. This print gives a good idea of the masquerades of Florence. Besides the harlequins and punchinellos, which the French have in such numbers, the other characters are very various and well kept up.

All ranks, without exception, are turned into ridicule. A carriage filled with porters has a judge dressed in a long robe and large wig, for a coachman. A physician is mounted on a lean ass, with panniers and cages filled with cats, and carrying a long staff, from which some large dead rats are suspended, while a scroll on the top of it bears the words *Remedi di topi*, 'antidotes against rats:' to these may be added doctors with asses' heads. The spectators themselves form a spectacle; the windows of the houses, and the balconies of the palaces, are all ornamented with rich tapestry, and graced with brilliant company. The people cover the tiles of the houses, and on these aerial theatres engage in games, from which Italian confidence and address take away all danger, and which afford a very diverting appearance.

The spectacle which we ourselves saw was very agreeable. The carriages, which throng the road, give great brilliancy to the scene; they are filled with masks who answer the joy and acclamations of the multitude by throwing them cakes and *confetti*, and by sprinkling showers of perfumed water from little syringes towards the spectators who line the windows and the balconies: some of the carriages contain musicians, and others are in the shape of triumphal cars, ornamented with different symbols.

In 1874 Henry James was far less impressed with what he called 'that languid organism known as the Florentine Carnival':

I encountered the line of carriages in the square before Santa Croce, of which they were making the circuit.

They rolled solemnly by, with their inmates frowning at each other in apparent wrath at not finding each other more amusing. There were no masks, no costumes, no decorations, no throwing of flowers or sweetmeats. It was as if each carriageful had privately resolved to be inexpensive, and was rather discomfited at finding that it was getting no better entertainment than it gave. The middle of the piazza was filled with little tables, with shouting mountebanks, mostly disguised in battered bonnets and crinolines, offering chances in raffles for plucked fowls and kerosene lamps. I have never thought the huge marble statue of Dante, which overlooks the scene, a work of the least refinement; but, as it stood there on its high pedestal, chin in hand, frowning down on all this cheap foolery, it seemed to have a great moral intention.

In his *Ilex and Olive* Michael Swan, then in his early twenties, gives an account of a visit to Santa Croce in 1947:

It was half-past two and the sun was glaring in the piazza . . . In the shadow on the top step of the church a young man was asleep with his head slumped on his shoulder and his mouth wide open. I tried to open the enormous door but it was locked, so I sat in another shadow and waited for the sacristan to open it. Just as I had fallen into a doze I was woken by the drawing of bolts and through the door peered a young, smiling, bespectacled monk. I got up and he politely ushered me into the church; I had gone only four steps before he spoke to me, asking if I were German. I told him I was English and he pointed to my hair, which had been bleached by the sun, and said, 'You look like a German, tee-hee-hee' – his laugh was like a zany's. I was wearing short trousers to reduce the fatigue of sightseeing in the intense heat, and he looked at my legs. I looked down, too, as he did so, to see what extraordinary thing he had seen in them and as I did so he suddenly bent down and plucked at a bunch of hair on my left calf. Before I could say anything and by way of explanation he pulled up his cassock and revealed a pair of white and quite hairless legs. 'Look,' he said, 'I have no

hair at all on my legs.' I was, however far more interested
in the fact that he supported his socks with a pair of
inferior and secular suspenders. 'You're lucky,' he went
on, 'you have hair on your legs – I don't,' and his red face
beamed benevolently. Suddenly his right index finger
was stuck in my stomach with a little noise and a laugh.
He talked for a little in French, attempted to pull a few
more hairs from my legs and then offered me a historical
leaflet. His salesmanship was eccentric but successful. I
left him to examine the church which is vast and, immediately, of little interest. The wooden beams which
support the roof are barbarous. It is the First Church of
the Franciscans and has a Franciscan simplicity; no side
chapels, except in the chancel, little ornamentation. Apart
from the Giottos and the stained glass it is the tombs
which are of most interest. Michelangelo lies here, on a
spot chosen by himself because from it he might see,
through the open door, the cupola of the Cathedral. But
the interest of the tombs is sentimental rather than aesthetic, and soon I was in the little Capella Peruzzi looking
at the miraculous Giotto frescoes. It was, however, a
pleasure too exquisite to last; suddenly I felt an index
finger between my third and fourth rib and a little sound
accompanied it.

'You like Giotto, tee-hee-hee?' inquired the sacristan.

'Yes,' I replied, simply and sharply.

He asked me if he might take me for a tour round the
gallery – a circumambulation which I did not relish and
managed to refuse. Then he noticed my camera. Bless-
edly he seemed never to have seen a similar camera; I
handed it to him and he examined it most earnestly. '*Magnifico! Magnifico!*' he mumbled to himself and while he
continued to examine it I returned to Giotto. When I
had finished he asked me very seriously if he might take
a photograph and beamed when I agreed. We went into a
chapel and he reverently placed me on the first step of the
altar with a Virgin and Child by Andrea della Robbia
behind me. Unfortunately the photograph turned out a
complete blank.

The North–eastern Quarter

OR SAN MICHELE

The church of Or San Michele, originally San Michele in Orto
or San Michele in the orchard, was erected in 1380. There is
dispute as to its architect, with Taddeo Gaddi, Orcagna and
Francesco Talenti and his son Simone all having claims to have
built it. Richard Lassels describes a visit:

> Going from the Piazza towards the Duomo, we were
> presently stopped by the church of St Michael, a square
> flat church, whose outside is adorned with rare statues, if
> not of gold, yet worth their weight in gold. The best are,
> that of S. Matthew in brass made by Laurentius Cion; that
> of S. Thomas in brass touching the side of our Saviour,
> with great demonstrations of diffidence in his looks, is of
> Andrea Verrocchio's hand. That of S. George in marble is
> compared to the best in Rome, and hath been praised both
> in prose and verse.

Some two hundred years later, Hawthorne was to describe
his own visit:

> We went into the church of San Michele, and saw in its
> architecture the traces of its transformation from a market
> into a church. In its pristine state it consisted of a double
> row of three great open arches, with the wind blowing
> through them, and the sun falling aslantwise into them,

while the bustle of the market, the sale of fish, flesh or fruit went on within, or brimmed over into the streets that enclosed them on every side. But, four or five hundred years ago, the broad arches were built up with stone-work; windows were pierced through and filled with painted glass; a high altar, in a rich style of pointed Gothic, was raised; shrines and confessionals were set up; and here it is, a solemn and antique church, where a man may buy his salvation instead of his dinner . . .

It appears that a picture of the Virgin used to hang against one of the pillars of the market-place, while it was still a market, and in the year 1292, several miracles were wrought by it, insomuch that a chapel was consecrated for it. So many worshippers came to the shrine that the business of the market was impeded, and ultimately the Virgin and St Michael won the whole space for themselves. The upper part of the edifice was at that time a granary, and is still used for other than religious purposes. This church was one spot to which the inhabitants betook themselves much for refuge and assistance during the great plague described by Boccaccio.

Ouida's *Pascarel* contains a characteristically overwrought but perceptive passage about the church and about one of its chief glories, Donatello's statue of *St George* – in complete armour but without sword or lance, bare-headed, and leaning on his shield, which displays the cross.

Or San Michele would have been a world's wonder had it stood alone, and not been companioned with such wondrous rivals that its own exceeding beauty scarce ever receives full justice.

Surely that square-set strength, as of a fortress, towering against the clouds, and catching the last light always on its fretted parapet, and everywhere embossed and enriched with foliage, and tracery, and figures of saints, and the shadows of vast arches, and the light of niches gold-starred and filled with divine forms, is a gift so perfect to the whole world, that, passing it, one should need say a prayer for the great Taddeo's soul.

Surely nowhere is the rugged, changeless, mountain force of hewn stone piled against the sky, and the luxuriant, dream-like, poetic delicacy of stone carven and shaped into leafage and loveliness, more perfectly blended and made one than where Or San Michele rises out of the dim, many-coloured, twisting streets, in its mass of ebon darkness and of silvery light.

The other day under the walls of it I stood, and looked at its Saint George, where he leans upon his shield, so calm, so young, with his bared head and quiet eyes.

'That is our Donatello's,' said a Florentine beside me – a man of the people, who drove a horse for hire in the public ways, and who paused, cracking his whip to tell his tale to me. 'Donatello did that, and it killed him. Do you know that? When he had done that Saint George he showed it to his master. And the master said, "It wants one thing only." Now, this saying our Donatello took gravely to heart, chiefly of all because his master would never explain where the fault lay; and so much did it hurt him, that he fell ill, and came nigh to death. Then he called his master to him. "Dear and great one, do tell me before I die," he said, "what is the one thing my statue lacks." The master smiled, and said, "Only – speech." "Then I die happy," said our Donatello. And he – died – indeed, that hour.'

Now, I cannot say that the pretty story is true; it is not in the least true; Donatello died when he was eighty-three, in the street of the Melon; and it was he himself who cried, 'Speak, then – speak!' to his statue, as it was carried through the city. But whether true or false the tale, this fact is surely true, that it is well – nobly and purely well – with a people, when the men amongst it who ply for hire on its public ways think caressingly of a sculptor dead five hundred years ago, and tell such a tale standing idly in the noonday sun, feeling the beauty and the pathos of it all.

'Our Donatello' still for the people of Florence – 'Our own little Donatello' still, as though he were living and working in their midst today, here in the shadow of the

Stocking-Makers' street, where his Saint George keeps watch and ward.

Because of the ravages of the weather, *St George* no longer keeps watch and ward in his original position but is now in the Bargello. A bronze copy of the marble is now in the niche.

THE CATHEDRAL, THE BAPTISTERY, THE CAMPANILE OF GIOTTO

Florence at the end of the thirteenth century was a city of growing commercial and political importance – and swelling civic pride. Santa Reparata, the cathedral deemed sufficient at the time of Dante's birth in 1265, was now held by the Signoria to be 'crudely built and too small for such a city.' Such a city as Florence had become plainly needed a new cathedral, one to rival those at Siena and Pisa, one which would, in the words of the Signoria, 'possess the utmost and most sumptuous magnificence.' With this hyperbolic mandate as his guide, the master architect Arnolfo di Cambio conceived an enormous new cathedral rising, according to the French model, from cloverleaf foundations. Arnolfo, who died in 1302, just as those foundations were being laid and the courses rising upon them, did not live to see his plans brought to fruition. But then no one involved in the planning did. The present façade, by Emilio de Fabris, dates only from 1887, a part of its cost having been born by Thomas Trollope's friend Stanley Sloane, who had first arrived in Italy as tutor to the Russian Bourtourlin family and had subsequently made a fortune out of copper mines near Volterra.

An early view of the Duomo is given in Richard Lassels's *The Voyage of Italy* (1670):

On the top of it stands mounted a fair cupola (or *tholus*) made by Brunelleschi, a Florentine. This was the first cupola in Europe; and therefore the more admirable for having no idea after which it could be framed; and for being the idea of that of St Peter's in Rome, after which so many young cupolas in Rome, and elsewhere, have been made since. Hence it is said that Michael Angelo coming now and then to Florence (his native country) while he was making the cupola in Rome of St Peter's church, and viewing attentively this cupola of Florence, used to say of it: *Come te non voglio, meglio di te non posso.* [Similar to thee I will not; better than thee I cannot]. It's said also that Brunelleschi, making this cupola, caused taverns, cook shops and lodgings to be set in it, that the workmen might find all things necessary there, and not spend time in going up and down . . .

Near the close of the eighteenth century, William Beckford made the observation, repeated by many writers after him, that 'The architect seems to have turned his building inside out; nothing in art being more ornamented than the exterior, and few churches so simple within.' He continues:

The nave is vast and solemn, the dome amazingly spacious, with the high altar in its centre, inclosed by a circular arcade near two hundred feet in diameter. There is something imposing in this decoration, as it suggests the idea of a sanctuary, into which none but the holy ought to penetrate. However profane I might feel myself, I took the liberty of entering, and sat myself down in a niche. Not a ray of light reaches this sacred inclosure, but through the medium of narrow windows, high in the dome and richly painted.

Viewing the Duomo and its surroundings in 1860, George Eliot wrote in her diary:

Apart from its venerable historical glory, the exterior of the Duomo is pleasant to behold when the wretched unfinished facade is quite hidden. The soaring pinnacles over the doors are exquisite; so are the forms of the windows in the great semi-circle of the apsis; and on the side where especially the white marble has taken on so rich and deep a yellow, that the black bands cease to be felt as a fault. The entire view on this side, closed in by Giotto's tower, with its delicate pinkish marble, its delicate Gothic windows with twisted columns, and its tall lightness carrying the eye upward, in contrast with the mighty breadth of the dome, is a thing not easily to be forgotten . . .

One of the most vivid scenes in *Romola* takes place in the Duomo, with Savonarola preaching to a crowded and rapt congregation. Having escaped from prison and seeking sanctuary, old Baldassare enters the Duomo:

He had expected to see a vast nave empty of everything but lifeless emblems – side altars with candles unlit, dim pictures, pale and rigid statues – with perhaps a few worshippers in the distant choir following a monotonous chant. That was the ordinary aspect of churches to a man who never went into them with any religious purpose.

And he saw, instead, a vast multitude of warm, living faces, upturned in breathless silence towards the pulpit, at the angle between the nave and the choir. The multitude was of all ranks, from magistrates and dames of gentle nurture to coarsely-clad artisans and country people. In the pulpit was a Dominican friar, with strong features and dark hair, preaching with the crucifix in his hand.

The Dominican friar is Savonarola; and he exhorts his congregation in the style, no doubt familiar to George Eliot from her youth, of some non-conformist preacher of mid-Victorian times. Seemingly as much intoxicated with his eloquence as the crowds ranged before him, Savonarola reaches his peroration:

'Listen, O people, over whom my heart yearns, as the heart of a mother over the children she has travailed for! God is my witness that but for your sakes I would willingly live as a turtle in the depths of the forest, singing low to my Beloved, who is mine and I am his. For you I toil, for you I languish, for you my nights are spent in watching, and my soul melteth away in very heaviness. O Lord, thou knowest I am willing – I am ready. Take me, stretch me on thy cross: let the wicked who delight in blood, and rob the poor, and defile the temple of their bodies, and harden themselves against thy mercy – let them wag their heads and shoot out the lip at me: let the thorns press upon my brow, and let my sweat be anguish – I desire to be made like thee in thy great love. But let me see the fruit of my travail – let this people be saved! . . . Come, O blessed promise; and behold, I am willing – lay me on thy altar: let my blood flow and the fire consume me; but let my witness be remembered among men, that iniquity shall not prosper for ever.'

Baldassare, the victim of an oppressive tyranny, thrills to Savonarola's denunciation of it:

Among all the human beings present, there was perhaps not one whose frame vibrated more strongly than his to the tones and words of the preacher; but it had vibrated like a harp of which all the strings had been wrenched away except one. That threat of a fiery inexorable vengeance – of a future into which the hated sinner might be pursued and held by the avenger in an eternal grapple, had come to him like the promise of an unquenchable fountain to unquenchable thirst.

Baldissare feels at one with the speaker, as he cries out within him: 'Let my blood flow; let the fire consume me!' Then he too, along with everyone else in the vast cathedral, bursts into sobs.

W. D. Howells was little impressed by the Duomo, calling it 'a temple to damp the spirit, dead or alive, by the immense impression of stony bareness, of drab vacuity, which one receives from its interior, unless it is filled with people.' Mark Twain was even less impressed, his natural egalitarianism outraged by the contrast between the poverty of the average Florentine and the richness of the church:

Look at the grand Duomo of Florence – a vast pile that has been sapping the purses of her citizens for five hundred years and is not nearly finished yet. Like all other men, I fell down and worshipped it, but when the filthy beggars swarmed around me the contrast was too striking, too

suggestive, and I said, 'O, sons of classic Italy, *is* the spirit
of enterprise, of self-reliance, of noble endeavour, utterly
dead within ye? Why don't you rob your church?' Three
hundred happy, comfortable priests are employed in that
cathedral.

Ruskin was appalled by the contrast between the sublimity
of the buildings which make up the Piazza and the squalor of
the daily life within it:

Of living Greek work there is none after the Florentine
Baptistery; of living Christian work, none so perfect as
the Tower of Giotto; and, under the gleam and shadow of
their marbles, the morning light was haunted by the
ghosts of the Father of Natural Science, Galileo; of Sacred
Art, Angelico, and the Master of Sacred Song, Dante.
Which spot of ground the modern Florentine has made
his principal hackney coach stand and omnibus station.
The hackney coaches, with their more or less farmyard-
like litter of occasional hay, and smell of variously mixed
horse-manure, are yet in more permissible harmony with
the place than the ordinary populace of a fashionable
promenade would be, with its cigars, spitting, and harlot-
planned fineries: but the omnibus place of call being in
front of the door of the tower, renders it impossible to
stand for a moment near it, to look at the sculptures of the
eastern or southern side; while the north side is enclosed
with an iron railing, and usually encumbered with lumber
as well: not a soul in Florence ever caring now for sight of
any piece of its old artist's work; and the mass of strangers
being on the whole intent on nothing but getting the
omnibus to go by steam; and so seeing the cathedral in
one swift circuit, by glimpses between the puffs of it.

On these comments Henry James took issue with Ruskin, as
he was often to do:

This fact [that 'the little square in front of the Cathedral
. . . is now the resort of a number of hackney-carriages
and omnibuses'] is doubtless lamentable, and it would be
a hundred times more agreeable to see among people who

have been made the heirs of as priceless a work of art as the sublime campanile some such feeling about it as would keep it free even from the danger of defilement. A cab-stand is a very ugly and dirty thing, and Giotto's tower should have nothing in common with such conveniences. But there is more than one way of taking such things, and the sensitive stranger who has been walking about for a week with his mind full of the sweetness and suggestiveness of a hundred Florentine places may feel at last in looking into Mr Ruskin's little tracts that, discord for discord, there isn't much to choose between the importunity of the author's personal ill-humour and the incongruity of horse-pails and bundles of hay.

When Dickens visited the piazza of the Duomo, he noticed 'an irregular kind of market' being held there, with 'stores of old iron and other small merchandise set out on stalls.' He also noticed, set into the pavement, the *Sasso di Dante* or 'Stone of Dante', marking the place where legend has it that Dante sat and gazed at the Cathedral. He puts a jocular reference to the *Sasso* in *Little Dorrit*: '. . . Dante – known to that gentleman [Mr Sparkler] as an eccentric man in the nature of an Old File, who used to put leaves round his head, and sit upon a stool for some unaccountable purpose, outside the cathedral at Florence.'

The *Sasso di Dante* inspired several English poets, among them Wordsworth, who, visiting Florence with Crabb Robinson in 1837, sat on the *Sasso* and then wrote a sonnet about the experience:

Under the shadow of a stately Pile,
The dome of Florence, pensive and alone,
Nor giving heed to aught that passed the while,
I stood, and gazed upon a marble stone,
The laurelled Dante's favourite seat. A throne,
In just esteem, it rivals; though no style
Be there of decoration to beguile
The mind, depressed by thought of greatness flown.
As a true man, who long had served the lyre,
I gazed with earnestness, and dared no more.

But in this breast the mighty Poet bore
A Patriot's heart, warm with undying fire.
Bold with the thought, in reverence I sate down,
And, for a moment, filled that empty Throne.

The *Sasso* is now let into a nearby wall, to prevent undue obstruction of the pavement. Beside it is a café, much frequented by tourists in search of restoration and relief, called *Il Sasso di Dante*.

Still in Ouida's day (*Pascarel*, 1873), as in Dickens's, the piazza of the Duomo was a centre not merely for reverential tourists but for the day-to-day life of a populous and busy city:

About the Duomo there is stir and strife at all times; crowds come and go; men buy and sell; lads laugh and fight; piles of fruit blaze gold and crimson; metal pails clash down on the stones with shrillest clangour; on the steps boys play at dominoes, and women give their children food, and merry-makers join in carnival fooleries; but there in the midst is the Duomo all unharmed and undegraded, a poem and a prayer in one, its marbles shining in the upper air, a thing so majestic in its strength, and yet so human in its tenderness, that nothing can assail and nothing equal it.

On the flank of the Duomo stands the Campanile of Giotto – compared by Hippolyte Taine, 'erect, isolated', to the Tour Saint Michel in Bordeaux and the Tour St Jacques in Paris. When George Eliot visited it in 1860, tourists were still permitted to climb to its top: 'This evening we have been mounting to the top of Giotto's tower – a very sublime getting-upstairs indeed – and our muscles are much astonished at the unusual exercise . . .' [George Eliot to Charles L. Lewes, 27 May 1861].

Originally it had been planned that the tower, already 250 feet high, should have a 30-foot spire. It was to the lack of this spire that Longfellow alluded when he wrote:

In the old Tuscan town stands Giotto's tower,
    The lily of Florence blossoming in stone, –
    A vision of delight, and a desire,

The builder's perfect and centennial flower
That in the night of ages bloomed alone,
But wanting still the glory of the spire.

Browning also alluded to the lack of a spire in his philosophic commentary on Vasari, 'Old Pictures in Florence':

Then one shall propose in a speech (curt Tuscan,
    Expurgate and sober, with scarcely an 'issimo,')
To end now our half-told tale of Cambuscan,
    And turn the bell-tower's alt to altissimo:
And fine as the beak of a young beccaccia
    The Campanile, the Duomo's fit ally,
Shall soar up in gold full fifty braccia,
    Completing Florence, as Florence Italy.

Shall I be alive that morning the scaffold
    Is broken away, and the long-pent fire,
Like the golden hope of the world, unbaffled
    Springs from its sleep, and up goes the spire
While 'God and the People' plain for its motto,
    Thence the new tricolour flaps at the sky?
At least to foresee that glory of Giotto
    And Florence together, the first am I!

Ruskin thought that the Campanile was 'the model and mirror of perfect architecture,' and instructed readers of his *Mornings in Florence*: 'Of representations of human art under heavenly guidance, the series of bas-reliefs which stud the base of this Tower of Giotto must be held certainly the chief in Europe . . . Read but these inlaid jewels of Giotto's once with patient following, and your hour's study will give you strength for all your life.'

The spirit of Dante haunts the Baptistery, as it does no other building in Florence: '*il mio bel San Giovanni*' he calls it, and in the fifteenth canto of *Il Paradiso* his ancestor Cacciaguida tells him: '. . . in your ancient Baptistery Christian and Cacciaguida I became' (i.e. like Dante himself and countless other Florentines, he had been baptized there). In Canto XXV of *Il Paradiso*, Dante makes a reference to his own baptism:

If ever it happen that the sacred song
   Whereto both heaven and earth have set a hand,
   Whereby I am lean these many years and long,
O'ercome the cruelty which keeps me banned
   From the fair sheepfold where I slept, a lamb,
   Foe to the wolves that raven through the land,
With different voice now, nor with fleece the same,
   Shall I return, poet, and at the font
   Of my baptizing shall the chaplet claim
Because into the faith that makes the account
   Of souls to God I won then . . .

It was in the Duomo that, in 1817, the fourteen-year-old Harriet Charlotte Beaujolais, then in Florence with her widowed mother, Lady Charlotte Campbell, attended the wedding of the second daughter of the Grand Duke to the Prince de Carignan – who later became the luckless King Carlo Alberto of Sardinia. This is the account – her misspellings retained – that this precocious girl wrote in her journal:

We went with Miss de la Chaux [her Swiss governess, nicknamed 'Tiranna'] to see what we could. As we were very early nothing had even begun and we chose excellent places upon a temporary platform which had been erected for the occasion around the choir. Opposite the alter there were placed two large arm chairs with cushions at their feet and a table opposite all covered with red velvet. On the right were placed three other chairs one of which was placed on a raised step. On the left there was a small throne. Beyond these seats were ranged rows of benches leaving a space in the middle. Some of these for the court were covered with red cloth. Several English soon came in all dressed or attempting to be dressed in full feathers – such a vulgar representation of our nation I never saw. Mamma and Lady Octavia Law were the only decent ones. Presently the whole of the choir was illuminated with an innumerable quantity of wax tapers. The italian Ladies who sat on the benches placed in front were particularly well dressed with a great profusion of jewels and very good taste. They disgraced the English.

In front of both the alters there were seated a numerous band of musicians who played for a short time. Suddenly a general silence prevailed and the Prince de Carignan followed by several aid de camps &c entered the church. Behind them was the Princess holding her brother's arm and behind them the Grand Duke and his elder daughter who is deformed. The Prince and Princess seated themselves on the chairs opposite the alter, the Grand Duke upon one of those placed on the right, his son at his side and the hunch back daughter next to him. In a few minutes the arch Bishop of Florence entered and seated himself on an arm chair placed on the upper step of the alter. The Prince and Princess placed themselves kneeling at his feet. After a few ceremonies which it was impossible to distinguish the Princess rose and made a curtesy to her father as an indication of asking his leave to marry the Prince. There was then a ring given I could not distinguish by whom and they both rose the ceremony being over. Immediately a Sardinian Princess got up and in the most goodnatured smiling manner began to remove a large fine veil from the Princesses head to mark that she was no longer a damsel. The Archbishop retired for a few minutes and the Prince and Princess retired to their seats. High Mass was then performed during all which time the Princess and her sister remained kneeling and seemed to follow the service with great attention. The Prince looked very uneasy and his new spouse cried all the time although she did her utmost to appear calm. I felt moved at the whole scene and what must have been the feelings of so young a person being only 16 upon so imposing an occasion. Being united for life to a man must ever be an awful step but particularly when every circumstance was united to add to these feelings. The immense crowds who were assembled to gaze upon the scene, the dead silence which prevailed at intervals only interrupted by the trembling voice of the Archbishop, and next the stunning peals of the organ beside the general effect of the Catholic rites were indeed enough to move the hearts of any one. I was extremely delighted when it was over for during the

ceremony I was too much overpowered to enjoy it
thoroughly. I do not think I shall easily forget so striking a
scene.

To anyone who might question the right of this youthful
but far from artless young writer to be included in this book, I
can only reply that her *Journey to Florence in 1817* seems to me to
have as much right to be classified as a work of literature
as Daisy Ashford's *The Young Visiters*, which it so much
resembles in its ardour, its innocence, its snobbery, and the
sharpness of its perceptions.

SAN LORENZO

On June 19, Nathaniel Hawthorne recorded in his Journal:

This forenoon we have been to the church of St Lorenzo,
which stands on the site of an ancient basilica, and was
itself built more than four centuries ago. The facade is still
an ugly height of rough brickwork . . .

His wife Sophia has described the same visit:

The church is undergoing repairs within and without,
and heaps of rubbish were all around. Upon entering I
was very much disappointed in the general effect of the
interior. Indeed it is difficult to be reconciled to the plain
walls, after being accustomed to the magnificent mosaics
of marbles in all Roman churches.

Like most visitors, however, the Hawthornes were pro-
foundly impressed by the new sacristy. Hawthorne wrote of
the statue of Lorenzo de' Medici:

The statue that sits above these two later allegories
[Morning and Evening] is like no other that ever came
from a sculptor's hand. It is the one work worthy of
Michel Angelo's reputation, and grand enough to vindi-
cate for him all the genius that the world gave him credit
for. And yet it seems a simple thing enough to think of or

to execute; merely a sitting figure, the face partly over-shadowed by a helmet, one hand supporting the chin, the other resting on the thigh. But after looking at it a little while, the spectator ceases to think of it as a marble statue; it comes to life, and you see that the princely figure is brooding over some great design, which, when he has arranged his own mind, the world will be fain to execute for him. No such grandeur and majesty have elsewhere been put into human shape. It is all a miracle; the deep repose, and deep life within it. It is as much a miracle to have achieved this as to make a statue that would rise up and walk. The face, when one gazes earnestly into it, beneath the shadow of its helmet, is seen to be calmly sombre; a mood which, I think, is generally that of the rulers of mankind, except in moments of vivid action.

Samuel Rogers wrote twice about this statue of Lorenzo, once in verse and once in prose:

> Nor then forget that Chamber of the Dead,
> Where the gigantic shapes of Night and Day,
> Turned into stone, rest everlastingly;
> Yet still are breathing, and shed round at noon
> A twofold influence – only to be felt –
> A light, a darkness, mingling each with each;
> Both, and yet neither. There, from age to age,
> Two ghosts are sitting on their sepulchres.
> That is the Duke Lorenzo. Mark him well.
> He meditates, his head upon his hand.
> What from beneath his helm-like bonnet scowls?
> Is it a face, or but an eyeless skull?
> 'Tis lost in shade; yet, like the basilisk,
> It fascinates and is intolerable.
> His mien is noble, most majestical!
> Then most so when the distant choir is heard
> At morn or eve – nor fail thou to attend
> On that thrice-hallowed day, when all are there;
> When all, propitiating with solemn songs,
> Visit the Dead. Then wilt thou feel his power.

In prose Rogers wrote:

I am no longer my own master. I am become the slave of a demon. I sit gazing, day after day, on that terrible phantom, the Duke Lorenzo in M. Angelo's chapel. All my better feelings would lead me to the Tribune and the lovely forms that inhabit there. I can dwell with delight on the membra formosa of the Wrestlers, the Fawn and the Apollo, on the sunshine of Titian, the soul of Raphael; but the statue loses none of its influence. He sits, a little reclining from you, his chin resting upon his left hand, his elbows on the arm of his chair. His look is calm and thoughtful, yet it seems to say a something that makes you shrink from it, a something beyond words. Like that of the Basilisk it fascinates – is intolerable.

. . . The visage of Lorenzo under the shade of that scowling and helmet-like bonnet is scarcely visible. You can just discern the likeness of human features; but whether alive or dead, whether a face or a skull, that of a mortal man or a Spirit from heaven or hell, you cannot say. His figure is gigantic and noble, not such as to shock belief or remind you that it is but a statue. It is the most real and unreal thing in stone that ever came from the chisel.

A comparison of these two passages shows how Rogers worked up a spontaneous record in prose into a highly artificial piece of verse. Who would deny that the prose version is far more effective?

Mark Twain, who almost invariably viewed things from a human, not an artistic, standpoint, was less impressed:

They have a grand mausoleum in Florence, which they built to bury our Lord and Saviour and the Medici family in. It sounds blasphemous, but it is true, and there they *act* blasphemy. The dead and damned Medicis who cruelly tyrannised over Florence and were her curse for over two hundred years, are salted away in a circle of costly vaults, and in their midst the Holy Sepulchre was to have been set up. The expedition sent to Jerusalem to seize it got into trouble and could not accomplish the burglary, and so the centre of the mausoleum is vacant now. They say the entire mausoleum was intended for the Holy Sepulchre, and was only turned into a family burying place after the Jerusalem expedition failed – but you will excuse me. Some of those Medicis would have smuggled themselves in sure. – What *they* had not the effrontery to do was not worth doing. Why, they had their trivial, forgotten exploits on land and sea pictured out in grand frescoes (as also did the Doges of Venice) with the Saviour and the Virgin throwing bouquets to them out of the clouds, and the Deity himself applauding from his throne in Heaven! And who painted these things? Titian, Tintoretto, Paul Veronese, Raphael – none other than the world's idols, the 'old masters.'

Andrea del Sarto glorified his princes in pictures that must save them for ever from the oblivion they merited, and they let him starve – a thing by no means to be regretted. Raphael pictured such miscreants as Catherine de Medicis seated in heaven and conversing familiarly with the Virgin Mary and the angels (to say nothing of higher personages), and yet my friends abuse me because I am a little prejudiced against the old masters – because I fail sometimes to see the beauty that is in their productions. I cannot help but see it, now and then, but I keep on protesting against the grovelling spirit that could persuade those masters to prostitute their noble talents to the adulation of such monsters as the French, Venetian, and Florentine princes of two and three hundred years ago, all the same.

I am told that the old masters had to do these shameful things for bread, the princes and potentates being the only patrons of art. If a grandly gifted man may drag his pride and his manhood in the dirt for bread rather than starve with the nobility that is in him untainted, the excuse is a valid one. It would excuse theft in Washingtons and Wellingtons, and unchastity in women as well.

But somehow I cannot keep that Medici mausoleum out of my memory. It is as large as a church; its pavement is rich enough for the pavement of a King's palace; its

great dome is gorgeous with frescoes; its walls are made
of – what? Marble? – plaster? – wood? – paper? No. Red
porphyry – verde antique – jasper – oriental agate –
alabaster – mother-of-pearl – chalcedony – red coral –
lapis lazuli! All the vast walls are made wholly of these
precious stones, worked in, and in and in together in
elaborate patterns and figures, and polished till they glow
like great mirrors with the pictured splendours reflected
from the dome overhead. And before the statue of one of
these dead Medicis reposes a crown that blazes with
diamonds and emeralds enough to buy a ship-of-the-line
almost – if they are genuine. These are the happy things
the Government has its evil eye upon, and a happy thing it
will be for Italy when they melt away in the public
treasury.

And now – . However, another beggar approaches. I
will go out and destroy him, and then come back and
write another chapter of vituperation . . .

Byron's robust view of the Medici Chapel was that it
consisted of 'fine frippery in great slabs of various expensive
stones, to commemorate fifty rotten and forgotten carcases.'

For aesthetic, and not political or humanitarian reasons,
Augustus Hare also withheld his admiration, in a judgement
of astonishing perversity:

The want of architectural power in Michelangelo is nowhere more definitely shown than in these monuments.
The narrow niches in which the Medici are confined
would make it impossible for them to stand upright, and
the disproportionate figures below are slipping off the
pitiable pedestals which support them.

Of the figure of *Night*, Giovanni Battista Strozzi wrote:

> Carved by an Angel, in this marble white
> Sweetly reposing, lo, the Goddess
>   Night!
> Calmly she sleeps, and so must living be:
> Awake her gently; she will speak to thee.

To this Michelangelo replied with a quatrian of his own:

Grateful is sleep, whilst wrong and shame survive;
More grateful still in senseless stone to live;
Gladly both sight and hearing I forego;
Oh, then awake me not! Hush! – whisper low.

[Trans. J. C. Wright]

Swinburne devoted a whole poem to San Lorenzo. In his lines on the figure of *Night* he echoed both Strozzi and Michelangelo:

Is not thine hour come to wake, O slumbering Night?
Hath not the Dawn a message in thine ear?
Though thou be stone and sleep, yet shalt thou hear
When the word falls from heaven – Let there be light.
Thou knowest we would not do thee the despite
To wake thee while the old sorrow and shame were
near;
We spake not loud for thy sake, and for fear
Lest thou shouldst lose the rest that was thy right,
The blessing given thee that was thine alone,
The happiness to sleep and to be stone:
Nay, we kept silence of thee for thy sake
Albeit we knew thee alive, and left with thee
The great good gift to feel not nor to see;
But will not yet thine Angel bid thee wake?

[In San Lorenzo]

William Wetmore Story (1819–95), the American sculptor and writer, who was long resident in Italy and whose personality was such that it attracted to him every foreign visitor of note, has left an account of the exhumation of the royal bodies which, in 1791, Ferdinand III had had 'piled together pell-mell in the subterranean vaults of the chapel, caring scarcely to distinguish one from another.' There they remained, uncared for and protected from invasion only by two wooden doors.

. . . But shame then came over those who had custody of the place, and it was determined to put them in order. In 1818 a rumour was current that the Medicean coffins had been violated and robbed of all the articles of value which they contained; but it was not until thirty-nine years afterwards, in 1857, that an examination into the fact was made. It was then found that the rumour had been well founded.

The forty-nine coffins containing the remains of the family were taken down one by one, and a sad state of things was exposed. Some of them had been broken into and robbed, some of them were the hiding-places of rats and every kind of vermin; and such was the nauseous odour they gave forth, that at least one of the persons employed in taking them down lost his life by inhaling it. In many of them nothing remained but fragments of bones and a handful of dust; but where they had not been stolen, the splendid dresses, covered with jewels, the wrought silks and satins of gold embroidery, the helmets and swords, crusted with gems and gold, still survived the dust and bones that had worn them in their splendid pageants and ephemeral days of power; and in many cases, where everything that bore the impress of life had gone, the hair remained, almost as fresh as ever.

Some, however, had been embalmed, and were in a fair preservation; and some were in a dreadful state of putre-faction. Ghastly and grinning skulls were there, adorned with crowns of gold. Dark and parchment-dried faces were seen, with thin golden hair, rich as ever, and twisted with gems and pearls and golden nets. The cardinals still wore their mitres and red cloaks and splendid rings. On the breast of Cardinal Carlos [son of Ferdinand I] was a beautiful cross of white enamel, with the effigy of Christ in black, and surrounded with emeralds, and on his hand a rich sapphire ring. On that of Cardinal Leopold, the son of Cosimo II, over the purple pianeta was a cross of amethysts, and on his finger a jacinth set in enamel. The dried bones of Vittoria della Rovere Montefeltro were draped in a dress of black silk of beautiful texture, trimmed with black and white lace, with a great golden medal on her breast, and the portrait of her as she was in life lying on one side, and her emblems on the other; while all that remained of herself was a few bones.

Anna Luisa, the Electress Palatine of the Rhine, daughter of Cosimo III, lay there, almost a skeleton, robed in a rich violet velvet, with the electoral crown surmounting a black, ghastly face of parchment – a medal of gold, with her name and effigy, on one side, and on her breast a crucifix of silver; while Francesco Maria, her uncle, lay beside her, a mass of putrid robes and rags. Cosimo I and Cosimo II had been stripped by profane hands of all their jewels and insignia; and so had been Eleonora de Toledo and Maria Christina, and many others, to the number of twenty.

The two bodies which were found in the best preservation were those of the Grand-Duchess Giovanna d'Austria, the wife of Francisco I, and their daughter Anna. Corruption had scarcely touched them, and they lay there fresh in colour as though they had just died. The mother, in her red satin, trimmed with lace, her red silk stockings and high-heeled shoes, the earrings hanging from her ears, and her blonde hair as fresh as ever; and equally well-preserved was the body of the daughter. And so, centuries after they had been laid there, the truth became evident of the rumour that ran through Florence at the time of their death, that they had died of poison. The arsenic which had taken them from their life had preserved their bodies. Giovanni delle Bande Nere was also there – the bones scattered and loose within his iron armour, and his rusty helmet with the vizor down.

Visiting San Lorenzo in October 1901, E. M. Forster confessed in a letter to the musicologist E. J. Dent: 'I got ready all the appropriate sentiments for the New Sacristy [the Medici Chapel], and they answered very well. More spontaneous perhaps were my feelings at seeing the cloisterful of starved and maimed cats.'

It was in the Piazza San Lorenzo that, in June 1860, while rummaging among the junk offered for sale at one of the many stalls, Browning came on the 'square yellow book' that was to provide the story of the murder which was to inspire what

many would regard as the greatest of all his works, *The Ring
and the Book*. Browning describes the book as follows:

> Small-quarto size, part print part manuscript:
> A book in shape but, really, pure crude fact
> Secreted from man's life when hearts beat hard,
> And brains, high-blooded, ticked two centuries since.

On 'that memorable day', having paid a lira for his
purchase, Browning first

> . . . leaned a little and overlooked my prize
> By the low railing round the fountain-source
> Close to the statue, where a step descends

and then, absorbed

> Still read I on, from written title-page
> To written index, on, through street and street,
> At the Strozzi, at the Pillar, at the Bridge;
> Till, by the time I stood at home again
> In Casa Guidi by Felice Church,
> Under the doorway where the black begins
> With the first stone slab of the staircase cold,
> I had mastered the contents, knew the whole truth
> Gathered together, bound up in this book . . .

In his *Ilex and Olive* Michael Swan describes how in 1948, in
the immediate aftermath of the war, he bought something
very different in the same piazza:

> Today in the market place in front of San Lorenzo, where
> Browning bought his yellow book, I bought a packet of
> Pall Mall cigarettes from a *ragazzo*, which seemed to
> symbolise modern Italy perfectly. The packet was red and
> shiny and neatly cellophaned with a U.S.A. guarantee
> label, but inside were twenty miserable weeds, smelling
> of everything save tobacco, though each was printed with
> the words 'Pall Mall.' I was told later that a factory in Bari
> manufactures this product, packet and all, and supplies
> the *ragazzi* from Venice to Calabria. The Government,
> knowing how little effective its measures would be

against this racket, produces its own version of Camels and Pall Malls, with the agreement of the American Government, and sells them reasonably in the normal way. But anyway, there in a packet of cigarettes is the *bella figura* and the maggot of Italy today.

That was a period when the English could still patronize and despise the Italians.

SAN MARCO

The Convent of San Marco is noted for two associations: one with Savonarola and the other with Fra Angelico.

'In heaven,' said Pius VII, 'I shall know the explanation of three great mysteries – the Immaculate Conception, the suppression of the Society of Jesus, and the death of Savonarola.'

In *Romola* George Eliot pictures Savonarola on his knees in the monastery of which he became the prior in 1490 and in which he preached with such success that even in winter the square was thronged for hours before its doors were opened:

It was an hour of relaxation in the monastery, and most of the cells were empty. The light through the narrow windows looked in on nothing but bare walls, and the hard pallet and the crucifix. And even behind that door at the end of the long corridor, in the inner cell opening from an ante-chamber where the Prior usually sat at his desk or received private visitors, the high jet of light fell on only one more object that looked quite as common a monastic sight as the bare walls and hard pallet. It was but the back of a figure in the long white Dominican tunic and scapulary, kneeling with bowed head before a crucifix. It might have been any ordinary Fra Girolamo, who had nothing worse to confess than thinking of wrong things when he was singing *in coro*, or feeling spiteful when Fra Benedetto dropped the ink over his own miniatures in the breviary he was illuminating – who had no higher thought than that of climbing safely into Paradise up the narrow ladder of prayer, fasting, and obedience. But under this particular white tunic there was a heart beating with a consciousness inconceivable to the average monk, and perhaps hard to be conceived by any man who has not arrived at self-knowledge through a tumultuous inner life: a consciousness in which irrevocable errors and lapses from verity were so entwined with noble purposes and sincere beliefs, in which self-justifying expediency was so inwoven with the tissue of a great work which the whole being seemed as unable to abandon as the body was unable to abandon glowing and trembling before the objects of hope and fear, that it was perhaps impossible, whatever course might be adopted, for the conscience to find perfect repose.

Savonarola was not only in the attitude of prayer, there were Latin words of prayer on his lips; and yet he was not praying. He had entered his cell, had fallen on his knees, and burst into words of supplication, seeking in this way for an influx of calmness which would be a warrant to him that the resolutions urged on him by crowding thoughts and passions were not wresting him away from the Divine support; but the previsions and impulses which had been at work within him for the last hour were too imperious; and while he pressed his hands against his face, and while his lips were uttering audibly, '*Cor mundum crea in me*' his mind was still filled with the images of the snare his enemies had prepared for him, was still busy with the arguments by which he could justify himself against their taunts and accusations.

Fra Angelico was a very different sort of man. Taine wrote of him:

Fra Angelico came to the convent before Savonarola, and his frescoes adorn the chapter-house, the corridors and the grey walls of the cells. He had lived aloof from the world, and amid new perturbations and doubts still lived the pure life absorbed in God inculcated by the *Fioretti* . . . His art is as primitive as his life; he had begun it with missal-work, which he really continued on these walls, for gold, vermilion, the brightest scarlets and most brilliant greens – all the medieval art of the illuminator shines in his work as though it were an old parchment . . . Around him all action is meditative, and every object gentle in hue. Day after day the unvarying hours bring before him the same dark lustre of the walls, the same severe folds of cowl and frock, the same rustling steps going to and fro between the chapel and the refectory. Delicate, indecisive sensations vaguely rise in this monotony, while tender dreams are like the perfume of a rose sheltered from the bitter winds and blooming far from the great highway noisy with the tread of men. The magnificance of eternity becomes visible, and the effort of the painter is centred on its expression . . .

The spiritual here has mastery; ponderable matter becomes transfigured; it has lost its mass, its substance is etherialised, and nothing remains but a vapour floating in azure splendour. In one instance the blessed ones go towards paradise over luxuriant meadows strewn with flowers white and red underneath beautiful trees in bloom. They are led by angels, and in saintly brotherhood form a circle, hand in hand. The burden of flesh no longer weighs them down, and light radiates from their heads as they glide through the air up to the flaming gate from which bursts a golden illumination, while above Christ, within a triple row of angels bowing before him like flowers, smiles upon the blessed from beneath his halo . . .

Although beautiful and ideal, Angelico's Christ, even in celestial triumph, is pale, thoughtful and somewhat emaciated. He is the eternal friend, the almost melancholy consoler of the *Imitation*, the poetic Lord of Mercy as the grieving heart imagines Him: He is in no way the over-healthy figure of the Renaissance painters. His long curling tresses and blonde beard mildly surround His features; sometimes He smiles faintly, while His gravity is always associated with gentle benignity . . . Near Him the Virgin, kneeling with downcast eyes, seems to be a young maiden who has just communicated . . . The

painter . . . cannot find colours pure enough or ornaments precious enough for his saints. He forgets that his
figures are but painted: he bestows on them the fond
devotion of a believer, a worshipper. He embroiders their
robes as if they were real, covering their mantles with
filigree as fine as the best goldsmith's work. He paints on
their copes small but perfect pictures; he delights in
delicately drawing their comely fair hair, or arranging
their curls, and severely marking the circular tonsure of
the monk. He lifts them into heaven for love and service;
and his art is the last blossom of the age of mysticism.

In his *Foreign Parts*, Henry James describes how he went to

the suppressed Convent of San Marco, paid my franc at
the profane little wicket which creaks away at the door
(no less than six custodians, apparently, are needed to
turn it, as if it had a recusant conscience), passed along the
bright, still cloister, and went in to look at Fra Angelico's
'Crucifixion', in that dusky chamber in the basement. I
looked long; one can hardly do otherwise. The fresco
deals with the highly pathetic, and after perceiving its
meaning you feel as little at liberty to go away abruptly as
you would to leave church during the sermon.

Having 'sat out the sermon, and departed, I hope, with the
gentle preacher's blessing', he went 'into the smaller refectory,
near by, to refresh my memory of the beautiful Last Supper of
Domenico Ghirlandaio.'

It would be putting things roughly to say that I felt as if I
had adjourned from a sermon to a comedy; but one may
certainly say that Ghirlandaio's theme, as contrasted with
the blessed Angelico's, was the dramatic, spectacular side
of human life.
 . . . The main idea with him has been the variety, the
brilliancy, the material charm of the scene, which finds
expression, with irrepressible generosity, in the access-
ories in the background. Instinctively he imagines an
opulent garden – imagines it with a good faith which

quite tides him over the reflection that Christ and his disciples were poor men and unused to sit at meat in palaces. Great full-fruited orange-trees peep over the wall before which the table is spread, strange birds fly through the air, and a peacock perches on the edge of the partition and looks down on the sacred repast. It is striking that, without any religious purpose at all intense, the figures, in their varied naturalness, have a dignity and sweetness of attitude which admits of numberless reverential constructions.

Having left the Ghirlandaio, James 'suddenly faltered and paused', as he was about to mount the stairs to 'the little painted cells of the Beato Angelico.' Then he decided: 'I wanted no more of him that day. I wanted no more macerated friars and spear-gashed sides.' He walked across the Piazza to the Accademia, where he looked at Botticelli's *Coronation of the Virgin*.

It was not one of the great works of art in San Marco which attracted the attention of Sophia Hawthorne but, as she was leaving the monastery,

a wooden image of Christ, sitting with bound hands, and the crown of thorns upon his head, from which blood was trickling over his figure. An expression of the utmost pain is in both face and form. A great many candles were burning around this distressing object, and a crowd of people were kneeling before it; and the whole chapel was filled with offerings from the devout – silver and gold hearts without number, chains and all kinds of trinkets; and watches (!) were hung round the neck and arms. It was the most extraordinary, repulsive, and even grotesque spectacle.

SPEDALE DEGLI INNOCENTI

The *Spedale degli Innocenti* (Foundling Hospital) in the Piazza della SS. Annunziata was founded in 1421. It contains a number of excellent pictures, among them an *Adoration of the*

Magi by Ghirlandaio. In his *Italian Hours* Henry James describes a copyist at work on this masterpiece. Museums used once to be full of such copyists – Reggie Temple, friend of so many writers of the first half of this century, at once comes to mind. Now, when photographic reproduction has attained a degree of accuracy surpassing even theirs, they have virtually disappeared.

> It [the *Adoration*] hangs in an obscure chapel, far aloft, behind an altar, and though now and then a stray tourist wanders in and puzzles awhile over the vaguely glowing forms, the picture is never really seen and enjoyed. I found an aged Frenchman of modest mien perched on a little platform beneath it, behind a great hedge of altar-candlesticks, with an admirable copy all completed. The difficulties of his task had been well-nigh insuperable, and his performance seemed to me a real feat of magic. He could scarcely move or turn, and could find room for his canvas but by rolling it together and painting a small piece at a time, so that he never enjoyed a view of his *ensemble*. The original is gorgeous with colour and bewildering with decorative detail, but not a gleam of the painter's crimson was wanting, not a curl in his gold arabesques. It seemed to me that if I had copied Ghirlandaio in such conditions I would at least maintain for my own credit that he was the finest painter in the world. 'Very good of its kind,' said the weary old man with a shrug of reply for my raptures; 'but oh how far short of Raphael!' However that may be, if the reader chances to observe this consummate copy in the so commendable Museum devoted in Paris to such works, let him stop before it with a due reverence; it is one of the patient things of art. Seeing it wrought there, in its dusky nook, under such scant convenience, I found no bar in the painter's foreignness to a thrilled sense that the old art-life of Florence isn't yet extinct. It still at least works spells and almost miracles.

SANTISSIMA ANNUNZIATA

The church of the Santissima Annunziata was founded in the thirteenth century, but has been constantly altered and modernized over the centuries. John Evelyn described his visit as follows:

> After dinner we went to the church of the Annunciata [sic], where the Duke and his Court were at their devotions, being a place of extraordinary repute for sanctity; for here is a shrine that does great miracles, proved by innumerable votive tablets, covering almost the walls of the whole church. This is the image of Gabriel who saluted the Blessed Virgin, and which the artist finished so well that he was in despair of performing the Virgin's face, whereupon it was miraculously done for him while he slept; but others say it was painted by St Luke himself. Whoever it was, infinite is the devotion of both sexes to it. The altar is set off with four columns of oriental alabaster, and lighted by thirty great silver lamps. There are innumerable other pictures by rare masters. Our Saviour's passion in brasse tables inserted in marble is the work of John di Bologna and Baccio Bandinelli . . .

The huddle of indifferent memorial slabs in the cloisters caused Albert Camus (1913–60) to reflect as follows:

> I remember how in Florence, in the cloister of the dead in Santissima Annunziata, I was transported by a feeling I believed to be dismay, but which was really only anger. I was reading the inscriptions on the tomb-stones and votive offerings. One had been a tender father and faithful husband; another, both the best of husbands and a shrewd businessman. A young woman, paragon of all virtues, spoke French 'like a native.' Then there was a young girl who was the future hope of her parents, 'but joy in this world is fleeting.' And yet I was not struck by any of this. According to the inscriptions, they were all resigned to the idea of death, and without any perplexities, seeing that they had accepted other duties. That day, some children had invaded the cloisters and played leapfrog on

the tombstones that were intended to perpetuate their
virtues. Night fell; I sat on the ground against a column.
A priest passing by smiled at me. The muffled playing of
an organ came from inside the church and the warm tone
of parts of the general tune emerged in between the
shouting of the children. Alone, leaning against the
column, I felt like someone gripped at the nape of the neck
shouting his faith as the last word. Everything inside me
rebelled against such resignation. 'It is necessary,' read the
inscription. But it is not and my rebellion was right. That
same joy that proceeded indifferent and enraptured like a
pilgrim wandering in the world; it was necessary to
follow it step by step. But for all the rest I did not want it. I
said no to it with all my strength.

The tombstones taught me that it was useless and that
life goes 'with sunrise and sunset.' But still today I cannot
see what uselessness my rebellion removes, and can see
perfectly well instead what it adds.

In the middle of the piazza stands Giambologna's statue of
the Grand Duke Ferdinand. This statue is interesting for a
reason additional to the eminence of its sculptor, since it is to it
that Browning refers in his poem 'The Statue and Bust.'
According to the poet, Ferdinand ordered the statue to be set
here so that it could gaze for all eternity at the della Robbia bust
of the woman whom he had loved in vain. The della Robbia
bust has now vanished. Here, in the poem, Ferdinand himself
is speaking of his commission to John of Douay (as Giambologna, a Belgian, was originally called):

> John of Douay shall effect my plan,
> Set me on horseback here aloft,
> Alive, as the crafty sculptor can,
>
> In the very square I have crossed so oft:
> That men may admire, when future suns
> Shall touch the eyes to a purpose soft,
>
> While the mouth and the brow stay in bronze –
> Admire and say 'when he was alive
> How he would take his pleasure once!'

In *Romola* George Eliot vividly evokes the Peasants' Fair which was held annually in the piazza:

At each of the opposite inlets he [Tito] saw people struggling into the piazza, while above them paper lanterns, held aloft on sticks, were waving uncertainly to and fro. A rude monotonous chant made a distinctly traceable strand of noise, across which screams, whistles, gibing chants in piping boyish voices, the beating of drums, and the ringing of little bells, met each other in confused din. Every now and then one of the dim floating lights disappeared with a smash from a stone launched more or less vaguely in pursuit of mischief, followed by a scream and renewed shouts. But on the outskirts of the whirling multitude there were groups who were keeping this vigil of the Nativity of the Virgin in a more methodical manner than by fitful stone-throwing and gibing. Certain ragged men, darting a hard sharp glance around them while their tongues rattled merrily, were inviting country people to game with them on fair and open-handed terms; two masquerading figures on stilts, who had snatched lanterns from the crowd, were swaying the lights to and fro in meteoric fashion, as they strode hither and thither; a sage trader was doing a profitable business at a small covered stall, in hot *berlingozzi* [ring-shaped cakes], a favourite farinaceous delicacy; one man standing on a barrel, with his back firmly planted against a pillar of the loggia in front of the Foundling Hospital [Spedale degli Innocenti], was selling efficacious pills, invented by a doctor of Salerno, warranted to prevent toothache and death by drowning; and not far off, against another pillar, a tumbler was showing off his tricks on a small platform; while a handful of 'prentices, despising the slack entertainment of guerrilla stone-throwing, were having a private concentrated match of that favourite Florentine sport at the narrow entrance of the Via de' Febbrai.

Porta Pinti: The Protestant Cemetery

Perhaps because its art and artefacts, its people and its palaces, proved to be a tonic to the soul, Florence came to be regarded as some sort of palliative for bodily ills as well. In this it could only disappoint, however, for the city's cruel climate – torrid in summer, dank in winter – carried off far more ailing visitors than it ever cured. With its tombstones recording the deaths of so many foreign visitors in their early years, the Protestant Cemetery provides a stark demonstration of this fact.

By all accounts it was once a lovely spot, sheltered by the old walls of the city. But these having long since been removed, it has now become little more than an outsize traffic-island, with buses, cars, and motor-bicycles roaring about it and its air acrid with exhaust fumes.

Here is the tomb of Elizabeth Barrett Browning, sculpted by Lord Leighton, its grey casket flanked by box-hedges. It is perhaps appropriate that Arthur Hugh Clough (1819–61), a victim of typhoid fever, should also be buried here, since he fretted himself to a shadow in unrequited love for Florence Nightingale and it was after the city, her birthplace, that she was named. Matthew Arnold wrote *Thyrsis* in commemoration of Clough's death, and some verses from it are inscribed on the stone. Shortly before his own death, Arnold, a frequent visitor to Florence, was thinking of retiring there – 'It is the most beautiful place I know,' he wrote to the American Minister, Charles K. Tuckerman.

The remains of Walter Savage Landor are also in the cemetery, the tomb engraved with Swinburne's:

> And thou, his Florence, to thy trust
>   Receive and keep,
> Keep safe his dedicated dust,
>   His sacred sleep.

> So shall thy lovers, come from far,
>   Mix with thy name,
> As morning-star with evening-star,
>   His faultless fame.

The North-western Quarter

VIA TORNABUONI

Arnold Bennett found the shops of the Via Tornabuoni –
which might be described as the Bond Street, Rue de Rivoli,
or Fifth Avenue of Florence – 'rather disappointing.' But
Augustus Hare called it 'the gayest and handsomest street in
Florence, where the best clubs and caffès are, and where the
most beautiful flowers are sold at the street corners'; and
W. D. Howells wrote of it:

> Via Tornabuoni is charming, and merits to be observed
> for the ensemble it offers of the contemporary Florentine
> expression, with its alluring shops, its confectioners and
> cafés, its florists and milliners, its dandies and tourists,
> and, ruggedly massing up out of their midst, the mighty
> bulk of the old Strozzi Palace, medieval, sombre, superb,
> tremendously impressive of the days when really a man's
> house was his castle. Everywhere in Florence the same
> sort of contrast presents itself in some degree, but
> nowhere quite so dramatically as here.

Of the Palazzo Strozzi in particular and of Florentine palazzi
in general Madame de Staël wrote in her novel of Italian life,
Corinne:

> The palaces of the leading families of Florence were built,
> in effect, like fortresses, from which they could defend

themselves; one can still see, on their outsides, the iron
rings from which each side could hang out its standards;
in short, everything is arranged with the object of maintaining individual forces, rather than of uniting them in
the common interest. One might say that the city has
been built for civil war.

Having commented on 'the Corinthian elegance of its cortile' and 'the massive strength of its facade, composed of what
the Italians call "*bozze di pietra forte*"' [blocks of rough-hewn
stone], Lady Morgan in her *Italy* goes on to declare that the

> great interest attached to this noble and ancient palace is
> that it was raised and inhabited by Filippo Strozzi, the
> Cato of his age, and by his strong-minded and ambitious
> wife, the famous Clarice de' Medici. When the rank, the
> wealth, the high consideration in which this illustrious
> citizen was held, induced the people to give him the title
> of *Messire*, he observed: 'My name is Filippo Strozzi; I am
> a Florentine merchant and no more: who gives me a title
> insults me.' Yet at the moment he held the Popes and
> Cardinals of the house of Medici at bay.

In the Via Tornabuoni stood Doney's Café, now recently,
sadly and inexplicably closed to make way for a shoe-shop.
Tourists had been frequenting it literally for centuries. Visiting Florence, the Goncourt brothers spent much of their time
there when not avidly sightseeing. It was where Herman
Melville, James Russell Lowell, and Ralph Waldo Emerson all
took their breakfasts when staying at the Hotel du Nord in the
Via delle Terme. Stendhal also often went there for breakfast.
In 1858, touring Europe for his health, the young American
dilettante writer J. De Forest described the café as then con-
sisting of three saloons, with cream-coloured columns and
marble-topped tables. He noted

> the white uniforms of Austrian officers, the easy travel-
> ling-coats of English tourists, and the noisy waiters,
> rushing about like incarnations of perpetual motion, and
> shouting the orders of the guests with the vehemence of
> sea captains in a hurricane.

The *fioraia* or flower-girl at Doney is, he comments, of a special species.

> She drops a bouquet on your table, fixes it in your button-hole; then, with a quick glance in your eye and a flattering smile, she trips hastily away; but at your departure, while you are stepping into the railway station or the diligence office, thinking in the joy of a good conscience that all your creditors are satisfied, you suddenly see before you the *fioraia*, smiling, wishing you *Buon viaggio*, presenting her final bouquet, and awaiting the reward of her floral benevolence.

In *Aurora Leigh*, Elizabeth Barrett Browning describes Doney, at about the same period when de Forest was so frequent a customer:

> Underneath,
> The river, just escaping from the weight
> Of that intolerable glory, ran
> In acquiescent shadow murmurously:
> And up, beside it, streamed the festa-folk
> With fellow-murmurs from their feet and fans
> (With *issimo* and *ino* and sweet poise
> Of vowels in their pleasant scandalous talk)
> Returning from the grand-duke's dairy-farm
> Before the trees grew dangerous at night
> (For, 'trust no tree by moonlight', Tuscans say),
> To eat their ice at Doni's tenderly, –
> Each lovely lady close to a cavalier
> Who holds her dear fan while she feeds her smile
> On meditative spoonfuls of vanille,
> He breathing hot protesting vows of love,
> Enough to thaw her cream, and scorch his beard.

The English governess, Ellen, who is the heroine of Lettice Cooper's Florentine novel *Fenny* – its time-scheme straddles the last War – frequently meets friends, English or Italian, in the café. Early on in the novel, it is while she is strolling along the Via Tornabuoni that she makes the momentous decision – the year is 1933 – to have her hair bobbed:

This was the first time that Ellen had been alone in
Florence. She had not brought her guide-book, and
without it did not know how to find the things she
wanted to see. She sauntered along the Via Tornabuoni
looking in the shop windows. It was one of the fashionable hours. Elegant women – Italian, English, American –
strolled on the pavement, shining cars nosed their way
along the street. Elderly ladies in pairs, with elaborately
veiled hats and antique summer dresses, tottered towards
Doney's for their five o'clock cup of tea. It amused Ellen
to watch this decorative world, but when she came
opposite to a mirror in a shop window she was struck by
the incongruity of her own sober figure, in the grey tweed
coat and skirt, with her grey hat tipping forward as usual
on her coils of hair. A few doors farther on she came to a
hairdresser's, where there was a notice in the window that
they spoke French and English. She went in and asked
them to cut off her hair.

The first snips of the scissors seemed to denude her of a
good deal of what had so far been her life . . .

Later, in 1937, an excursion to Doney's with her two
charges, Shand and Donata, leads to Ellen (or Fenny, as her
charges call her) seeing rampant Fascism at close quarters:

When they came out of the café, the police had cleared
the street of cars, and the procession was passing, cheered
by spectators packed on the pavements and in the shop
doorways and the windows above. A group of young
Fascists went by, military and smart in their uniform
jackets and top boots. They were boys of Shand's age or
less. Some of them looked very hot, the sweat rolled
down their solemn young faces under the peaked caps,
but they carried themselves proudly, their limbs swing-
ing in perfect time, their heads erect under the swaying
banners with their portraits of the Duce, the Roman wolf,
the fasces and the ever-repeated inscription, 'Credere,
obedire, combattere.'

'How well they march!' Donata said with exaggerated

fervour and a mischievous glance at her governess's unsmiling face.

Ellen saw Shand on the opposite pavement. In his flannel trousers, sandals and open-necked shirt – clothes which he always wore untidily – he could not have looked a more complete contrast to his marching contemporaries. He was frowning at them with open hostility. Behind the marching boys there was a brief gap in the procession between their rear rank and the leaders and the foremost banners of the *squadristi*, who followed them. Through this gap, as the movement of the procession brought it opposite to him, Shand slouched coolly across the road.

Luckily there were at the moment no policemen nor Blackshirts outside the door of Doney's. A young man wearing a party badge shook his fist at Shand, and began to pour out a torrent of abuse. He evidently thought him English, for the word 'sanctions' kept on recurring. Two or three of the bystanders joined in, and there was a movement towards them from the back of the crowd. Ellen pushed Donata inside Doney's and pulled Shand after her.

As sad as the demise of Doney is that of the restaurant the Buca di Lapi, also in the Via Tornabuoni and also much frequented by writers. Arnold Bennett describes a visit with typical relish:

Here the cooking is done in full view of the audience. Each dish specially prepared for each client. All by one man. About 35, dark, personable, extraordinarily quick and graceful. If he left his recess for a moment to go upstairs he would slide down the rail to come back again. Charcoal stove. He blew it up constantly with a fan. Sparks fly. He puts on charcoal with his hand. Everything goes through that hand. He would fan with one hand and stir with the other. He made an omelette in a moment: very quick his gesture in turning it over like a pancake, in the pan. Very careful and slow in making our coffee. Orders called out in a loud voice by the landlord or the

boy waiter – who was not dressed as a waiter. All
professional conversation very loud and constantly going
on. Things not in stock, such as ham, sent for and
brought down in paper. When a dish is ready the chef
would plank it down on a ledge and whistle, or call out its
name. When we arrived the landlord was finishing his
dressing in the further saloon which was darkened. Later
the boy waiter – perhaps his son – took a pair of loose cuffs
from a hat-hook and slipped them on, at once giving
himself an air of grande toilette. Still later, the landlord,
evidently bethinking himself, did the same from another
hook. About 10 or 12 or 15 customers, and all cooked by
one man.

Off the Via Tornabuoni runs the Borgo Santi Apostoli. No.
19 is the Palazzo Usimbardi (Acciaoli), the beautiful sixteenth-
century façade of which was destroyed in the last War. During
the nineteenth century the palazzo became the Grand Hotel
Royal, where such literary figures as Dickens, Longfellow,
and Swinburne put up.

Santa Maria Novella

The chief Dominican church of Florence is Santa Maria
Novella. The building was begun in 1278, on a site that before
the erection of a third set of walls around Florence was actually
outside the city boundaries. As a result the church was first
known as Santa Maria tra le Vigne, or St Mary among the
Vineyards. *La sposa* – the bride – was the nickname given to it
by Michelangelo, who thus conveyed the radiant innocence of
a supreme example of Tuscan Gothic architecture.

The chief literary interest of this church is that it is here that
Boccaccio set the first scene of the *Decameron*. Longfellow
referred to this connection when noting in his Journal:

At Florence I took lodgings in a house which fronts upon
the Piazza Novella. In front of my parlour windows was
the venerable Gothic church of Santa Maria Novella, in
whose gloomy aisles Boccaccio has placed the opening

scenes of his *Decamerone*. There, when the plague was raging in the city, one Tuesday morning after mass, 'the seven ladies, young and fair,' held council together, and resolved to leave the infected city and flee to their rural villas in the environs, where they might 'hear the birds sing, and see the green hills, and the plains, and the fields covered with grain and undulating like the sea, and trees of species manifold.'

Of all the pictures within the church, none in the nineteenth century excited a greater diversity of opinion than 'Cimabue's' *Madonna*. (Subsequently ascribed to Cimabue's pupil Duccio, it is now to be seen in the Uffizi.) Lady Morgan calls it 'a horrible monster.' Hawthorne is hardly more complimentary:

I could see no charm whatever in the broad-faced Virgin, and it would relieve my mind and rejoice my spirit if the picture were borne out of the church in another triumphal procession (like the one which brought it here) and reverently burnt.

Elizabeth Barrett Browning was far more complimentary:

Ascend the right stair from the farther nave
   To muse in a small chapel scarcely lit
By Cimabue's Virgin. Bright and brave
   That picture was accounted, mark, of old;
A king stood bare before its sovran grace,
   A reverent people shouted to behold
The picture, not the king, not even the place
   Containing such a miracle grew bold,
Named the glad Borgo from that beauteous face
   Which thrilled the artist, after work, to think
His own ideal Mary-smile should stand
   So very near him, – he, within the brink
Of all that glory, let in by his hand
   With too divine a rashness! Yet none shrink
Who come to gaze here now; albeit 'twas planned
   Sublimely in the thought's simplicity:
The Lady, throned in empyreal state,
   Minds only the young Babe upon her knee,

While sidelong angels bear the royal weight,
   Prostrated meekly, smiling tenderly
Oblivion of their wings; the Child thereat
   Stretching his hand like God. If any should,
Because of some stiff draperies and loose joints,
   Gaze scorn down from the height of Raphaelhood
On Cimabue's picture, – Heaven anoints
   The head of no such critic, and his blood
The poet's curse strikes full on and appoints
   To ague and cold spasms for evermore.
A noble picture! worthy of the shout
   Wherewith along the streets the people bore
Its cherub-faces, which the sun threw out,
   Until they stooped and entered the church door.

The Piazza of Santa Maria Novella provides the setting for two passages in Anatole France's *Le Lys Rouge* (The Red Lily). Reading this novel, one realizes how much influence both it and its author must have had on Aldous Huxley. Some of its passages are, indeed, hardly distinguishable from ones in Huxley's own novel about aristocratic, rich, and intellectual *émigré* life in Tuscany, *Those Barren Leaves*.

In each extract from *Le Lys Rouge*, a contrast is drawn between the simplicity of an Italian cobbler and the sophistication of the foreign visitors, to the disadvantage of the latter. The Choulette of the two passages is an elderly, drink-sodden poet, clearly modelled on Verlaine:

The next day, as they were coming out of Santa Maria Novella, and crossing the square, where, as in an ancient circus, stand two obelisks of marble, Madame Marmet said to Countess Martin: 'I think I see Monsieur Choulette.'

Sitting in a cobbler's booth, pipe in hand, Choulette was gesticulating rhythmically, and appeared to be reciting verses. The Florentine shoemaker, as he worked with his awl, was listening with a good-natured smile. He was a little bald man, a favourite type in Flemish pictures. On the table, among the wooden lasts, nails, pieces of leather and balls of wax, was a basil plant. A sparrow with a false leg, made of a bit of match, was hopping gaily from the old man's shoulder to his head.

Delighted at such a sight, Madame Marmet stood on the threshold and called Choulette, who was reciting in a soft, singing voice, and asked him why he had not come with her to visit the Cappella degli Spagnuoli.

He rose and replied:

'Madame, you are occupied with vain imaginings. I am concerned with life and reality.'

He shook hands with the cobbler, and followed the two ladies.

'On my way to Santa Maria Novella,' he said, 'I saw this old man leaning over his work, holding the last between his knees as if in a vice, and stitching clumsy shoes. I felt that he was simple and good. I said to him in Italian, 'Father, will you drink a glass of Chianti wine with me?' He was quite willing. He went to fetch a bottle and glasses, while I minded his shop.'

And Choulette pointed to two glasses and a bottle standing on the stove.

'When he returned, we drank together; I repeated good words of obscure meaning, the music of which delighted him. I shall return to his booth. I shall learn from him how to make shoes and live a contented life. After that I shall never know sadness, which arises solely from discontent and idleness.'

Countess Martin smiled.

'Monsieur Choulette, I am not discontented and yet I am not gay. Must I also learn to make shoes?'

Choulette replied gravely:

'Not yet.'

When they reached the Oricellai Gardens, Madame Marmet dropped on to a seat. At Santa Maria Novella she had carefully examined the serene frescoes of Ghirlandajo, the choir-stalls, the virgin of Cimabue, and the pictures in the monastery. She had taken great pains in honour of her husband's memory, who was said to have loved Italian art. She was tired. Choulette sat down beside her and said:

'Could you tell me, Madame, if it is true that the Pope has his robes made by Worth?'

Countess Martin and Madame Marmet again visit Santa Maria Novella, on this occasion in the company of a spinster English writer, resident in Florence, called Vivian Bell – a character modelled on the real-life Vernon Lee, whom France had met and admired. Once again the cobbler is at work:

Coming out of the church, they passed the booth of the cobbler whom Choulette had adopted as his master. The good man was patching a countryman's boots. The pot of basil was at his side, and the sparrow with the wooden leg chirped close by.

Madame Marmet asked the old man if he were quite well, if he had enough work to do, and if he were happy. To all these questions he replied the charming Italian 'Yes,' the *Si* coming musically from his toothless mouth. She made him tell them his sparrow's story. One day the poor little creature had put his foot into the boiling wax.

'I made my little friend a wooden leg out of a match, and now he is able to perch on my shoulder as of old.'

'He is a kind old man,' said Miss Bell, 'who teaches M. Choulette wisdom. At Athens there was a cobbler, named Simon, who wrote works on philosophy and was a friend of Socrates. I have always thought M. Choulette resembled Socrates.'

Thérèse asked the shoemaker to tell them his name and story. His name was Serafino Stoppini, and he came from Stia. He was old. His life had been full of trouble.

He put back his spectacles on to his forehead, revealing his blue kindly eyes, growing dim beneath their reddened lids.

'I had a wife and children, now I am alone. I have known things, which now I have forgotten.'

. . . 'His tools, a handful of nails, the tub in which he soaks the leather, and a pot of basil are all he has in the world,' thought Thérèse, 'and yet he is happy.'

'This plant smells sweet, and soon it will flower,' she said.

'If the poor little thing flowers, it will die,' he replied.

There is a reference both to Michelangelo's *la sposa* and to France's 'two obelisks of marble' in Elizabeth Barrett Browning's *Aurora Leigh*, in which she writes of:

> Maria Novella's Place
> In which the mystic obelisks stand up
> Triangular, pyramidal, each based
> On a single trine of brazen tortoises,
> To guard that fair church, Buonarotti's Bride,
> That stares out from her large blind dial-eyes,
> Her quadrant and armillary dials, black
> With rhythms of many suns and moons, in vain
> Inquiry for so rich a soul as his . . .

These 'mystic obelisks' were erected to mark the goals of the chariot races held in the piazza under Cosimo I and his successors on the Eve of St John. Fenimore Cooper has left us a description of these races in his *Gleanings in Europe*:

The games are called the *corsi dei cocchi*. There are two small obelisks on opposite extremities of the square, and the temporary circus is constructed by their means. A cord is stretched from one to the other; a sort of amphitheatre is formed by scaffoldings around the whole, the royal and diplomatic boxes being prepared near the goal. As there is much scenic painting, a good parade of guards both horse and foot, a well-dressed population, and a background of balconies garnished by tapestry and fine women, to say nothing of roofs and chimneys, the general effect is quite imposing.

The falling off is in the chariots. The ancient vehicle was small and had but two wheels; whereas these were large and clumsy, had four wheels, and unusually long and straggling perches, – an invention to keep them from upsetting. In other respects the form was preserved, and the charioteers were in costume.

Four chariots, to use the modern language, entered for the race. The start was pretty fair, and the distance twice round the obelisks. If you ask me for the effect, I shall tell you that, apart from the appliances – such as the court, the guards, the spectators and the dresses, and perhaps I might add the turns, – one may witness the same any fine evening in New York, between two drunken Irish cartmen who are on their way home. There was certainly a little skill manifested at the turns, and it was easy to see that betting should have been on the outside chariot; for those nearer to the obelisks were obliged to go considerably beyond them before they could come round, while the one farthest from the poles just cleared them. This outside chariot won the race, the charioteer having the sagacity not to make his push before the last turn.

After the chariot-races we had the *corso dei barberi* or a race between barbs. The horses were without riders, and the track was the longest street of the town. To this amusement everyone who could went in a carriage, and the *corso* of vehicles was much the most interesting part of the exhibition. Two lines are made, and the coaches move in opposite directions through the same street, on a walk. Of course, everybody sees everybody, – and pretty often the somebodies see nobodies, for the mania to make one on these occasions is so strong, that half the artisans are abroad in carriages, as well as their betters. The royal equipages moved in the line, the same as that of the milliner. When we were well tired of looking at each other, the grand duke went into a gallery prepared for him, and the race was run. The latter does not merit a syllable; but so strong is the rage for sporting, that I heard some Englishmen betting on the winner.

Piazza dell' Unità

Near Santa Maria Novella and the railway station lies the Piazza dell' Unità, in which is situated the Hotel Baglioni. Having categorized this hotel as Expensive, the Fodor entry continues 'Large, comfortable rooms; Renaissance decor in public room; roof garden.' It is in the lift of the Hotel Baglioni that, in Mario Soldati's 1955 *The Confession*, there occurs an incident which is to cause the hero, Clemente Perrier, four-teen-year-old pupil at a Jesuit school in Turin, to agonize over his vocation for the priesthood. Clemente is obsessed with a remembered image:

of a plump, blonde woman, with rounded eyes, pouting lips, and that sad, jaded expression which, much more effectively than any other, stimulates the imagination and arouses the desire. Clemente had seen the woman only once, and then only for a few minutes. The autumn before, in Florence, he had found himself alone with her in a lift in the Hotel Baglioni. But afterward, thinking every day of what happened – for ten minutes in the morning as he lazed in the warmth of his bed, for ten minutes in the afternoon during the initial stupor of his siesta, and for ten minutes each night before falling off to sleep – he had passed that single, swift impression in slow motion before his eyes and had ended by increasing its duration. The blonde woman had made a long journey with him. Shut up, just the two of them, in that tepid and isolated lift as in the compartment of an old-fashioned train, standing close to each other, without fear of wit-nesses, they had risen mile after mile, hour after hour, in the tallest of skyscrapers. Once again Clemente saw that white pudgy hand, with scarlet sharply pointed nails and on one finger a huge pearl ring, place itself on the panel and push the button which would make the lift start to go up.

He seemed to remember that he had pretended a mo-ment's distraction and, as though he, too, wanted to push the button, had placed his hand over hers and felt its warm softness. But, as often happened to him in such fantasies, he was not completely sure whether he hadn't merely confined himself to desiring that contact and, having quickly conceived the trick by which to obtain it and yet lacking the courage to act, he had cherished it, afterwards, as something that had actually taken place, even to the point of deceiving his own memory.

Clemente saw again the black velvet dress that clung to

the woman's figure: the pinkish, plump legs that stood
out against the sharp black of the skirt's hem, the black
satin slippers with diamond buckles (it did not occur to
him to think, even about these gems on her slippers, that
they might be false), the naked arms, the deep slit down
her back – all that flesh which the velvet cloth, the pearl
necklace, and the other jewels endowed with the arcane,
heavy preciousness of an idol, an idol who stood very
close to him and in whom, he sensed, lived his happiness,
yet whom a superior and cruel will prohibited his hands
from even touching ever so lightly.

Clemente remembered the rise and fall of her breasts as
she breathed, and the faint pulsations that ran along the
folds of her velvet dress, at the waist and over the belly.

But, above all, he had been fascinated by her eyes, dark,
shining, and like a doll's. Now and then her heavy lids
would lower and her eyes would shut tightly; the skin all
around them would become wrinkled and the woman's
face then suggested the fulfilment of a pleasure, yet with
that almost ugly, almost sad grimace which comes
from great sensual experience and a knowledge of all its
refinements.

Even now when, returning to that scene for the
thousandth time, Clemente travelled up the woman's
body and at last saw again that exquisite, withered face,
those eyes that seemed closed in pleasure, his blood
would pound in his veins.

He would have liked to slake himself in that sweetness,
that sadness, that knowledge and enjoyment of life which
he felt he lacked. And he imagined finding himself again
in the lift and flinging himself without a word at the
woman's feet, embracing her legs, her knees, begging to
be taken, subjected, dominated, crushed.

He had thought of becoming her little servant and,
with the idea of greater humiliation and voluptuousness,
of wearing the absurd red uniform of the hotel bellboys.
No longer for anyone would he be Clemente Perrier, the
boy who studied with the Jesuits, the boy in whose
family's living-room among the lady friends and artillery

officers, on the seventh and the twenty-first of every month (the days of his mother's receptions), they would chat about, saying: 'He is very intelligent', 'shows a great deal of promise,' and 'will go far.' Yes, he could just hear them: 'But, my dear, you ought to have seen how excited he became, and at his age, in front of Michelangelo's *Moses* and the Duomo in Florence, during the trip he got as a reward last autumn,' and so on. No, he would vanish from the world. They'd search for him in vain. He'd go to that woman's country, which, he imagined, was either Hungary or Sweden. He'd become her servant for life. Nobody could ever track him down again. At the start he would forget everything, even his surname. Then at last he would feel annulled in her, sacrificed, her slave, and therefore happy.

Piazza della Repubblica

So that the present-day Piazza della Repubblica – originally the Piazza Vittorio Emmanuele – and the streets around it could be erected in all their empty grandeur, the accretions of two thousands years of history were swept away at the end of the last century and the beginning of this. The site of the Roman forum, later to become the site of the Mercato Vecchio, the Old Market, was transformed into an area of restaurants, cafés, shops, and hotels. The people who had lived in this area, once regarded as a slum, were relocated, usually against their will, in new housing especially built for them outside the Porta San Frediano.

George Eliot's *Romola* contains a description of the Mercato Vecchio as it was at the time of Savonarola:

This piazza, though it had been the scene of a provision-market from time immemorial, and may, perhaps, says fond imagination, be the very spot to which the Fesulean ancestors of the Florentines descended from their high fastness to traffic with the rustic population of the valley, had not been shunned as a place of residence by Florentine wealth. In the early decades of the fifteenth century, which was now near its end, the Medici and other power- ful families of the *popolani grassi*, or commercial nobility, had their houses there, not perhaps finding their ears much offended by the loud roar of mingled dialects, or their eyes much shocked by the butchers' stalls, which the old poet Antonio Pucci accounts a chief glory, or *dignita*, of a market that, in his esteem, eclipsed the markets of all the earth beside. But the glory of mutton and veal (well attested to be the flesh of the right animals; for were not the skins, with the heads attached, duly displayed accord- ing to the decree of the Signoria?) was just now wanting to the Mercato, the time of Lent not being yet over. The proud corporation, or 'Art,' of butchers was in abeyance, and it was the great harvest-time of the market- gardeners, the cheese-mongers, the vendors of macaroni, corn, eggs, milk, and dried fruits: a change which was apt to make the women's voices predominant in the chorus. But in all seasons there was the exceptional ringing of pots and pans, the chinking of the money-changers, the tempting offers of cheapness at the old-clothes stalls, the challenges of the dicers, the vaunting of new linens and woollens, of excellent wooden-ware, kettles and frying- pans; there was the choking of the narrow inlets with mules and carts, together with much uncomplimentary remonstrance in terms remarkably identical with the insults in use by the gentler sex of the present day, under the same imbrowning and heating circumstances. Ladies and gentlemen, who came to market, looked on at a larger amount of amateur fighting than could easily be seen in these later times, and beheld more revolting rags, beggary, and rascaldom, than modern householders could well picture to themselves. As the day wore on the hideous drama of the gaming-house might be seen here by any chance open-air spectator – the quivering eager- ness, the blank despair, the sobs, the blasphemy, and the blows . . .

But still there was the relief of prettier sights: there were brood-rabbits, not less innocent and astonished than those of our own period; there were doves and singing-birds to be bought as presents for the children; there were even kittens for sale, and here and there a handsome *gattuccio*, or 'Tom,' with the highest character for mousing; and, better than all, there were young, softly-rounded cheeks and bright eyes, freshened by the start from the far-off *castello* at daybreak, not to speak of older faces with the unfading charm of honest goodwill in them, such as are never quite wanting in scenes of human industry. And high on a pillar in the centre of the place – a venerable pillar, fetched from the Church of San Giovanni – stood Donatello's statue of Plenty, with a fountain near it, where the good wives of the market freshened their utensils, and their throats also; not because they were unable to buy wine, but because they wished to save the money for their husbands.

The buildings now standing in and around the Piazza are of the kind described by Browning when he wrote:

They are stone-faced, white as a curd, there's something to
    take the eye!
Houses in four straight lines, not a single front awry!
Green blinds as a matter of course, to draw when the sun
    gets high,
And the shops with fanciful signs which are painted
    properly.

Writing in 1912, in his *A Wanderer in Florence*, E. V. Lucas commented:

In talking to elderly persons who can remember Florence forty and fifty years ago I find that nothing so distresses them as the loss of the old quarter for the making of this new spacious piazza; and probably nothing can so delight the younger Florentines as its possession, for having nothing to do in the evenings, they do it chiefly in the Piazza Vittorio Emmanuele. Chairs and tables spring up like mushrooms in the roadway, among which too few waiters distribute those very inexpensive refreshments which seem to be purchased rather for the right to the seat that they confer than for any stimulation. It is extraordinary to the eyes of the thriftless English, who are never so happy as when they are overpaying Italian and other caterers in their own country, to notice how long these wiser folk will occupy a table on an expenditure of fourpence.

If for 'very inexpensive refreshments' one substitutes 'very expensive refreshments', this passage has in no way dated.

In D. H. Lawrence's *Aaron's Rod*, set in the period immediately after the First World War, the piazza is described as 'the centre of Florence by night' – as, indeed, it still remains today. Aaron comes to a 'large, brilliantly-lighted café' on a Sunday evening, to find the place full.

Men. Florentines, many men sat in groups and in twos and threes at the little marble tables. They were mostly in dark clothes or black overcoats. They had mostly been drinking just a cup of coffee – others, however, glasses of wine or liquor. But mostly it was just a little coffee-tray with a tiny coffee pot and a cup and saucer. There was a faint film of tobacco smoke. And the men were all talking: talking, talking with that peculiar intensity of Florentines.

Aaron cannot find a table. But then Argyle – the character based on Norman Douglas – bobs up and suggests that Aaron join him and his friends. The little group of foreigners discuss the political unrest of the time and the likelihood that (as one of them puts it) 'Some form of Socialism is bound to come, no matter how you postpone it or try variations.'

Suddenly their erudite, sometimes rancorous discussion is literally blown apart:

CRASH!
There intervened one awful minute of pure shock, when the soul was in darkness.
Out of this shock Aaron felt himself issuing amid a mass of terrible sensations: the fearful blow of the explosion, the noise of glass, the hoarse howl of people, the rushing of men, the sudden gulf, the awful gurgling whirlpool of horror in the social life.

He stood in agony and semi-blindness amid a chaos. Then as he began to recover his consciousness, he found himself standing by a pillar some distance from where he had been sitting: he saw a place where tables and chairs were all upside down, legs in the air, amid debris of glass and breakage: he saw the cafe almost empty, nearly everybody gone: he saw the owner, or the manager, advancing aghast to the place of the debris: he saw Lilly standing not far off, white as a sheet, and as if unconscious. And still he had no idea of what had happened. He thought perhaps something had broken down. He could not understand.

Lilly began to look round. He caught Aaron's eye. And then Aaron began to approach his friend.

'What is it?' he asked.

'A bomb,' said Lilly.

The manager, and one old waiter, and three or four youths had now advanced to the place of debris. And now Aaron saw that a man was lying there – and horror, blood was running across the floor of the cafe. Men began now hastily to return to the place. Some seized their hats and departed again at once. But many began to crowd in – a black eager crowd of men pressing to where the bomb had burst – where the man was lying. It was rather dark, some of the lamps were broken – but enough still shone. Men surged in with that eager, excited zest of people, where there has been an accident. Grey carabinieri, and carabinieri in the cocked hat and fine Sunday uniform pressed forward officiously.

'Let us go,' said Lilly.

And he went to the far corner, where his hat hung. But Aaron looked in vain for his own hat. The bomb had fallen near the stand where he had hung it and his overcoat.

'My hat and coat?' he said to Lilly.

Lilly, not very tall, stood on tiptoe. Then he climbed on a chair and looked around. Then he squeezed past the crowd.

Aaron followed. On the other side of the crowd excited

angry men were wrestling over overcoats that were
mixed up with a broken marble table-top. Aaron spied his
own black hat under the sofa near the wall. He waited his
turn and then in the confusion pressed forward to where
the coats were. Someone had dragged out his, and it lay
on the floor under many feet. He managed, with a
struggle, to get it from under the feet of the crowd. He felt
at once for his flute. But his trampled, torn coat had no
flute in its pocket. He pushed and struggled, caught sight
of a section and picked it up. But it was split right down,
two silver stops were torn out, and a long thin spelk of
wood was curiously torn off. He looked at it, and his
heart stood still. No need to look for the rest.

He felt utterly, utterly overcome – as if he didn't care
what became of him any further. He didn't care whether
he were hit by a bomb, or whether he himself threw the
next bomb, and hit somebody. He just didn't care any
more about anything in life or death. It was as if the reins
of his life slipped from his hands, and he would let
everything run where it would, so long as it did run.

There is a parallel between this passage and that in E. M.
Forster's *A Room With a View* in which the heroine, Lucy,
witnesses the stabbing of a man. In each the act of violence
takes place in a popular and crowded piazza; in each case it
disrupts an atmosphere of happiness and relaxation; and in
each case it transforms the protagonist's life.

It was in the Gambrinus, for a long time the café in the piazza
most popular with writers, that in December 1895 André Gide
met Gabriele d'Annunzio:

. . .d'Annunzio indulges with obvious greediness in little
vanilla ices served in small cardboard boxes. He sits
beside me and talks gracefully and charmingly without, it
seems to me, paying any special attention to the role he is
playing. He is short; from a distance his face seems
ordinary or already familiar, so devoid is he of any
exterior sign of literature or genius. He wears a little
pointed beard which is pale blond and talks with a clearly
articulated voice, somewhat cold, but supple and almost

caressing. His eyes are rather cold; he is perhaps rather cruel, but perhaps it is simply the appearance of his delicate sensuality that makes him seem so. He is wearing a black derby, quite unaffectedly.

. . . I say to him laughingly: 'But you have read everything!' 'Everything,' he replies gracefully. 'I believe one has to have read everything. We read everything,' he continues, 'in the constantly renewed hope of finally finding the masterpiece that we are all awaiting so eagerly.' He does not much like Maeterlinck, whose language strikes him as too simple. Ibsen displeases him by 'his lack of beauty.' 'What do you expect?' he says, as though to excuse himself; 'I am a Latin.'

. . . When I expressed my amazement that his great erudition allows him so sustained and so perfect a literary production – or that his work as a writer allows him the time to read so much: 'Oh,' he says, 'I have my own method for reading quickly. I am a terrible worker; nine or ten months in the year without stopping I work twelve hours a day. I have already produced twenty books.'

Moreover he says this without boasting at all and quite simply. In this way the evening is prolonged without difficulty.

Some ten days later, Gide again met d'Annunzio at Gambrinus:

He tells me that he has never known insomnia, or at least never had to suffer from it. Fencing and riding keep him from it. He fences a great deal and often rides. Tomorrow he is to go to Vinci, Leonardo's village; it is a pilgrimage, he says, and invites me to accompany him. If I were not such a poor horseman, I should have taken pleasure in riding with him. Talking of irony, he says that he cannot endure it, that in using irony you oppose yourself to things whereas it is only through love that you penetrate them, and that is essential . . .

With his meals he drinks only water; this is a hard worker's practice. On the other hand, he says that he drinks ten or twelve cups of tea a day. This morning, excusing himself for coming to the table in riding-habit, his elegance, his suave assurance and his unselfconsciousness were charming.

Four years later, the electorate of Florence gave the *coup de grâce* to d'Annunzio's already ailing political career, when he stood for the San Giovanni district in a general election precipitated by the murder of King Umberto II by an anarchist called Bresci. In his biography of d'Annunzio, *The Poet as Superman*, Anthony Rhodes summarizes the situation as follows:

> The electors of the Via Tornabuoni and the Via Strozzi were suspicious of a man who went from the ultra-conservatism of the Right, to the ultra-radicalism of the Left, particularly as he had large outstanding accounts in their shops. His new adversary, Cambray-Digny, was quick to sense this and an attack was made on his private life. D'Annunzio was accused of adultery, polygamy, theft, incest, sodomy, simony, murder and cannibalism.

Not surprisingly, he was defeated.

THE CASCINE

English guide-books often call the Cascine the Hyde Park of Florence; French guide-books, its Bois de Boulogne. Before the First World War E. V. Lucas wrote of it: 'Here the wealthy Florentines drive, the middle-classes saunter and ride bicycles, the poor enjoy picnics, and the English take country walks.' Except that it is now not only the wealthy who drive their cars up and down its avenues, that the bicycles are all too often and all too noisily motor ones, that those who enjoy their picnics tend to bring transistor radios with them and leave an extraordinary amount of litter behind them, and jogging for many people has taken the place of walking, the Cascine has little changed.

In the seventeenth and eighteenth centuries, when Florence was still a small, compact city, to go out to the Cascine was similar to going out to Richmond Park or Wimbledon Common from London at the same period. This is how the Cascine

in 1732 was described by Joseph Spence (1699–1768), chiefly
now remembered for the bright, impartial light which his
posthumously published *Andecdotes* throws on Pope, his
circle, and his antagonists:

At a little way out of the gate that we live next to . . . is a
place made for the pleasure of the Grand Duke and his
good subjects. You go to it through a range of vast Scotch
fir-trees: on your left hand is a long run of groves and
pretty artificial islands full of arbours, and on the right lie
the vineyards and cornfields interspersed, which is the
manner all about Florence (as in Lombardy). This leads
into a large beautiful meadow. The walk of firs is continued on, all the length of it; the groves and woods, with a
variety of a thousand different walks on the left, beyond
which, all along, runs the river Arno. These woods are at
last brought rounding to join the fir-walk, and so termin-
ate the meadow. This meadow all our autumn was almost
as fresh a green as we have in England (a very uncommon
thing here), and was all sprinkled with wild crocuses as
thick as the stars in heaven. Many of the trees in the
woody part wanted to show another crop of leaves, and
the wild vines that are very frequent in it hung over your
head from tree to tree with their glistening black bunches
of grapes, that were left there for the happiness of the
birds that inhabit those woods very plentifully . . .

Very different from this rural scene is that described by
Charles Lever more than a hundred years later in 1856:

On one side the gentle river stealing past beneath the
shadowing foliage; on the other, the picturesque mountains towards Fiesole, dotted with its palaces and terraced
gardens. The ancient city itself is partly seen, and the
massive Duomo and the Palazzo Vecchio proudly tower
above the trees. What other people of Europe have such a
haunt? What other people would know so thoroughly
how to enjoy it?
    . . . Although a choice military band was performing
with exquisite skill the favourite overtures of the day, the

noise and tumult of conversation almost drowned their notes. In fact, the Cascine is to the world of society what the Bourse is to the world of trade. It is the great centre of all news and intelligence, where bargains of intercourse are transacted, the scene of past pleasures is revived, and where the plans of future enjoyment are canvassed. The great and wealthy are there to see and meet with each other. Their proud equipages lie side by side, like great liners; while phaetons, like fast frigates, shoot swiftly by, and solitary dandies flit past in varieties of conveyance to which sea craft can offer no analogies. All are busy, eager and occupied. Scandal holds here its festival, and the misdeeds of every capital of Europe are now being discussed. The higher themes of politics occupy but few: the interests of literature attract still less. It is essentially of the world they talk, and it must be owned that they do it like adepts. The last witticism of Paris – the last duel at Berlin – who has fled from his creditors in England – who has run away from her husband at Naples – all are retailed with a serious circumstantiality that would lead one to believe that gossip maintained its own correspondent in every city of the Continent. Moralists might fancy, perhaps, that in the tone these subjects are treated there might mingle a reprobation of the bad, and a due estimate of the opposite if it ever occurred at all; but no. Never were censors more lenient – never were critics so charitable. The transgressions against good breeding, the *gaucheries* of manner, the solecisms in dress, language, or demeanour, do indeed meet with sharp reproof and cutting sarcasm; but in recompense for such severity, how gently they deal with graver offences. For the felonies they can always discover 'the attenuating circumstances'; for the petty larcenies of fashion they have nothing but whipcord.

Lever himself was guilty of committing 'petty larcenies of fashion' because of the boisterous and showy manner in which he drove through the crowded avenues of the Cascine, with his numerous children, brilliantly attired, accompanying him on horseback. More than one onlooker remarked sarcastically that he must be Franconi, then famous as an equestrian in the Cirque Parisienne.

Elizabeth Barrett Browning provides a similar evocation of a place which, in the nineteeth century, was part Ranelagh and part Vauxhall:

> You remember down at Florence our Cascine
>   Where the people on the feast-day walk and drive,
> And through the trees, long-drawn in many a green way,
>   O'er-roofing hum and murmur like a hive,
>   The river and the mountains look alive.
>
> You remember the piazzone there, the stand-place
>   Of carriages alive with Florentine beauties,
> Who lean and melt to music as the band plays,
>   To smile and chat with some one who afoot is,
>   Or on horseback, in observance of male duties?
>
> 'Tis pretty, in the afternoons of summer,
>   So many gracious faces brought together!
> Call it rout, or call it concert, they have come here,
>   In the floating of the fan and of the feather,
>   To reciprocate with beauty and fine weather.

The 'carriages alive with Florentine beauties' could already be seen in the Cascine when Tobias Smollett visited it in 1765.

Here, in the summer evenings, the quality resort to take the air in their coaches. Every carriage stops and forms a little separate conversazione. The ladies sit within, and the *cicisbei* stand on the foot-boards, on each side of the coach, entertaining them with their discourse. It would be no unpleasant enquiry to trace this sort of gallantry to its original, and investigate all its progress. The Italians, having been accused of jealousy, were resolved to wipe off the reproach, and seeking to avoid it for the future, have run into the other extreme. I know that it is generally assumed that the custom of choosing *cicisbei* was calculated to prevent the extinction of families, which would otherwise often happen in consequence of marriages

founded upon interest, without any mutual affection in
the contracting parties. How far this political considera-
tion may have weighed against the jealous and vindictive
temper of the Italians, I will not pretend to judge; but
certain it is, every married lady in this country has her
cicisbeo, or *servente*, who attends her every where, and on
all occasions; and upon whose privileges the husband dare
not encroach, without incurring the censure and ridicule
of the whole community. For my part I would rather be
condemned for life to the gallies than exercise the office of
cicisbeo, exposed to the intolerable caprices and dangerous
resentment of an Italian virago. I pretend not to judge the
national character from my own observation; but if the
portraits drawn by Goldoni are taken from nature, I
would not hesitate to pronounce the Italian women the
most haughty, insolent, capricious, and revengeful
females on the face of the earth. Indeed, their resentments
are so cruelly implacable, and contain such a mixture of
perfidy, that, in my opinion, they are very unfit subjects
for comedy, whose province it is rather to ridicule folly
than to stigmatize such atrocious vice.

Alexandre Dumas – who spent a year in Florence in 1840,
renting the Villa Palmieri in Via Giovanni Boccaccio – also
evokes a picture of easy-going dalliance in the Cascine:

Of their own accord, and without one telling them, the
coachmen take the road to the Piazzale. They halt there
without one's even being obliged to make them a sign.

The reason is that the Piazzale of Florence offers one
something which perhaps no other town in the world can
offer: a kind of open-air *salon*, in which everyone makes
or receives visits. It goes without saying that the visitors
are men. The women remain in their carriages, the men
go from one to another and, some on foot, some on
horseback and some, more familiar, standing on the
pavement, converse at the carriage doors.

It is in the Piazzale that life is lived each evening, that
glances are exchanged, that meetings are fixed.

Among all these carriages the flower-girls thread their

path, handing out bouquets of roses and violets. Next day the same flower-girls will turn up in the cafés to demand their payment. In doing so, they will present each gentleman with a carnation.

Visiting the Cascine on Ascension Day in 1912, Arnold Bennett noted:

I saw a number of people with little cages containing crickets or grasshoppers which, I am told, are on sale in hundreds or thousands in the Cascine on Ascension Day morning.

The Cascine as a place of popular celebration, of picnics and sport, of assignation and amorous intrigue is very different from the Cascine which, wild and deserted, inspired Shelley to write his *Ode to the West Wind*.

L'Oltrarno

Partly lying on the south bank of the Arno and partly climbing up the hill of San Giorgio, the quarter of Oltrarno was not originally part of the city itself. For long chiefly inhabited by the poor, it began to be settled in the thirteenth century by a few rich and noble families, among them the Bardi. At the junction of the Via dei Bardi, now a fashionable and much-frequented street, and the Ponte Vecchio used to stand the Casa Ambrogi, guest house of the British envoy Horace Mann, who there put up Horace Walpole and Gray in 1740. Sadly, this palazzo was among the buildings blown up by the retreating Germans in 1944.

Via de' Bardi

It is in the Via de' Bardi that the family of George Eliot's heroine Romola lives. The novelist writes of it as follows:

> The Via de' Bardi . . . extends from the Ponte Vecchio to the Piazza de' Mozzo at the head of the Ponte alle Grazie; its right-hand line of houses and walls being backed by the rather steep ascent which in the fifteenth century was known as the hill of Bogoli, the famous stone-quarry whence the city got its pavement – of dangerously un-stable consistence when penetrated by rains; its left-hand buildings flanking the river, and making on their

northern side a length of quaint, irregularly pierced
facade, of which the waters give a softened, loving reflection as the sun begins to decline towards the western
heights. But quaint as these buildings are, some of them
seem to the historical memory a too modern substitute
for the famous houses of the Bardi family, destroyed by
popular rage in the middle of the fourteenth century.

They were a proud and energetic stock, these Bardi:
conspicuous among those who clutched the sword in the
earliest world-famous quarrels of Florentines with
Florentines, when the narrow streets were darkened with
the high towers of the nobles, and when the old tutelar
god Mars, as he saw the gutters reddened with neighbours' blood, might well have smiled at the centuries of
lip-service paid to his rival, the Baptist. But the Bardi
hands were of the sort that not only clutch the sword-hilt
with vigour, but love the more delicate pleasure of finger-
ing minted metal: they were matched, too, with true
Florentine eyes, capable of discerning that power may be
won by other means than by rending and riving, and by
the middle of the fourteenth century we find them risen
from their original condition of *popolani* to be possessors,
by purchase, of lands and strongholds, and the feudal
dignity of Counts of Vernion, disturbing to the jealousy
of their republican fellow-citizens. These lordly purchases are explained by our seeing the Bardi disastrously
signalised a few years later as standing in the very front of
European commerce – the Christian Rothschilds of that
time – undertaking to furnish specie for the wars of our
Edward the Third, and having revenues 'in kind' made
over to them; especially in wool, most precious of
freights for Florentine galleys. Their august debtor left
them with an august deficit, and alarmed Sicilian creditors made a too sudden demand for the payment of
deposits, causing a ruinous shock to the credit of the Bardi
and of the associated houses, which was felt as a commercial calamity all along the coasts of the Mediterranean.
But, like more modern bankrupts, they did not, for all
that, hide their heads in humiliation; on the contrary, they

seem to have held them higher than ever, and to have been
amongst the most arrogant of those grandees . . . who
drew upon themselves the exasperation of the armed
people in 1343. The Bardi, who had made themselves fast
in their street between the two bridges, kept these narrow
inlets, like panthers at bay, against the oncoming gonfa-
lons of the people, and were only made to give way by an
assault from the hill behind them. Their houses by the
river, to the number of twenty-two (*palagi e case grandi*),
were sacked and burnt, and many among the chief of
those who bore the Bardi name were driven from the city.
But an old Florentine family was many-rooted, and we
find the Bardi maintaining importance and rising again
and again to the surface of Florentine affairs in a more or
less creditable manner, implying an untold family history
that would have included even more vicissitudes and
contrasts of dignity and disgrace, of wealth and poverty,
than are usually seen on the background of wide kinship.

The Pitti Palace and the Boboli Gardens

Arnold Bennett thought that the Pitti Palace looked like 'a
rather expensive barracks'; but George Eliot described its
architecture as 'a wonderful union of Cyclopean massiveness
with stately regularity', and Taine wrote of it: 'I doubt if there
is a more monumental palace in the whole of Europe; I have
never seen one that left me with a comparable impression of
grandeur and simplicity.'
Less than a hundred years after Ammannati had completed
the building, originally the residence of Luca Pitti, for the
Medici Duke Cosimo and his wife Eleonora of Toledo, John
Evelyn visited it in the 1640s. Little has changed since his
description:

> The Palace of Pitti was built by the family, but of late
> greatly beautified by Cosimo with huge square stones of
> the Doric, Ionic, and the Corinthian orders, with a terrace
> at each side having rustic uncut balustrades, with a foun-
> tain that ends in a cascade seen from the great gate, and so

forming a vista to the gardens. Nothing is more admirable than the vacant stayrecase, marbles, statues, urnes,
pictures, courte, grotto, and waterworkes. In the quad-
rangle is a huge jetto of water in a volto of 4 faces, with
noble statues at each square, especially the Diana of por-
phyrie above the grotto. We were here shew'd a prodi-
gious greate load-stone.

Evelyn also toured the Boboli Gardens, which had been laid
out for Duke Cosimo behind the palace:

The garden has every variety, hills, dales, rocks, groves,
aviaries, vivaries, fountaines, especialy one of five jettos,
the middle basin being one of the longest stones I ever
saw. Here is everything to make such a paradise delight-
full. In the garden I saw a rose grafted on an orange-tree.
There was much topiary worke, and columns in
architecture about the hedges. The Duke has added an
ample laboratorye, over against which stands a Fort on a
hill where they told us his treasure is kept. In this Palace
the Duke ordinarily resides, living with his Swiss guards,
after the frugal Italian way, and even selling what he can
spare of his wines, at the cellar under his very house,
wicker bottles dangling over even the chief entrance into
the Palace, serving for his vinter's bush.

In that once immensely popular historical novel *John
Inglesant*, J. H. Shorthouse (1834–1903) imagines the court of
Evelyn's wine-merchant autocrat of a Duke in a hyper-
bolically romantic manner. Inglesant, an English Roman
Catholic, arrives in Florence in 1651, on a secret errand for the
Royalist cause, and is invited to the Pitti Palace:

The saloons were crowded and very hot, and when
Inglesant left the supper room and came into the brilliant
marble hall lighted with great lustres, where the Court
was at play, he was more excited than was his wont. The
Court was gathered at different tables – a very large one in
the centre of the hall and other smaller ones around. The
brilliant dresses, the jewels, the beautiful women, the
reflections in the numberless mirrors, made a dazzling

and mystifying impression on his brain. The play was
very high and at the table at which Inglesant sat down
especially so. He lost heavily and this did not tend to calm
his nerves; he doubled his stake, with all the money he had
with him, and lost again.

As he rises from the table, a page hands him a 'delicately
perfumed note,' from an Italian woman, Lauretta, who needs
his help and with whom he has already fallen in love. She
summons him to the Grand Duchess's lodgings.

They [Inglesant and the page] passed through many
corridors and rooms richly furnished until they reached
the lodgings of the Grand Duchess. The night was sultry,
and through the open windows above the gardens the
strange odours that are born of darkness and of night
entered the palace. In the dark arcades the nightingales
were singing, preferring gloom and mystery to the light
in which all other creatures rejoice; and in the stillness the
murmur of brooks and the splash of the fountains op-
pressed the air with an unearthly and unaccustomed
sound. Around the casements festoons of harmless and
familiar flowers and leaves assumed wild and repulsive
shapes, as if transformed into malicious demons who
made men their sport. Inglesant thought involuntarily of
those plants that are at enmity with man, which are used
for enchantments and for poisoning, and whose very
scent is death; such saturnine and fatal flowers seemed
more at home in the lovely Italian night than the innocent
plants which witness to lovers' vows, and upon which
divines moralize and preach. The rooms of the Duchess
were full of perfume of the kind that enervates and dulls
the sense. It seemed to Inglesant as though he were
treading the intricate pathways of a dream, careless as to
what befell him, yet with a passionate longing which
urged him forward, heedless of a restraining voice which
he was even then half-conscious that at other times he
should have heard. The part of the palace where he was
seemed deserted, and the page led him through more than
one anteroom without meeting any one, until they

reached a curtained door, which the boy opened, and
directed Inglesant to enter. He did so, and found himself
at once in the presence of Lauretta, who was lying upon a
low seat at the open window. The room was lighted by
several small lamps in different positions, giving an ample, yet at the same time soft and dreamy light. Lauretta
was carelessly dressed, yet, in the soft light, and in her
negligent attitude, there was something that made her
beauty the more attractive, and her manner to Inglesant
was unrestrained and clinging. Her growing affection,
the urgency of her need, and the circumstances of the
hour, caused her innocently to speak and act in a way the
most fitted to promote her brother's atrocious purpose.

'Cavaliere,' she said, 'I have sent for you because I have
no friend but you. I have sent for you to help me against
my own family . . .'

Although in 1785 Mrs Piozzi (Thrale) thought the Grand
Duke's court informal she had little doubt that Leopold I was
an autocrat:

Our Grand Duke lives with little state for aught I can
observe here; but where there is least pomp, there is
commonly most power . . . He tells his subjects when to
go to bed, and who to dance with, till the hour he chooses
they should retire to rest, with exactly that sort of old-
fashioned paternal authority that fathers used to exercise
over families in England before commerce had run her
levelling plough over all ranks, and annihilated even the
name of subordination. If he hear of any person living
long in Florence without being able to give a good
account of his business there, the Duke warns him to go
away; and if he loiters after such warning given, sends
him out. Does any nobleman shine in pompous equipage
or splendid table; the Grand Duke enquires soon into his
pretensions, and scruples not to give personal advice and
add grave proofs with regard to the management of each
individual's private affairs, the establishment of their
sons, the marriage of their sisters etc. When they appeared
to complain of this behaviour to me, I know not, replied

I, what to answer: one has always read and heard that the
Sovereigns ought to behave in despotic governments like
the *fathers of their family* . . . 'Yes, Madam,' replied one of
my auditors, with an acuteness truly Italian, 'but this
Prince is our *father-in-law* . . .'

By the time of Stendhal's visit in 1817, the Grand Duke of
the day, Ferdinand III, was a far less autocratic figure:

Grand-Duke Ferdinand, realising full well that he could
command neither enough soldiers nor enough courtiers
to live a happy life surrounded by the general execration
of his subjects, has chosen rather to become a most
familiar monarch, and you may meet him strolling un-
accompanied through the streets of Florence. His Highness the Grand-Duke has three Ministers, of whom one,
Prince Neri Corsini, is a dyed-in-the-wool reactionary,
whilst the other two, signor Fossombroni, a geometer of
noted reputation, and signor Frullani, are very reasonable
beings; His Highness foregathers with them but once a
week, and in fact takes little or no hand in the government
of his domain. Year by year it is his habit to commission
some thirty thousand francs' worth of pictures from the
studios of those excruciating painters whom the public
(which admires them) sees fit to designate for such an
honour; likewise, year by year, he purchases a fine estate
or two. Granted only that Heaven sees fit to preserve this
supremely *reasonable* being, whom it has thus pleased her
to bestow upon the Duchy, I am convinced that, in the
end, he will prosper to undertake the government of his
Tuscan subjects *free and for nothing*.

In 1817 the fourteen-year-old Charlotte Harriet Beaujolais
Campbell wrote in her journal of a visit of her mother and her
older sister Eleanor to the Grand Duke:

At 12 in the morning they were at the Palazzo Pitti and
with a few other English all of whom are really a disgrace
to the nation. Mr Dorkins [in fact, Dawkins, Secretary at
the British Legation] led them into the room where the
Grand Duke was standing. He spoke to nobody but

Mamma and the Miss Berries [two inseparable sisters, intimates of Horace Walpole] whom he knew some years ago. He merely said that he was glad that mamma was come to Florence at the time of his daughter's marriage as it would make every thing appear more gay to her. He then bowed saying he would detain them no longer but hoped· to see them very often. There are about twenty other English who have the impudence to present themselves at this court because it is foreign whereas in England they would not dare to show their noses. This is a disgusting forwardness and the Grand Duke scarcely bowed to them . . .

Some dozen years later, James Fenimore Cooper was presented at court:

Ten was the hour at which I presented myself at the Pitti, in an ordinary morning-dress, wearing shoes instead of boots. I was shown into an ante-chamber, where I was desired to take a seat. A servant soon after passed through the room with a salver, bearing a chocolate-cup and a bit of toast, a proof that his imperial highness had just been making a light breakfast. I was then told that the grand duke would receive me.

The door opened on a large room, shaped like a parallelogram, which had the appearance of a private library, or cabinet. There were tables, books, maps, drawings, and all the appliances of work. The library of the palace, however, is another part of the edifice, and contains many thousands of volumes, among which are some that are very precious, and their disposition is one of the most convenient, though not the most imposing as to show, of any library I know.

The grand duke was standing alone at the upper end of a long table that was covered by some drawings and plans of the *Maremme*, a part of his territories in reclaiming which he is said to be now much occupied. As I entered, he advanced and gave me a very civil reception. I paid my compliments, and made an offering of a book I had caused to be printed in Florence. This he accepted with great politeness; and then he told me, in the simplest manner, that 'his wife' was so ill, she could not see me that morning. I had a book for her imperial highness also, and he said that it might be left at Poggio Imperiale.

As soon as these little matters were disposed of, the grand duke walked to a small round table, in a corner, near which stood two chairs, and, requesting me to take one, he seated himself in the other, when he began a conversation that lasted near an hour. The prince was, as before, very curious on the subject of America, going over again some of the old topics. He spoke of Washington with great respect, and evidently felt no hostility to him on account of his political career. Indeed, I could not trace in the conversation of the prince the slightest evidence of a harsh feeling, distrust, or jealousy towards America; but, on the other hand, I thought he was disposed to view us kindly, – a thing so unusual among political men in Europe as to be worthy of mention. He left on my mind, in this interview, the same impression and integrity of feeling as the other. . . .

He observed that fewer Americans travelled now than formerly, he believed. So far from this, I told him, the number had greatly increased within the last few years. 'I used to see a good many,' he answered, 'but now I see but few.' I was obliged to tell him what is the truth, – that most of those who came to Europe knew little of courts, that they did not give themselves time to see more than the commoner sights, and that they were but indifferent courtiers. He spoke highly of our ships, several of which he had seen in Leghorn, and on board of one or two of which he had actually been. . . .

I found him better informed than usual on the subject of our history; though, of course, many of his notions had the usual European vagueness. He seemed aware, for instance, of the great difficulty with which we had to contend in the revolution, for the want of the commonest munitions, such as arms and powder. He related an anecdote of Washington connected with this subject, with a feeling and spirit that showed his sympathies were

on the right side of that great question, on whichever side
his policy might have been.

We had some conversation on the subject of the dis-
covery of America, and I took the occasion to compliment him on there having been a Florentine [Amerigo
Vespucci] concerned in that great enterprise; but he did
not seem disposed to rob Columbus of any glory on
account of his own countryman, though he admitted that
the circumstances in a degree connected his own town
with the event.

At length he rose, and I took my leave of him, after
thanking him for the facilities afforded me in Tuscany.
When we separated, he went quietly to his maps; and as I
turned at the door to make a parting salute, I found his
eyes on the paper, as if he expected no such ceremony.

Thomas Trollope and his indomitable mother attended the
weekly balls given by the Grand Duke. Florence at that period
was, as he remarked, 'an especially economical place for those
to whom it was pleasant to enjoy during the whole of the gay
season as many balls, concerts and other entertainments as
they could possibly desire, without the necessity, or indeed the
possibility, of putting themselves to the expense of giving
anything in return.' There were weekly balls at the club of the
Florentine aristocracy, the Casa dei Nobili; the foreign ministers were constantly giving balls; and from time to time some
wealthy grandee would also give one. But 'perhaps the
pleasantest of all these were the balls at the Pitti', since 'they
were so entirely *sans gêne*.'

No court dress was required save on the first day of the
year, when it was *de rigueur*. But absence on that occasion
in no way excluded the absentee from the other balls.
Indeed, save to a newcomer, no invitations to foreigners
were issued, it being understood that all who had been
there once were welcome ever after. The Pitti balls were
by no means concluded, but rather divided into two,
by a very handsome and abundant supper, at which, to
tell tales out of school (but then the offenders have no

doubt mostly gone over to the majority), the guests used
to behave abominably. The English would seize the plates
of *bonbons* and empty the contents bodily into their coat
pockets. The ladies would do the same with their pocket-
handkerchiefs.

But the Duke's liege subjects carried on their depre-
dations on a far bolder scale. I have seen large portions of
fish, sauce and all, packed up in a newspaper, and
deposited in a pocket. I have seen fowls and ham share the
same fate, without any newspaper at all. I have seen jelly
carefully wrapped in an Italian countess's laced *mouchoir*! I
think the servants must have had orders not to allow
entire bottles of wine to be carried away, for I never saw
that attempted, and can imagine no other reason why. I
remember that those who affected to be knowing old
hands used to recommend one to specially pay attention
to the Grand Ducal Rhine wine, and remember, too,
conceiving a suspicion that certain of these connoisseurs
based their judgement in this matter wholly on the knowledge that the Duke possessed estates in Bohemia!

Apparently the Americans behaved better than the other
nationalities: 'I never saw an American pillaging the supper
table; though I may add that American ladies would accept any
amount of *bonbons* from English blockade-runners.'

More than a century before, in 1740, Horace Walpole had
commented on the manner in which even the most affluent
and elegant people were not above filching food from the table
of their host.

. . . A large palace finely illuminated; there were all the
beauties, all the jewels, and all the sugar-plums of
Florence. Servants loaded with large chargers full of
comfits heap the tables with them, the women fall on
with both hands, and stuff their pockets and every creek
and corner about them.

In his *Life of Charles Lever*, Lever's first biographer, W. J.
Fitzpatrick quotes a Mrs M – 's account of Lever's behaviour as
a guest at these balls at the Pitti:

In one part of the palace card-playing would be going on, while the intoxicating whirl of the dance held sway in another. When deep in his game of whist and with me as his partner, he often, on hearing some favourite air struck up, flung down his cards, saying, 'I must give my little wife a turn;' which having done, he rapidly resumed his place at the table. The polka was the dance of which he was most fond. Mrs Lever was so small and he so fat that in heeling and toeing it he cut a rather comical figure, but all admired his abiding love for her; and he certainly looked supremely happy in her companionship. As his too solid belt of flesh increased, he gradually relinquished dancing, and remarked that nothing short of an Irish jig could tempt him to the effort.

Mrs Trollope was the only person in these gatherings before whom 'he seemed to collapse', so that he would transparently manoeuvre not to have her as his partner at whist, while she no less transparently coveted this position.

Of the treasures on show in the Pitti Palace, writers have been impressed by a variety of pictures and statues. For Swinburne the supreme painter here was Andrea del Sarto. Remarking that 'his life was corroded by the poisonous solvent of love, and his soul burnt into ashes' – this was clearly intended as a recommendation – he added that 'At Florence only can one trace and tell how great a painter and how various Andrea was. There only, but surely there, can the spirit and presence of the things of time on his immortal spirit be understood.' Hawthorne was drawn to a picture, *The Fates*, then ascribed to Michelangelo; 'As regards the interpretation of this, or of any other profound picture, there are likely to be as many interpretations as there are spectators. Each man interprets the hieroglyphic in his own way; and the painter perhaps had a meaning which none of them have reached; or possibly he put forth a riddle without himself knowing the solution.' Sophia Hawthorne was particularly taken by Titian's *Portrait of Ippolito de' Medici*, describing it as 'superb'. She goes on:

He is in a Hungarian dress, buttoned up to the throat,
which is very becoming, when a handsome head and face
are shut off in that way. He stands with a wonderful
dignity and grace, and his features and style of head are of
fascinating beauty, though I am sure he is not a good man.
He looks dark and treacherous, with a princely state,
worthy of a higher character.

While the Hawthornes were going round the palace, a
military band struck up in the piazza, as it used to do each
afternoon, and so 'glorified the common day and added life to
the painted forms and faces. We came down and went into the
magnificent Cortile . . . and walked round it, listening to the
music.'

John Addington Symonds was rhapsodic about Giorgione's
Concert of Music:

Of the indisputed pictures by Giorgione, the grandest is
the *Monk at the Clavichord* [as he called it]. The young
man has his fingers on the keys; his head is turned away
towards an old man standing near him. On the other side
of the instrument is a boy. These two figures are but foils
and adjuncts to the musician in the middle; and the whole
interest of his face lies in its concentrated feeling – the very
soul of music, passing through his eyes.

For Henry James, viewing a dozen Titian portraits 'of
unequal interest', the best was that of

that formidable young man in black, with the small
compact head, the delicate nose and the irascible blue eye.
Who was he? What was he? '*Ritratto virile*' [male portrait]
is all the catalogue is able to call the picture. 'Virile!
Rather!' you vulgarly exclaim. You may weave what
romance you please about it, but a romance your dream
must be. Handsome, clever, defiant, passionate, dangerous, it was not his fault if he hadn't adventures and to
spare. He was a gentleman and a warrior, and his adventures balanced between camp and court. I imagine him
the young orphan of a noble house, about to come into
mortgaged estates. One wouldn't have cared to be his

guardian, bound to paternal admonitions once a month over his precocious transactions with the Jess or his scandalous abduction from her convent of such and such a noble maiden.

William Beckford (1759–1844) – who spent October 1780 in Florence in the course of a sumptuous Grand Tour – described a visit to the Boboli Gardens as follows:

I walked to one of the bridges across the Arno, and surveyed the hills at a distance, purpled by the declining sun. Its mild beams tempted me to the garden of Boboli which lies behind the Palazzo Pitti, stretched out on the side of the mountain. I ascended terrace after terrace, robed by a thick underwood of bay and myrtle, above which rise several nodding towers, and a long sweep of venerable wall, almost entirely covered by ivy. You would have been enraptured with the broad masses of shade and dusky alleys that opened as I advanced, with white statues of fauns and sylvans glimmering amongst them; some of which pour water into sarcophagi of the purest marble, covered with antique relievos. The capitals of columns and ancient friezes are scattered about as seats.

On these I reposed myself, and looked up at the cypress groves spiring above the thickets; then, plunging into their retirements, I followed a winding path, which led me by a series of steep ascents to a green platform overlooking the whole extent of wood with Florence deep beneath, and the tops of the hills which encircle it, jagged with pines; here and there a convent, or villa, whitening in the sun. This scene extends as far as the eye can reach.

Still ascending I attained the brow of the mountain, and had nothing but the fortress of Belvedere, and two or three open porticoes above me. On this elevated situation, I found several walks of trellis-work, clothed with luxuriant vines, that produce to my certain knowledge the most delicious clusters. A colossal statue of Ceres, her hands extended in the act of scattering fertility over the prospect, crowns the summit, where I lingered to watch the landscape fade, and the bright skirts of the western sun die gradually away,

Then descending alley after alley and bank after bank, I came to the orangery in front of the palace, disposed in a grand amphitheatre, with marble niches relieved by dark foliage, out which spring tall aerial cypresses. The spot brought the scenery of an antique Roman garden full into my mind. I expected every instant to be called to the table of Lucullus hard by, in one of the porticoes, and to stretch myself on his purple triclinias; but waiting in vain for the summons till the approach of night, I returned delighted with a ramble that had led me so far into antiquity . . .

Shelley was hardly less rhapsodic. Florence, seen from the eminence of the Belvedere, was for him 'a smokeless city' – which it certainly is not today. He remarked on 'a Babylon of palaces and gardens', making up another city outside the then narrow confines of the city itself; on 'the etherial mountain-line, hoary with snow and intersected by clouds'; on 'the cypress groves whose obeliskine forms of intense green pierce the grey shadow of the wintry hill that overhangs them'; on the cypresses of the garden, which 'form a magnificent fore-ground of accumulated verdure' – 'pyramids of dark leaves and shining cones rising out of the mass, beneath which are cut, like caverns, recesses which conduct into walks.'

The narrator of Henry James's early tale (1879) *The Diary of a Man of Fifty* visits the Boboli Gardens and the Pitti Palace on the day after his arrival in Florence. His previous visit, when he fell in love with an Italian aristocrat, long since dead, was twenty-seven years before; but, contrary to what everyone has warned him, he finds 'Everything is so perfectly the same that I seem to be living in my youth all over again; all the forgotten impressions of that enchanting time come back to me.'

I wandered for an hour in the Boboli Gardens; we [he and the Italian girl] went there several times together. I re-membered all those days individually; they seem to me as yesterday. I found the corner where she always chose to sit – the bench of sun-warmed marble, in front of the screen of ilex, with that exuberant statue of Pomona just beside it. The place is exactly the same, except that poor Pomona has lost one of her tapering fingers. I sat there for half-an-hour, and it was strange how near to me she seemed. The place was perfectly empty – that is, it was filled with *her*. I closed my eyes and listened; I could almost hear the rustle of her dress on the gravel. Why do we make such an ado about death? What is it after all but a sort of refinement of life? She died ten years ago, and yet, as I sat there in the evening stillness, she was a palpable, audible presence. I went afterwards into the gallery of the palace, and wandered for an hour from room to room. The same great pictures hung in the same places and the same dark frescoes stretched above them. Twice, of all, I went there with her; she had a great understanding of art. She understood all sorts of things. Before the Madonna of the Chair I stood a long time. The face is not a particle like hers, and yet it reminded me of her. But everything does that. We stood and looked at it together once for half-an-hour; I remember perfectly what she said.

Of Raphael's *La Madonna della Seggiola* – a tondo – George Eliot wrote that it 'leaves me, with all its beauty, impressed only by the grave gaze of the infant.'

It was at the back of the Pitti Palace that, in 1644, John Evelyn inspected 'the Prince's Cavalarizzo', moved there, some years previously, from the back of the Signoria.

. . . The Prince has a stable of the finest horses of all countries, Arabs, Turks, Barbs, Gennets, English, &c, which are constantly exercised in the *manège*.

Near the 'Cavalarizzo' was a place where he kept several wild beasts, as wolves, catts, beares, tygers and lions. They are loose in a deep wall'd court, and therefore to be seen with more pleasure than at the Tower of London, in their grates. One of the lions leaped to a surprising height to catch a joynt of mutton which I caused to be hung downe.

Visiting the same place a few years later, Richard Lassels recorded how the Grand Duke and his court would amuse themselves by leaning over the pit and watching the animals scrapping among themselves. When they had become bored with the contest, the lions would be driven back to their lairs by 'a fearful machine of wood made like a great Green Dragon which a man within it rowles upon wheels, and holding out two lighted torches at the eyes of it, frights the fiercest beast thereby into his den.'

The Natural History Museum

The Museo di Fisica e di Storia Naturale (now the Museo Zoologico 'La Specola'), situated at 17 Via Roma, beyond the Pitti Palace, exercised on visitors of the nineteenth century a fascination which it has lost for modern ones. We tend either boldy to outface death or else to avert our eyes from it; they tended morbidly to flirt with it.

Longfellow chiefly noticed 'the representation in wax of some of the appalling scenes of the plague'. The artist, he noted, was a Sicilian by the name of Zumbo. Zumbo, he decided,

> must have been a man of the most gloomy and saturnine imagination, and more akin to the worm than most of us, thus to have revelled night and day in the hideous mysteries of death, corruption, and the charnel-house. It is strange how this representation haunts one. It is like a dream of the sepulchre, with its loathesome corpses, with 'the blackening, the swelling, the bursting of the trunk – the worm, the rat, and the tarantula at work.' You breathe more freely as you step out into the open air again; and when the bright sunshine, and the crowded, busy streets next meet your eye, you are ready to ask, is this indeed a representation of reality? Can this pure air have been laden with pestilence? Can this gay city have ever been a city of the plague?

Dickens remarks that the Natural History Museum is

> famous throughout the world for its preparations in wax; beginning with models of leaves, seeds, plants, inferior

animals; and gradually ascending, through separate
organs of the human frame, up to the whole structure of
that wonderful creation, exquisitely presented, as in recent death. Few admonitions of our frail mortality can be
more solemn and more sad, or strike so home upon the
heart, as the counterfeits of Youth and Beauty that are
lying there, upon their beds, in their last sleep.

Sophia Hawthorne found much at which to marvel: the
'wax models of rare exotics and fruits'; the collection of stuffed
birds – 'the parrots in a corner looked like a fierce autumnal
sunset'; the 'two real pearls still upon an oyster where they
grew, more beautiful than any in the British Museum'; the
skeletons of animals, the models of their interiors 'very curious and very horrid.' Above all, she was impressed by the
relics of Galileo, among them 'one of his fingers, pointing
upward.' Another finger, she records, is in the Laurentian
Library, adding: 'How little he dreamed, when he sat in
prison, that even his fingers would become precious relics for
posterity! But I wish he had kept firm, and not denied the truth
he had discovered. That is an endless grief to me.'

SANTO SPIRITO

A visit to the Brunelleschi church of Santo Spirito – Luther
preached there on his way to Rome as an Augustinian monk –
caused Sophia Hawthorne to write some tart comments on the
Italian priesthood at that period:

To rest, I went to the Church of Santo Spirito, so
beautiful with its majestic colonnades and ruby lights
forever burning at the superb altar of Florentine mosaic;
and I sat there in peace and quiet for an hour. Meanwhile
the priests came in, as once before when I was there, and
chanted their evening service, but I could not see them
from my seat. There were several persons, saying their
prayers, with their rosaries, in the nave, and acolytes were
crossing in the distance, with lamps and salvers and
copes, but with no sound. All was still, except the voices

of the chanters, rising and falling like waves in a summer
sea. If there were always heart and truth in those monks
and prelates, real, religious worship, how deep would be
our emotions during those imposing functions! But I am
always sensible of hollowness and emptiness in every
ceremony I see; and especially with the ennui and inward
disgust of the priests themselves, who seem very anxious
to get through the endlessly repeated task, so as to go and
eat and drink and be merry. Yet there are doubtless many
among them truly devout. The appearance of the clergy
in Florence is almost invariably repulsive and gross, and
they are said to be peculiarly depraved. They are mostly
fat, with flabby cheeks, chins and throats, of very earthly
aspect. There is nothing to compare them to but hogs,
and they merely need to stoop upon their hands to be
perfect likenesses of swine, so that the encounter of one of
them in the street gives one a faint sensation. It is shocking
that such men are in holy garb, set apart from the constant
worship of God, and, under cover of superior sanctity,
becoming the most corrupt of human beings. Such blasphemy of the Holy Spirit seems to blot out the sun, and
poison the air; but I think there must be good persons
among them to bear witness – or how could these monasteries uphold themselves? 'A lie cannot stand,' says our
great philosopher.

To the immediate west of San Spirito lies the working-class,
once slummy but now rapidly improving district Borgo San
Frediano. It is in this district that many of the novels of Vasco
Pratolino (1913–   ), best of Florentine novelists of this
century, are set:

Sanfrediano is the unhealthiest section of the city; in the
heart of its streets, as densely populated as ant-hills, are
located the Central Refuse Dump, the public dormitory,
the barracks. The greater part of its slums is the home of
rag-pickers, and of those who cook the intestines of cattle
to make their living from them and from the broth that is
their product.
      . . . The houses are ancient because of their stones, and

even more because of their squalor. One banked up against another, they form an immense block . . . The happy, bickering clamour of the people brings these places to life: the sounds of the second-hand man and the rag-picker, the worker in the nearby repair shops, the office clerk, the artisan who works in gold, or in marble, or with furs. And even the women, most of them, have a job. Sanfrediano is a little republic of women who do work at home . . .

The Sanfrediani are sentimental and pitiless at once: their idea of justice is symbolized by the enemy's remains hung to a lamp-post; and their idea of Paradise, summed up in a proverb, is poetic and vulgar: a Utopian place where there is an abundance of millet and a shortage of birds.

Since Pratolini wrote these words in the 1950s, the Borgo San Frediano, like the East End of London, has undergone great changes. It now certainly contains more antique-dealers than rag-pickers and more restaurateurs than cookers of intestines.

SAN MINIATO

Many people would claim that the Romanesque basilica of San Miniato al Monte is the most beautiful church in Florence, and some that it is the most beautiful church in the whole of Italy. Yet, when Oscar Wilde visited it in 1875, at the age of twenty-one, it induced in him not aesthetic delight but theatrical self-laceration:

> See, I have climbed the mountainside
> Up to this holy house of God,
> Where once the Angel-Painter trod
> Who saw the heavens opened wide,
>
> And throned upon the crescent moon
> The Virginal white Queen of Grace,
> Mary! Could I but see thy face,
> Death would not come at all too soon.

> O crowned of God with thorns and pain!
> Mother of Christ! O mystic wife!
> My heart is weary of this life
> And oversad to sing again.
>
> O crowned by God with love and flame!
> O crowned by Christ the Holy One!
> O listen ere the setting sun
> Show to the world my sin and shame!

The last quatrain is chillingly prophetic.

Nineteen years later, in May 1894, shortly before the libel action that was to precipitate his ruin, Wilde was once again in Florence, this time with Alfred Douglas. Gide, who constantly swung between discretion and recklessness, was disconcerted when, in a café, he ran into the famous English writer in the company of (as he wrote circumspectly to Paul Valéry) 'another poet of a younger generation'.

While in Florence on this second occasion, Wilde renewed an acquaintanceship with Vernon Lee and her brother, the poet Eugene Lee-Hamilton. Mary Berenson, who eight years before had been enchanted by 'the fair Oscar' – seated next to him at a dinner-party, she had 'simply revelled in his witty aphorisms about America and England and Art and Novels and all manner of subjects' – was the intermediary, taking Wilde to call with her. Next day she recorded of the visit:

> It was a great success. Oscar talked like an angel, and they all fell in love with him – even Vernon, who had hated him almost as bitterly as he had hated her. He, on his part, was charmed with her – he likes people without souls, or else with great peace in their souls, and when he met her before he found her restless and self-assertive. But yesterday he admitted that she had grown less strenous.

By now Mary Berenson's admiration of Wilde was no longer whole-hearted. 'Oscar says such extraordinarily clever and subtle things, I can't help liking to talk to him, but he is so untrustworthy, on the other hand, so utterly lacking in any kind of character with which I have sympathy, but it is a "mingled cup".'

The Environs

FIESOLE

Leigh Hunt wrote that his almost daily walk was to Fiesole, through a path skirted with wild myrtle and cyclamen. There he could stop at the cloister of the Doccia, and sit 'on the melancholy platform behind it, reading or looking through the pines down to Florence.'

Milton and Galileo give a glory to Fiesole beyond even its starry antiquity: nor perhaps is there a name eminent in the best annals of Florence to which some connections cannot be traced with this favoured spot. When it was full of wood, it must have been eminently beautiful. It is at present full of vines and olives, but this is not wood, *woody*.

Hunt and his family were staying in the nearby village of Maiano, now subsumed into Fiesole itself. The ground floor of the villa which they had rented was occupied by 'a Hebrew family' of jewellers, 'who partook the love of music in common with their tribe.' The little girls 'declaimed out of Alfieri' in the morning; and in the evening the parents 'led concerts in the garden.' Often there were visits from the priest, who would play 'a Christian game at cards with his Hebrew friends.' Hunt recounts how

one evening all the young peasantry in the neighbourhood assembled in the hall of the village, by leave of the proprietor (an old custom), and had the most energetic ball I ever beheld. The walls of the room seemed to spin round with the waltz, as though it would never leave off – the whirling faces all looking grave, hot, and astonished at one another. Among the musicians I observed one of the apprentices of my friend the bookseller, and evidence of a twofold mode of getting money not unknown in England. I recollected his face the more promptly, inasmuch as not many days previous he had accompanied me to my abode with a set of books, and astonished me by jumping on a sudden from one side of me to the other. I asked what was the matter, and he said, 'A viper, sir.' He seemed to think that an Englishman might as well settle the viper as the bill.

Of the panoramic view of Florence and the hills around it, Hunt said that it was 'a sight to enrich the eyes.' Charles Armitage Brown, Shakespearian scholar and friend of Keats, was a neighbour of Hunt's at the former convent of San Baldassare.

On the *Arx* (citadel) of the ancient city rests the church of S. Alessandro and Franciscan convent. To this Franciscan convent, the young American, Rowland Mallett, one of the leading characters of Henry James's *Roderick Hudson*, makes his way:

It was a day all benignant; the March sun felt like May, as the English poet [Browning] of Florence says; the thick-blossomed shrubs, the high-climbing plants that hung over the walls of villas and *podere* flung their odorous promise into the warm still air. He followed our friend, the winding, mounting lanes; lingered as he got higher beneath the rusty cypresses, beside the low parapets, where you look down on the charming city and sweep the vale of the Arno; reached the small square before the cathedral and rested a while in the massive, dusky church; then, climbing hither, pushed up to the Franciscan convent poised on the very apex of the great hill. He rang at the little gateway; a shabby, senile, red-faced brother admitted him, a personage almost maudlin with the milk of human kindness. There was a dreary chill in the chapel and the corridors, and he passed rapidly through them into the delightfully steep and tangled old garden which runs wild over the forehead of the mountain. He had been there before, he came back to it as to a friend. The garden hangs in the air, and you ramble from terrace to terrace and wonder how it keeps from slipping down, in full consummation of its dishonour and decay, to the nakedly romantic gorge beneath. It was just noon at Rowland's visit, and after roaming about a while he flung himself on the sun-warmed slab of a mossy stone bench and pulled his hat over his eyes. The short shadows of the brown-coated cypresses above him had grown very long, later on, and yet he had not passed through the convent. One of the monks, in a faded snuff-coloured robe, came wandering out into the garden, reading a greasy little breviary. Suddenly he approached the bench on which Rowland had stretched himself and paused for respectful interest. Rowland was still in possession, but seated himself now with his head in his hands and his elbows on his knees. He seemed not to have heard the sandalled tread of the good brother, but as the monk remained watching him he at last looked up. It was not the ignoble old man who had admitted him, but a pale, gaunt personage, of a graver and more ascetic and yet of a charitable aspect. Rowland's face might have borne for him the traces of extreme trouble; something he appeared mildly to con-sider as he kept his finger in his little book and folded his arms picturesquely across his breast. Was his attitude, as he bent his sympathetic Italian eyes, the mere accident of his civility or the fruit of an exquisite spiritual tact? To Rowland, however this might have been, it appeared a sort of offer of ready intelligence. He rose and approached the monk, laying his hand on his arm.

'My brother,' he said, 'did you ever see the Devil in person?'

The *frate* gazed gravely and crossed himself. 'Heaven forbid, my son!'

'He was here,' Rowland went on, 'here in this lovely

garden, as he was once in Paradise, half an hour ago. But have no fear; I drove him out.' And he stooped and picked up his hat, which had rolled away into a bed of cyclamen in vague suggestion of a positive scrimmage.

'You've been tempted, *figlio mio*?' asked the friar tenderly.

'Hideously!'

'And you've resisted – and conquered!'

'I believe I've conquered.'

'The blessed Saint Francis be praised. It's well done. If you like, we'll offer a mass for you.'

Rowland hesitated. 'I'm not of your faith.'

The *frate* smiled with dignity. 'That's a reason the more.'

'But it's for you then to choose. Shake hands with me,' Rowland added; 'that will do as well; and suffer me as I go out to stop a moment in your chapel.'

They shook hands and separated. The *frate* crossed himself, opened his book and wandered away in relief against the western sky. Rowland passed back into the convent and paused long enough in the chapel to look for the alms-box. He had had what is vulgarly called a great scare; he believed very poignantly, for the time, in Beelzebub and felt an irresistible need to subscribe to any institution that might engage to keep him at a distance.

At the end of October 1950, Noël Coward stayed in Fiesole with Derek Hill, in a villino which Bernard Berenson had put at the then youthful painter's disposal on his estate of I Tatti. On his arrival, Coward noted in his diary: 'Went to Derek's little house which is a dear little ice-house and very horrid indeed. It was pitch dark.' On the next day he recorded:

Cough not improved by freezing house. Woke feeling lousy. Bathroom *frigorifico* and no hot water. Just my dish. Derek took me over Berenson's villa. It is filled with priceless *objets d'art* and pictures – a great number of immensely famous Madonnas simpering in gold leaf. The car broke down so it was hours before we could get away.

On arrival at Derek's house, I made my great decision

and told Derek in no uncertain terms that I was leaving his bed and board in favour of the Excelsior Hotel on account of not wanting to catch pneumonia. He was very sweet about it. I packed like lightning and was out of that beastly little ice-box for ever. Began to relax at the Excelsior. Retired to my warm bed in a warm room with infinite relief.

On the following day Coward had dinner with Derek Hill, at an expensive restaurant in Florence. During it, he expressed his disapproval of 'the prissy, self-conscious academic beauty of Florence'. Hill subsequently executed the most truthful portrait in existence of Coward. So far from being 'very horrid indeed', the Berenson villino was charming, albeit primitive in its comforts.

Below Fiesole lies San Domenico and the Valle delle Donne, beloved of Landor:

> Here by the lake, Boccaccio's fair brigade
> Beguiled the hours and tale for tale repaid.

At the end of the tenth novel of the *Decameron*, when the men settle themselves to gambling, Madonna urges the women to come on an afternoon excursion with her:

'Ever since we have been here I have wished to show you a place not far off where I believe none of you has ever been: it is called La Valle delle Donne, and till today I have not had a chance to speak of it. It is yet early; if you choose to come with me, I promise that you will be pleased with your walk.' And they answered that they were all willing: so without saying a word to the gentlemen, they called one of their women to attend to them, and after a walk of nearly a mile they came to the place which they entered by a strait path where there burst forth a crystal stream, and they found it so beautiful and so pleasant, especially in those hot still hours of afternoon, that nothing could excel it: and as some of them told me later, the little plain in the valley was an exact circle, as though it had been described by a pair of compasses, as though it was indeed rather the work of Nature than of Man. It was about half a mile in

circumference surrounded by six hills of moderate
height, on each of which was a palace built in the form of a
little castle . . . And then what gave them the greatest
delight was the rivulet that came through the valley
which divided two hills and, running through the rocks,
fell suddenly and sweetly in a waterfall seeming, as it was
dashed and sprinkled in drops all about, like so much
quicksilver. Coming into the little plain beneath this fall,
the stream was received in a fine canal, and, running
swiftly to the midst of the plain, formed itself in a pool not
deeper than man's breast and so clear that you might see
the gravelly bottom and the pebbles intermixed, which
indeed you might count: and there were fishes there
also swimming up and down in great plenty; and the
water that overflowed was received into another little
canal which carried it out of the valley. There the ladies all
came together, and after praising the place, seeing the
basin before them, that it was very private, they agreed to
bathe. Bidding the maid to keep watch and to let them
know if anyone came nigh by, they stripped off their
clothes and went in, and it covered the beauty of their
bodies as a crystal glass conceals a rose. After they had
diverted themselves there for some time, they dressed
themselves again and returned, softly talking all the way
of the beauty of the place.

On his Italian tour in 1887, Thomas Hardy was always far
more interested in the Roman and Etruscan remains than in the
architecture and art of subsequent centuries. It is not surprising
therefore that the only poem which Florence inspired him to
write should have been 'In the Old Theatre, Fiesole'. This
Roman theatre was built at the end of the first century BC
and subsequently enlarged by Claudius and Septimius
Severus.

I traced the Circus whose grey stones incline
Where Rome and dim Etruria interjoin,
Till came a child who showed an ancient coin
That bore the image of a Constantine.

She lightly passed; nor did she once opine
How, better than all books, she had raised for me
In swift perspective Europe's history
Through the vast years of Caesar's sceptred line.

For in my distant plot of English loam
'Twas but to delve, and straightway there to find
Coins of like impress. As with one half blind
Whom common simples cure, her act flashed home
In that mute moment to my opened mind
The power, the pride, the reach of perished Rome.

THE CERTOSA

The Certosa (Charterhouse, or Carthusian monastery) di Val
d'Ema, reached until recently by tram through the suburbs of
Le Due Strade to Galluzzo, is now accessible by bus. But
Stendhal was obliged to go by other means:

This morning I hired a *sediolo* [gig] in order to visit the
famous Charterhouse which lies some two miles distant
from the walls of Florence. This consecrated building
stands upon a hill-top beside the highway to Rome; at
first glance you might well mistake it for a *palazzo* or a
gothic stronghold. As a structure, the mass is imposing;
yet the impression is very different from that which is left
upon the mind by the Grande Chartreuse, near Grenoble.
There is nothing *holy* about this edifice; nothing sublime,
nothing to exalt the spirit, nothing to fill the soul with
involuntary religious awe; rather is this a satire against
religion itself; the mind dwells willy-nilly upon the limit-
less treasuries of gold poured out in order to afford some
eighteen *fakirs* the grim satisfaction of mortifying the
flesh. It would be simpler, all in all, merely to lock them
away in a dungeon cell, and to convert this Charterhouse
into a common gaol to serve the whole of Tuscany. And
even so, with this new attribution, it might well still number no more than eighteen inmates, so dispassionately
do these people affect to calculate their interests, and so

little swayed are they by those surging tempests of the
heart which may send the most upright men headlong
toppling into the abyss.

Today Stendhal would certainly be even more disapprov-
ing. From the magnificent apartments in which Charles V,
Pius VI, and Pius VII were lodged, one now passes over to the
Farmacia, where postcards, chocolate, scent, and the liqueurs
of the place, many of them in majolica flasks, are on sale to
hordes of tourists.

The Certosa was the first stop on an energetic walk taken
by James Russell Lowell, with his friends Frank Shaw and
William Page, on the first of his three visits to Florence. From
the Certosa:

> We took a roundabout course among the hills, going first
> to Galileo's tower, and then to that of the Church of San
> Miniato which Michelangelo defended. Thence we de-
> scended steeply towards the Arno, crossed it by a ferry-
> boat, and then found ourselves opposite a *trattoria*. It was a
> warm October day, and we unanimously turned in at the
> open door. There were three rooms, one upstairs, where
> one might dine 'more obscurely and courageously', the
> kitchen, and the room in which we were. As I sat upon the
> corner of the bench, I looked out through some grape-
> trailers which hung waving over the door, and saw first
> the Arno, then, beyond it a hill on which stood a villa
> with a garden laid out in squares with huge walls of box
> and a clump of tall black cypresses in the middle, then, to
> the right of this, the ruined tower of San Miniato, and
> beyond it that from which Milton had doubtless watched
> the moon rising 'o'er the top of Fiesole.' This was my
> landscape. Behind me was the kitchen. The cook in his
> white linen cap was stirring alternately a huge cauldron of
> soup and a pan of sausages, which exploded into a sudden
> flame now and then, as if by spontaneous combustion. A
> woman wound up at short intervals a jack which turned
> three or four chickens before the fire, and attended a kind
> of lake of hot fat in which countless tiny fishes darted,
> squirmed, and turned topsy-turvy in a way so much more

active and with an expression of so much more enjoyment than is wont to characterize living, that you would
have said that they had now for the first time found their
element, and were created to revel in boiling oil. The
wine sold here was the produce of the vineyard which you
could see behind and on each side of the little *trattoria*. We
had a large loaf of bread, and something like a quart and a
half of pure cool wine for nine of our cents. During the
whole time I was in Florence, though I never saw anyone
drink water, I also never saw a single drunken man,
except some Austrian soldiers, and only four of these –
two of them officers . . .

THE PALACE OF PRATOLINO

Little now remains of the Palace of Pratolino, about 9 miles
from the Porta S. Gallo. It was built by Francesco de' Medici,
an outrageous voluptuary, for the beautiful Venetian, Bianca
Cappello, whom, having had her young husband murdered in
the street and having poisoned his own Duchess, Francesco
eventually married in 1578. Richard Lassels left an account of
the aquatic marvels to be found there:

Here we saw in the garden excellent grots, fountains,
water-works, shady-walks, groves and the like, all upon
the side of the hill. Here you have the Grot of Cupid with
the wetting-stools, upon which, sitting down, a great
spout of water comes full in your face. The Fountain of
the Tritons overtakes you too, and washeth you soundly.
Then being led about this garden, where there are stores
of fountains under the laurel trees, we were carried back
to the grots that are under the stairs and saw there many
giuochi d'aqua: as that of Pan striking up a melodious tune
upon his mouth-organ at the sight of his mistress, appear-
ing over against him: that where the Angel carries a
trumpet to his mouth and soundeth it; and where the
Country Clown offers a dish of water to a serpent, who
drinks it and lifteth up his head when he hath drunk: that
of the Mill which seems to break and grind olives: the

Paper Mill: the Man with the Grinding Stone: the
Saracen's Head gaping and spewing out water: the grot of
Galatea who comes out of a door in a sea-chariot with two
nymphs, and saileth awhile upon the water and so returns
again in at the same door: the curious Round Table
capable of twelve or fifteen men, with a curious fountain
playing constantly in the midst of it, and places between
every trencher, for every man to set his bottle of wine in
cold water: the Samaritan Woman coming out of her
house with her buckets to fetch water at the fountain, and
having filled her buckets, returns back again the same
way: in the meantime you see Smiths thumping, Birds
chirping in trees, Mills grinding: and all this is done by
water, which sets these little inventions awork, and
makes them move as it were of themselves: in the meantime an organ plays to you while you dine there in *fresco* at
that table, if you have meat. Then the neat bathing place,
the pillar of petrified water: and lastly, the great pond and
grotta before the house, with the huge Giant stooping to
catch at a rock, to throw it to heaven. This Giant is so big,
that within the very thigh of him is a great grot of water,
called the Grot of Thetis and Shell Fishes, all spouting
water.

At the beginning of the nineteenth century, Ferdinando of
Lorraine wantonly ordered that the villa, with its fountains
and *jeux d'eaux*, should be blown up. In 1872 the immensely
wealthy Russian Prince Demidoff bought the estate. The huge
park, eventually made over to the province, is now open to the
public.

BELLOSGUARDO

On the hill of Arcetri, south of Florence, rises the Torre del
Gallo, restored in 1904–6 in the style of the fourteenth century. From its tower Galileo made his observations; and it is
here that Milton is supposed to have visited him, subsequently
writing of

> . . . the moon, whose orb
> Through optic glass the Tuscan artist views
> At evening from the top of Fiesole,
> Or in Valdarno, to descry new lands,
> Rivers, or mountains in her spotty globe.

In his *Italy* Samuel Rogers has a passage about the meeting between the then aged and blind Galileo, forced by the Inquisition to live at Arcetri, outside the confines of the city, which he was only to reenter when his body was carried in for burial, and the still youthful and clear-sighted Milton:

> Nearer we hail
> Thy sunny slope, Arcetri, sung of old
> For its green vine; dearer to me, to most,
> As dwelt on by that great astronomer,
> Seven years a prisoner at the city-gate,
> Let in but in his grave-clothes. Sacred be
> His villa (justly it was called the Gem)!
> Sacred the lawn, where many a cypress threw
> Its length of shadow, while he watched the stars!
> Sacred the vineyard, where, while yet his sight
> Glimmered, at blush of morn he dressed his vines,
> Chanting aloud in gaiety of heart
> Some verse of Ariosto! – There, unseen,
> Gazing with reverent awe – Milton his guest,
> Just then come forth, all life and enterprise;
> *He* in his old age and extremity
> Blind, at noonday exploring with his staff;
> His eyes upturned as to the golden sun,
> His eyeballs idly rolling. Little then
> Did Galileo think whom he received:
> That in his hand he held the hand of one
> Who could requite him – who would spread his name
> O'er land and seas – great as himself, nay, greater;
> Milton as little that in him he saw,
> As in a glass, what he himself should be,
> Destined as soon to fall on evil days
> And evil tongues – so soon, alas! to live

In darkness, and with dangers compassed round,
And solitude.

The heroine of Ouida's *Pascarel* – a novel about the adventures of a troop of *commedia dell'arte* players – describes a visit to
the Torre del Gallo, and in so doing evokes the life of the
countryfolk around Florence in the age of Garibaldi:

. . . He took me up to the Star Tower of Galileo amongst
the winding paths of the hills, with the grey walls over-
topped by white fruit blossoms, and ever and again, at
some break in their ramparts of stone, the gleam of the
yellow Arno water, or the glisten of the marbles of the
City shining far beneath us, through the silvery veil of the
olive-leaves.

. . . The air was full of a dreamy fragrance; the bullocks
went on their slow ways with flowers in their leather
frontlets; the contadini had flowers stuck behind their ears
or in their waistbands; women sat by the wayside, singing
as they plaited their yellow curling lengths of straw;
children frisked and tumbled like young rabbits under the
budding maples; the plum-trees strewed the green landscape with flashes of white like newly fallen snow on
Alpine grass slopes; again and again amongst the tender
pallor of the olive woods there rose the beautiful flush of
rosy almond-tree; at every step the passer-by trod ankle
deep in violets.

. . . About the foot of the Tower of Galileo ivy and
vervain, and the Madonna's herb, and the white hexagons
of the stars of Bethlehem grew amongst the grasses;
pigeons paced to and fro, with pretty pride of plumage; a
dog slept on the flags; the cool, moist, deep-veined
creepers climbed about the stones; there were peach-trees
in all the beauty of their blossoms, and everywhere about
them were close-set olive-trees, with the ground between
them scarlet with the tulips and the wild rose bushes.

From a window a girl leaned out and hung a cage
amongst the ivy-leaves, that her bird might sing his
vespers to the sun.

Who will may see the scene today.

So little changed – so little, if at all, from the time when the feet of the great student wore the timber of the tower stairs, and the fair-haired scholar, who had travelled from the isles in the northern sea, came up between the olive stems to gaze thence on Vallombrosa.

The world has spoiled most of its places of pilgrimage, but the old Star Tower is not harmed as yet, where it stands amongst its quiet garden-ways and grass-grown slopes, up high amongst the hills, with sounds of dripping water on its court, and wild wood-flowers thrusting their bright heads through its stones.

. . . It is as peaceful, as simple, as homely, as closely girt with blossoming boughs and with tulip-crimsoned grasses now as then, when, from its roof, in the still midnights of far-off time, its master read the secret of the stars.

'The world has spoiled most of its places of pilgrimage.' Some hundred years after Ouida wrote this description, it has also spoiled much of the countryside around the Torre.

It was not far from the Torre, on the hill of Bellosguardo, that in the summer of 1858 Nathaniel Hawthorne rented what Henry James called

a picturesque old villa . . . a curious structure with a crenelated tower, which, after having in the course of its career suffered many vicissitudes and played many parts, now finds its most vivid identity in being pointed out to strangers as the sometimes residence of the celebrated American romancer.

The Villa Montauto was subsequently transformed into the castle of Monte Beni, the ancestral home of Donatello, the hero of *The Marble Faun* (or *Transformation*, as it was originally called in England).

MONTEGUFONI

When, in 1909, Sir George Sitwell bought the estate of Monte-gufoni, he sent a letter to his eldest son Osbert, who was later to guy and pillory his many oddities to such amusing effect in his many-volumed autobiography *Left Hand, Right Hand*. It began:

> My dearest Osbert,
> You will be interested to hear that I am buying in your name the Castle of Acciaiuoli (pronounced Accheeyawly) between Florence and Siena. The Acciaiuoli were a reigning family in Greece in the thirteenth century, and afterwards great Italian nobles. The castle is split up between many poor families, and has an air of forlorn grandeur. It would probably cost £100,000 to build today.

Sir George then gave a catalogue of the innumerable rooms, including a picture-gallery with frescoed portraits of the owners, a great saloon opening on to an interior courtyard, a library, and a museum. He concluded:

> We shall be able to grow our own fruit, wine, oil – even champagne! I have actually bought half the castle for £2,200; the other half belongs to the village usurer, whom we are endeavouring to get out. The ultimatum expires today, but I do not yet know the result. The purchase, apart from the romantic interest, is a good one, as it returns five per cent. The roof is in splendid order, and the drains can't be wrong, as there aren't any. I shall have to find the money in your name, and I do hope, my dear Osbert, that you will prove worthy of what I am doing for you, and you will not pursue that miserable career of extravagance and selfishness which already once ruined your family. – Ever your loving father,
>   GEORGE R. SITWELL

In June 1926, D. H. Lawrence visited Montegufoni. He wrote of the furnishings of the Castle in a letter to a friend, Mrs Otway:

> Sir G. [Sir George Sitwell] collects *beds*. . . . Room after room, and nothing but bed after bed. I said 'but do you put your guests in them?' – Oh! he said. They're not to sleep in. They're museum pieces. Also gilt and wiggly-

carved chairs. I sat on one. Oh! he said. Those chairs are not to sit in! – So I wiggled on the seat in the hopes that it would come to pieces.

In subsequent years Osbert, his brother Sacheverell, and his sister Edith were frequently to entertain their friends at Montegufoni. But 'the rarest of all houseparties' (Osbert Sitwell's own phrase) gathered there, in their enforced absence, in 1940. This consisted of such pictures, sent there from Florence for safe-keeping from the possible ravages of war, as Botticelli's *Primavera* and Uccello's *Battle of San Romano*. Osbert Sitwell records that all were undamaged, with the exception of Ghirlandaio's circular *Adoration of the Magi*, greatly admired by Ruskin. 'The Germans used it face upwards, as a table-top (though the table beneath had a top of its own), and it was stained in consequence with wine, food, and coffee, and with marks which the soldiers made on it with their knives.'

A Distant Retrospect

With rare exceptions – Byron was one – the love which nineteenth-century expatriate writers felt for Florence was passionate and unqualified. Of all the cities of Italy, it was the one which, lacking the religious oppressiveness of Rome and the hedonistic frivolity of Venice, they most favoured. With the coming of the twentieth century, however, a note of carping insinuated itself. Already in 1909 the Russian poet Alexander Blok (1880–1921) could address Florence with a mixture of disgust and pity:

> . . . Oh, laugh at yourself today, Bella,
> For your features have fallen in,
> Death's rotten wrinkles disfigure
> That once miraculous skin.
>
> The motorcars shout in your lanes,
> Your houses fill me with disgust;
> You have given yourself to the stains
> Of Europe's bilious yellow dust.

Although he and his wife spent so much time in Florence and its environs, Huxley could declare perversely that 'the spectacle of that second-rate provincial town with its repulsive Gothic architecture and its acres of Christmas card primitives made me almost sick.'

Dylan Thomas (1914–53), ensconced thanks to the generosity of his foolishly long-suffering patroness, the first wife of the historian A. J. P. Taylor, in the Villa del Beccaro in Scandicci in 1947, found Florence 'a gruelling museum' and eventually decided that he was 'sick . . . of drinking chianti in our marble shanty, sick of vini and contadini and bambini.'

Another English poet, Laurie Lee (1914–   ), also soon decided that he had had his fill of 'the lovely but indigestible city.' He had been tormented by the heat, in which 'the carved palaces quivered like radiators in the sun,' 'hot blasts of air, as from kitchen stoves, moved through the streets laden with odours of meat and frying oil' and 'in the cheaper cafés brick-faced British tourists sat sweating and counting their crumpled money.'

But despite such voices raised in irritation, exasperation, and even hatred, for most literary visitors the spell has remained as potent as it was for Ouida more than a hundred years ago:

The beauty of the past goes with you at every step in Florence. Buy eggs in the market, and you buy them where Donatello bought those which fell down in a broken heap before the wonder of the crucifix. Pause in a narrow street and it shall be that Borgo Allegri, which the people so baptized for the love of the old painter [Cimabue] and the new-born art. Stray into a great dark church at evening-time, where peasants tell their beads in the marble silence, and you are where the whole city flocked, weeping, at midnight, to look their last upon the dead face of their Michelangelo. Pace up the steps of the palace of the Signoria, and you tread the stone that felt the feet of him [Savonarola] to whom so bitterly was known 'com' e duro calle lo scendere e lo salir per l'altrui scale.' Buy a knot of March anemones or April arum lilies, and you may bear them with you through the same city ward in which the child Ghirlandajo once played amidst the golden and silver garlands that his father fashioned for the young heads of the Renaissance. Ask for a shoemaker, and you shall find a cobbler sitting with his board in the same old twisting, shadowy street-way where the old man Toscanelli drew his charts that served a fair-haired sailor of

Genoa, called Columbus. Toil to fetch a tinker through
the squalor of San Nicolo, and there shall fall on you the
shadow of the bell-tower, where the old sacristan saved to
the world the genius of Night and Day. Glance up to see
the hour of the evening, and there, sombre and tragical,
will loom above you the walls of the communal palace on
which the traitors were painted by the brush of Sarto, and
the tower of Giotto, fair and fresh in its perfect grace as
though angels had built it in the night just past . . .

It is this interpenetration of past and present which – albeit
nowadays all too often a source of friction and therefore
of discomfort – gives to Florence its unique interest and
distinctive charm.

Bibliography

Acton, Harold and Chaney, Edward, *Florence: A Traveller's Companion*, London, 1986
Acton, Harold, *Spectator*, 23 September 1989
Addison, Joseph, *Remarks on Several Parts of Italy etc.*, London, 1705
Aldington, Richard, *Pinorman*, London, 1954
Arnold, Matthew, *Letters (1848–88)*, ed. G. W. E. Russell, London, 1901
Beckford, William, *Dreams, Waking Thoughts, and Incidents, in a series of letters from various parts of Europe*, London, 1783, revised 1834
Bennett, Arnold, *Florentine Journal*, London, 1967
Berenson, Mary, *A Self-Portrait from her Letters and Diaries*, ed. Barbara Strachey and Jayne Samuels, London, 1983
Biagi, Guido, *Men and Manner of Old Florence*, London, 1919
Blok, Alexander, *The Twelve and Other Poems*, trans. Jon Stallworthy and Peter France, London, 1974
Boccaccio, *Life of Dante*, trans. Mrs Oliphant in *The Makers of Florence*, London, 1883
Boynton, Henry Walcott, *James Fenimore Cooper*, New York, 1931
Browning, Elizabeth Barrett, *Aurora Leigh*, London, 1857
——, *Casa Guidi Windows*, London, 1851
—— and Robert, *Letters*, London, 1899
Browning, Robert, *The Ring and the Book*, London, 1868–9
—— *The Complete Works*, 2 vols., London, 1915
Byron, Lord George Gordon, *Letters and Journals*, ed. Leslie A. Marchand, London, 1973–81
—— *Poems*, Oxford, 1945
Campbell, Harriet Charlotte Beaujolais, *A Journey to Florence in 1817*, ed. G. R. de Beer, London, 1951
Camus, Albert, essay in *Reflections on Florence*, ed. Simone Bargellini and Alice Scott, Florence, 1984
Castellan, Antoine Laurent, *Letters on Italy*, London, 1820
Cooper, James Fenimore, *Gleanings in Europe*, Italy, 1838

Cooper, Lettice, *Fenny*, London, 1953.

Coward, Noel, *Diaries*, ed. Graham Payn and Sheridan Morley, London, 1982

Cunard, Nancy, *Grand Man*, London, 1954

Dante, *Il Paradiso*, trans. Laurence Binyon, London, 1943

Day Lewis, C., 'Florence: Works of Art' from *Collected Poems*, London, 1954

Dentler, Clara Louise, *Famous Foreigners in Florence*, Italy, 1964

Dickens, Charles, *Little Dorrit*, London, 1855–7

—— *Pictures from Italy*, London, 1846

Dostoevsky, Anna, *Dostoevsky: Reminiscences*, London, 1926

Dostoevsky, Fyodor, *Letters*, London, 1961

Dowden, Edward, *Browning*, London, 1904

Downey, E., *Charles Lever, his Life and Letters*, London, 1906

Dumas, Alexandre, *Une Année à Florence*, Paris, 1851 (author's translation)

Eaton, Charlotte A., *Continental Adventures*, London, 1826

Eliot, George, *Journals and Letters*, ed. J. W. Cross, London, 1885

—— *Romola*, London, 1863

Evelyn, John, *Diary*, London, 1818

Fields, Anna, *Harriet Beecher Stowe*, London, 1898

Fitzpatrick, W. J., *The Life of Charles Lever*, London, 1879

Forest, J. de, *European Acquaintances*, New York, 1858

Forster, E. M., *A Room with a View*, London, 1908

—— *Selected Letters*, Vol. I, ed. Mary Lago and P. N. Furbank, London, 1983

Forster, J., *Walter Savage Landor*, London, 1869

France, Anatole, *Le Lys Rouge*, trans. *The Red Lily*, Winifred Stephens, London, 1908

Gardner, Edmund G., *The Story of Florence*, London, 1902

Gide, André, *Journals*, trans. Justin O'Brien, London, 1947

Gray, Thomas, *Letters*, ed. Mason, London, 1835–40

Hardy, Florence Emily, *The Life of Thomas Hardy 1840–1928*, London, 1962

Hare, Augustus J. C., *Florence*, London, 1896

Hawthorne, Nathaniel, *The Marble Faun*, London, 1860

—— *Passages from the French and Italian Notebooks*, London, 1871

Hawthorne, Sophia, *Notes in England and Italy*, London, 1851

Hazlitt, William, *Notes of a Journey Through France and Italy*, London, 1826

Holloway, Mark, *Norman Douglas*, London, 1976

Howells, W. D., *Tuscan Cities*, London, 1891

Hunt, Leigh, *Autobiography*, London, 1850

Hutton, Edward, *Florence*, London, 1952

—— *Country Walks About Florence*, London, 1908

Hutton, Laurence, *Literary Landmarks of Old Florence*, London, 1897

Huxley, Aldous, *Letters*, ed. Grover Smith, London, 1969

—— *Time Must Have a Stop*, London, 1945

James, Henry, *Foreign Parts*, London, 1883

—— *Italian Hours*, London, 1909
—— *Letters*, ed. Leon Edel, London, 1975–80
—— *Portrait of a Lady*, London, 1881
—— *Roderick Hudson*, London, 1876
—— *The Diary of a Man of Fifty*, London, 1879
—— (ed.), *William Wetmore Story and His Friends*, London, 1903
Johnson, Samuel, *Miscellanies*, ed. George Birkbeck Hill, Oxford, 1897
Kjetsaa, Geir, *Fyodor Dostoevsky: A Writer's Life*, London, 1988
Landor, Walter Savage, *Complete Poems*, 4 Vols., ed. Stephen Wheeler, London, 1933–6.
Lassels, Richard, *The Voyage of Italy*, London, 1670
Lawrence, D. H., *Letters*, ed. Aldous Huxley, London, 1932
—— *Aaron's Rod*, London, 1922
Lawrence, Frieda, *Not I, But the Wind*, London, 1935
Lee, Elizabeth, *Ouida, a Memoir*, London, 1914
Lee, Laurie, *I Can't Stay Long*, London, 1975
Lewis, Sinclair, *World So Wide*, London, 1951
Longfellow, Henry Wadsworth, *Outre-mer: A Pilgrimage Beyond the Sea*, Boston, 1833–4
Lowell, James Russell, *Letters*, ed. C. E. Norton, New York, 1894
Lucas, E. V., *A Wanderer in Florence*, London, 1912
Macaulay, Thomas Babbington, *Life and Letters* by George Otto Trevelyan, London, 1877
Maugham, H. Neville, *The Book of Italian Travel*, London, 1903
Maugham, William Somerset, *Then and Now*, London, 1967
Meyers, Jeffrey, *D. H. Lawrence*, London, 1990
Montaigne, Michel de, *Journal du voyage en Italie*, trans. William Hazlitt, London, 1842
Moore, Harry T., *The Priest of Love: A Life of D. H. Lawrence*, London, 1974
Morgan, Lady Sydney, *Italy*, London, 1821
Oliphant, Margaret, *The Makers of Florence*, London, 1883
Origo, Iris, *Images and Shadows*, London, 1970
Ouida (Marie Louise de la Ramée), *Pascarel*, London, 1873
Piozzi, Mrs (Thrale, Hester Lynch), *Observations and Reflections made in the course of a Journey through France, Italy and Germany*, 1789
Pratolini, Vasco, *The Girls of San Frediano*, trans. William Weaver, London, 1950
Proust, Marcel, *À la recherche du temps perdu: Du côté de chez Swann* and *Le côté de Guermantes*, 1913, trans. C. K. Scott Moncrieff, *Remembrance of Things Past: Swann's Way* and *The Guermantes Way*, London, 1922 and 1925
Rhodes, Anthony, *The Poet as Superman*, London, 1957
Rogers, Samuel, *Italy*, London, 1836
—— *The Italian Journal*, ed. J. R. Hale, London, 1956
Ruskin, John, *Mornings in Florence*, Orpington, 1875–7
—— *Praeterita*, London, 1885–9

—— *The Diaries of John Ruskin*, selected and edited by Joan Evans and John Howard Whitehouse, Oxford, 1956

Shelley, Percy Bysshe, *Letters*, ed. Roger Ingpen, London, 1909

Shorthouse, J. H., *John Inglesant*, London, 1881

Sitwell, Osbert, *Great Morning*, London, 1948

Smollett, Tobias, *Travels through France and Italy*, London, 1766

Soldati, Mario, *The Confession*, trans. Raymond Rosenthal, London, 1958

Spence, Joseph, *Letters from the Grand Tour*, ed. Slava Klima, Montreal–London, 1975

Staël, Madame de, *Corinne*, Paris, 1807 (author's translation)

Steegmuller, Francis, 'A Letter from Florence' in *Stories and True Stories*, Boston, 1972

Stendhal (Henri Beyle), *Rome, Naples and Florence*, London, 1959

Stirling, Monica, *The Fine and the Wicked*, Gollancz, 1957

Strelsky, Katherine, *Dostoevsky in Florence, The Russian Review*, Vol. XXIII, No. 2, April 1964

Swan, Michael, *Ilex and Olive*, London, 1949

Swinburne, Algernon Charles, *Songs Before Sunrise*, London, 1871

Symonds, John Addington, *Renaissance in Italy*, London, 1898

Taine, Hippolyte, *Italy*, trans. J. Durand, New York, 1875

Taylor, Katherine Kressman, *Diary of Florence in the Flood*, New York, 1967

Tennyson, Hallam, *Tennyson and His Friends*, London, 1911

Thomas, Dylan, *Selected Letters*, London, 1965

Trefusis, Violet, *Don't Look Round*, London, 1952

Treves, G. Artom, *The Golden Ring*, London, 1956

Trollope, Anthony, *He Knew He was Right*, London, 1869

Trollope, Thomas, *What I Remember*, London, 1887

Twain, Mark, *The Innocents Abroad*, Hartford, Connecticut, 1869

Walpole, Horace, *Letters*, ed. P. Toynbee, London, 1903–5

Waterfield, Lina, *Castle in Italy*, London, 1961

Williams, William Carlos, *A Voyage to Pagany*, New York, 1928

Acknowledgements

Acknowledgement is due to the following for kindly giving permission to reproduce copyright material: Lettice Cooper, *Fenny*, Virago, 1987. Extract reproduced by permission of Lettice Cooper; Noel Coward, *Diaries*, G. Payn, 1983. Extract reproduced by permission of Macmillan Ltd.; C. Day Lewis, *Collected Poems*, 1954. Extract reproduced by permission of the Peters Fraser & Dunlop Group Ltd.; E. M. Forster, *A Room with a View*, 1908. Extract reproduced by permission of Edward Arnold Ltd.; Aldous Huxley, *Letters*, 1969. Extract reproduced by permission of Mrs Laura Huxley and Chatto & Windus Ltd; Sinclair Lewis, *World So Wide*, 1951. Extract reproduced by permission of William Heinemann Ltd.; Somerset Maugham, *Then and Now*, 1967. Extract reproduced by permission of William Heinemann Ltd.; Anthony Rhodes, *The Poet as Superman*, Weidenfeld & Nicolson, 1957. Extract reproduced by permission of A. M. Heath Ltd.; Osbert Sitwell, *Left Hand! Right Hand!*, Macmillan, 1945. Extract reproduced by permission of David Higham Associates Ltd.; Mario Soldati, *The Confession*, 1958. Extract reproduced by permission of André Deutsch Ltd.; Michael Swan, *Ilex and Olive*, Home & Van Thal, 1949. Extracts reproduced by permission of Anna P. Swan and Curtis Brown Ltd.; Violet Trefusis, *Don't Look Round*, 1952. Extract reproduced by permission of the Estate of Violet Trefusis and Hutchinson Ltd.; William Carlos Williams, *A Voyage to Pagany*. Copyright © 1970 New Directions Publishing Corp. Extract reproduced by permission of New Directions.

Index